The Moral Psychology of Amusement

Moral Psychology of the Emotions

Series editor: Mark Alfano, Associate Professor of Philosophy, Macquarie University

How do our emotions influence our other mental states (perceptions, beliefs, motivations, and intentions) and our behavior? How are they influenced by our other mental states, our environments, and our cultures? What is the moral value of a particular emotion in a particular context? This series explores the causes, consequences, and value of the emotions from an interdisciplinary perspective. Emotions are diverse, with components at various levels (biological, neural, psychological, and social), so each book in this series is devoted to a distinct emotion. This focus allows the author and reader to delve into a specific mental state, rather than trying to sum up emotions en masse. Authors approach a particular emotion from their own disciplinary angle (e.g., conceptual analysis, feminist philosophy, critical race theory, phenomenology, social psychology, personality psychology, and neuroscience) while connecting with other fields. In so doing, they build a mosaic for each emotion, evaluating both its nature and its moral properties.

Other titles in this series:
The Moral Psychology of Forgiveness edited by Kathryn J. Norlock
The Moral Psychology of Pride edited by Adam J. Carter and Emma C. Gordon
The Moral Psychology of Sadness edited by Anna Gotlib
The Moral Psychology of Anger edited by Myisha Cherry and Owen Flanagan
The Moral Psychology of Contempt edited by Michelle Mason
The Moral Psychology of Compassion edited by Justin Caouette and Carolyn Price
The Moral Psychology of Disgust edited by Nina Strohminger and Victor Kumar
The Moral Psychology of Gratitude, edited by Robert Roberts and Daniel Telech
The Moral Psychology of Admiration, edited by Alfred Archer and André Grahle
The Moral Psychology of Regret edited by Anna Gotlib
The Moral Psychology of Hope edited by Claudia Blöser and Titus Stahl
The Moral Psychology of Amusement edited by Brian Robinson

The Moral Psychology of Amusement

Edited by
Brian Robinson

ROWMAN & LITTLEFIELD
Lanham • Boulder • New York • London

Published by Rowman & Littlefield
An imprint of The Rowman & Littlefield Publishing Group, Inc.
4501 Forbes Boulevard, Suite 200, Lanham, Maryland 20706
www.rowman.com

86-90 Paul Street, London EC2A 4NE

Selection and editorial matter copyright © 2021 by Brian Robinson

Copyright in individual chapters is held by the respective chapter authors.

All rights reserved. No part of this book may be reproduced in any form or by any electronic or mechanical means, including information storage and retrieval systems, without written permission from the publisher, except by a reviewer who may quote passages in a review.

British Library Cataloguing in Publication Information Available

Library of Congress Cataloging-in-Publication Data

Names: Robinson, Brian, 1978– editor.
Title: The moral psychology of amusement / edited by Brian Robinson.
Description: Lanham, Maryland : Rowman & Littlefield, [2021] | Series: Moral psychology of the emotions | Includes bibliographical references and index.
Identifiers: LCCN 2021025438 (print) | LCCN 2021025439 (ebook) | ISBN 9781786613295 (cloth) | ISBN 9781538161647 (paperback) | ISBN 9781786613301 (epub)
Subjects: LCSH: Comic, The—Moral and ethical aspects. | Wit and humor—Moral and ethical aspects. | Laughter—Moral and ethical aspects. | Comic, The. | Wit and humor—Philosophy. | Laughter. | LCGFT: Essays.
Classification: LCC BH301.C7 M67 2021 (print) | LCC BH301.C7 (ebook) | DDC 179—dc23
LC record available at https://lccn.loc.gov/2021025438
LC ebook record available at https://lccn.loc.gov/2021025439

Dedication

*Dedicated to my sons, James and Henry, who amuse
me in wonderful and new ways every day.
And in memory of Peter Glaser, the teacher who first
introduced me to both philosophy and the joy of puns.*

Contents

Introduction: The Moral Psychology of Amusement 1
Brian Robinson

PART I: AMUSEMENT AND MORAL JUDGMENTS 11

1. LOL: What We Can Learn from Forced Laughter 13
   Dan Shargel

2. An Interactional Sociolinguist Engages the Moral Psychology of Amusement 31
   Catherine Evans Davies

3. It's All Fun and Games until Someone Gets Hurt: Amusement's Negative Influence on Moral Judgment 45
   Nathan Stout

PART II: MORAL JUDGMENTS OF AMUSEMENT 63

4. Beyond a Joke: A Defence of Comic Moralism 65
   Alan Roberts

5. This Isn't Funny: It's Serious 75
   Brian Mondy

6. The Ethics of Humor 95
   Tristan Nash

PART III: SOCIAL MORAL JUDGMENTS OF AMUSEMENT — 107

7 You Shouldn't Have Laughed!: The Ethics of Derogatory Amusement — 109
   Andrew Morgan and Ralph DiFranco

8 Amused by the Outrageous: The Morally Tempering Effect of News Satire — 131
   Rasmus Rosenberg Larsen and David Sackris

9 *Eutrapelia* and the Normativity of Social Humor — 151
   Andrew Jordan and Stephanie Patridge

PART IV: ANCIENT PERSPECTIVES ON THE MORAL JUDGMENTS OF AMUSEMENT — 169

10 Amusement, Happiness, and the Good Life in Plato's Dialogues — 171
    Oksana Maksymchuk

11 Zhuangzi's Moral Psychology and Humor: The Playful Liberation of Self, Others, and Society — 189
    Carl Helsing

12 Starting from the Muses: Engaging Moral Imagination through Memory's Many Gifts — 211
    Guy Axtell

Index — 231

About the Contributors — 235

Introduction
The Moral Psychology of Amusement
Brian Robinson

Amusement is a funny thing. It is culturally universal yet amazingly elusive, being both difficult to define or even create. Still, at least the cause of amusement is easy to describe, given the widely accepted comedic principle that jokes are always funnier when explained. (You see, the reason it's amusing to joke about how many philosophers it takes to screw in a light bulb is . . .)

In all seriousness though, this volume focuses on the moral psychology of the emotion of amusement. It may seem an enjoyable, but a trivial diversion from the serious business of life. In truth, however, amusement is deadly serious and of tremendous importance to one's moral life. It can be argued that to live well requires amusement. Part of the project of the moral life is to consider the many moral complexities of living a human life in one's social milieu and the many potential pitfalls and perils, as well as the advantages of the good life and the aids to achieving it. Amusement is both. We can be amused in the wrong way. But amusement is one of the true joys of life as well, not to be completely eschewed. A life without any amusement hardly represents a good life. We can be amused by things we should not, at times we should not, or to an extent we should not. Alternatively, the amusement itself may be altogether fitting, but can nevertheless lull us into inattention to other matters that we should be focused on. We can amuse ourselves to death, either physical death or the death of the possibility of a morally good life. On the other hand, someone who never feels amusement (even when morally appropriate) does not seem to have lived a happy, flourishing life. Their life appears bereft of an emotional state that is part of what makes life worth living. Of course, this view assumes that there can be morally appropriate occasions to be amused, or perhaps even to seek it out. Whether that is correct is a matter worth considering, instead of merely assuming yay or nay.

Another motivation for this volume is to help fill a surprising gap in recent work on the philosophy and psychology of humor. The last decade has seen an increased interest in this topic (e.g., Amir, 2010; McGraw and Warren 2010; Martin and Ford, 2018; Gimbel 2018; Amir 2019; this is only a small sample). Yet a long-standing problem remains in this interdisciplinary investigation of humor. As Clark put it, "There can be no adequate account of the notion of humor without one of the notion of amusement" (1970, 142). Such an account of amusement itself has not been as forthcoming as one might hope or expect.

The chapters in this volume are the authors' musings on amusement. While none attempt to convey a complete account of amusement, each chapter examines different aspects of it. Part of the goal of this volume is to spur a future empirical and theoretical investigation into amusement.

This volume consists of twelve chapters divided into four equal sections. Before introducing them, it is worth discussing some general points about common assumptions made by each of the authors in this volume. The first governing assumption of this volume is that amusement is an emotion. This volume is part of a larger series on the moral psychology of various emotions, including joy, disgust, and anger. As such, the contributing authors and I proceed on the view that amusement is an emotion as well. (There have been challenges to this view, which I will respond to below.)

Second, this volume is an exploration of the moral psychology of amusement. To study amusement, it is necessary to examine it as a psychological phenomenon—since emotions are part of our psychology—and also not as an amoral psychological state, but as an inherently moral one. Our views of morality may affect what one finds amusing. Being amused may affect what we find morally permissible or reprehensible. We are emotionally complicated beings, and these emotions affect us in complicated ways, many of which have complicated relationships with moral questions. In other words, the second assumption is that we cannot examine the morality of amusement apart from its part in our psychology *and* we cannot engage in the psychological study of amusement apart from its moral complexities.

Lastly, this volume focuses on amusement specifically; it is not fundamentally about the philosophy or psychology of humor. Obviously, amusement and humor are very related. Amusement is typically (or even always, depending on whom you ask) the intended emotional state of humor. But they are distinct. It may be possible to produce humor that does not intend to induce amusement (Gimbel 2018). Likewise, it may be possible to be amused due to other stimuli besides humor. Nevertheless, many of the chapters here are informed by philosophy and psychology of humor, and the volume will be of interest to anyone in either field. At times in some chapters, humor and amusement have become so intertwined that they cannot be unraveled, and so in speaking about one, the authors are directly addressing the other as well. These two areas of research should be in conversation. In developing the moral psychology of amusement, many of the authors make connections back to philosophy or psychology of humor. A central aim of this volume is to advance this conversation.

And now for something completely different: a brief overview of the sections and chapters.

SECTION I: AMUSEMENT AND MORAL JUDGMENTS

Section I focuses on the nature of amusement itself and its relationship with our moral judgments. Dan Shargel starts things off in chapter 1, applying his enactive account of emotions to amusement specifically. His analysis of amusement is based on a study of amusement's conspicuous absence, that is, cases of forced laughter when no one was amused. In your next social interaction, especially with someone with whom you are not close, pay attention to how often you laugh when nothing was really funny or amusing. We do this a great deal for social effect. Most contemporary theories of emotion contend that emotions involve some judgment or perception. Shargel's enactive account of emotions, however, contends that emotions change what we can do. Amusement prepares us to act. Often, its social function is to prepare us for cooperative action with others with whom we've just been laughing. Social coordination is very important for social stability. It is so important that we often fake amusement by exhibiting forced laughter to try to bring about the same end.

Chapter 2 is written by Catherine Evans Davies, a sociolinguist, who engages in the moral psychology of amusement through the methods of ethnography. The chapter presents an autoethnographic study of her own uses of humorous language. Her chapter presents insights into how one can examine their own sense of humor, their own feelings of amusement. Davies's focus is to consider her own various humorous interactions with others to see if they were adaptive or maladaptive. Building from Martin (2003), adaptive uses of humor promote social cohesion or are self-enhancing. Maladaptive humor, on the other hand, attacks others or is self-defeating. The chapter, in short, is a master work with examples in how to make moral judgments of one's own amusement. Davies then builds on this analysis to consider the oft-employed "Just joking" defense. It is not uncommon for speakers to defend their sense of humor when social norms about what should be funny or amusing are changing, such as when it is no longer "politically correct" to joke about a particular group.

Section I then concludes with Nathan Stout in chapter 3 considering how amusement affects our moral judgments. As he notes, there is a long-standing debate in philosophy of humor about whether our moral judgments (i.e., whether something is morally acceptable or not) can or should affect what we find amusing. Stout takes that debate and flips it on its head. If I am amused, how does that affect my moral judgments of right and wrong? Am I less likely to consider something morally objectionable? These questions have not received enough attention in psychology or philosophy. Stout lays extensive groundwork for possible theoretical and empirical investigation. He presents two possible influences of amusement on our moral judgments, both ripe for further study. Stout proposes amusement may have a dispositional effect, disposing us to prosocial judgments (and behavior). Alternatively, amusement may distract us from what is morally important, misleading us to judgments we might not otherwise endorse.

SECTION II: MORAL JUDGMENTS OF AMUSEMENT

The next section directly addresses the moral boundaries of humor and amusement. Is amusement at humor morally permissible? If so, when is it morally permissible and (more importantly) when is it wrong to be amused by a piece of humor? Similar questions arise for making jokes aimed at amusing others. As mentioned, these are not new questions. The debate has been well canvased and views long articulated. This section aims to engage in this debate in new ways, sometimes by considering the question from the perspective of the morality of being amused instead of just the morality of whether or not to make certain jokes. Each chapter breathes new life into this discussion or dives deeper into the existing question.

Alan Roberts authors chapter 4 and opens this section with a clear summary of the three main views: comic moralism, comic immoralism, and comic amoralism. He then proceeds to offer a robust defense of comic moralism, the view that a moral judgment that something is morally impermissible (or even morally questionable) makes it less amusing. If I judge sexist attitudes to be morally objectionable, then according to comic moralism I will not be amused by sexist jokes (or at least not find them funny). Roberts's focus is on the merited-response argument that has been raised as an objection to comic moralism (Carroll 2014a, 2014b). His argument against this criticism is that it is based on an underdeveloped conception of amusement. By better understanding the nature of amusement especially in cases of so-called "gallows" or "black humor" (humor in the face of death or suffering) the merited-response argument loses its power against comic moralism.

In chapter 5, Brian Mondy engages with a common moral objection of humor. The alleged problem with humor is that it prompts one to be amused about a subject matter when instead it should be taken seriously. Jokes about racism or rape do not take the morally requisite seriousness of these moral evils. We are amused and laugh instead of being angered and prompted to action to bring about justice. Mondy explores this supposed dichotomy between amusement and seriousness, concluding that they are not necessarily diametrically opposed to one another. Some humor, instead of precluding seriousness, actually promotes taking a serious attitude to the subject matter joked about. He uses an example of an Iraqi comedy show joking about fake government checkpoints. Al-Qaeda actually did set up such fake checkpoints, which is a serious threat to people's safety. The show played on this fact, pranking celebrities by finding planted bombs in their car. The criticism is that such humor distracts from this serious problem by encouraging amusement instead. Mondy says that there are different kinds of seriousness, and they come in degrees. Sometimes humor can encourage both seriousness and amusement. In the case of the fake checkpoints, they can be regarded as both amusing and raising awareness about a serious problem.

Tristan Nash closes the section with chapter 6, in which he considers whether morality should place any restrictions on humor and amusement. Much of this debate, he argues, has confused two distinct conflicts. Morality can conflict with nonmoral considerations. Alternatively, morality can conflict with immoral considerations. Keeping these kinds of conflicts distinct is critical in considering the ethics of humor and amusement. He concludes that morality does set the outer bounds of what is morally acceptable humor and amusement. Within those bounds, however, morality is not a trump card that overrides any other considerations. Sorting out those bounds and what weight morality should be given in one's considerations requires practical wisdom.

SECTION III: SOCIAL MORAL JUDGMENTS OF AMUSEMENT

Section III focuses more on the larger role of amusement and humor in society generally. What social role does humor and amusement play? Some of these issues are touched on in previous chapters, but here they take center stage. Of particular concern is political satire. Does this form of humor cause more social harm than the amusement it provides? Part of my motivation as editor in having chapters consider this question is the following thought by famed comedic actor and director Mel Brooks, which he gave during a 2001 interview on the occasion of the revival of his movie *The Producers* that mocks Hitler and Nazis. He states, "If you stand on a soapbox and trade rhetoric with a dictator you never win. Rhetoric does not get you anywhere, because Hitler and Mussolini are just as good at rhetoric. But if you can bring these people down with comedy, they stand no chance" (Shute 2001).

Andrew Morgan and Ralph DiFranco take up this topic in chapter 7, starting with the comedic roasting of Sarah Huckabee Sanders, President Trump's former press secretary. Michelle Wolf, the comedian, made derogatory remarks about Huckabee Sanders for the sake of amusement. Morgan and DiFranco use this occasion to consider claims that one should not have laughed at derogatory humor. To that end, they develop an account of expressive derogation that is defined apart any psychological effects caused. Some derogatory humor and amusement (including some examples of subversive political or social satire), they assert, cannot be morally countenanced. They discuss the ethics of telling derogatory humor and being amused by derogatory humor separately. The moral permissibility of each is related but separate matters. A particular derogatory joke may not have been morally permissible, yet it still may be morally permissible to be amused by it so long as the amusement does not stem from a morally impermissible derogatory attitude. Even still, in such cases, it may be best to not laugh in public despite one's amusement.

In chapter 8, Rasmus Rosenberg Larsen and David Sackris focus entirely on news satire, such *The Daily Show* and *Last Week Tonight*. Such shows aim to generate amusement from the outrageous. Rosenberg Larsen and Sackris build on empirical research of the social effects of these shows, such as whether they increase young people's likelihood of voting. If so, then such findings would indicate that the humor is *both* amusing and outrageous: young viewers watch for the amusement but are outraged enough by those mocked that they vote when they otherwise would not have. As Rosenberg Larsen and Sackris point out, however, such attempts to empirically determine such social effects of satire have been inconclusive and methodologically challenged. Rosenberg Larsen and Sackris make suggestions about methodological improvements. They then, working from Prinz's sentimentalist moral psychology (Prinz 2006; 2006; 2015; 2016), present their own hypothesis that news satire has an attenuating effect on its viewers.

Andrew Jordan and Stephanie Patridge then wrap up section III with chapter 9, which focuses on social humor and *eutapelia*. They draw from Aristotle's development of *eutapelia* as a social virtue, perhaps best understood as wittiness. Their focus is not so much explication of Aristotle, as it is to use his account of wit as a social virtue to advance and develop their own fitting-attitude theory of humor and amusement (Jordan and Patridge 2017). Social humor that is not primarily an aesthetic act like stand-up but a social activity aiming for pleasing social interchanges appears prima facie to challenge their fitting-attitude theory. By employing Aristotle's *eutapelia*, they diffuse this challenge and contend that the normative constraints on social humor are different than other kinds of humor.

SECTION IV: ANCIENT PERSPECTIVES ON THE MORAL JUDGMENTS OF AMUSEMENT

The last section embraces more fully the turn to the past that Jordan and Patridge introduce. Moral psychology is best when engaging in cutting-edge scientific advancement that is informed by and in conversation with ancient perspectives. The somewhat recent situationist challenge to character traits and virtue ethics is a good example (Alfano 2016, 112–137). The moral psychology of amusement is no different. A variety of ancient sources provide insight into the same questions we explore today regarding the nature and ethics of amusement. The chapters in this last section seek to draw out some of these insights to inform contemporary theoretical and empirical research.

Oksana Maksymchuk presents chapter 10, which looks back to Plato's *Gorgias*, *Republic*, and *Theaetetus*. Plato's main objection to amusement is similar to what Mondy explored in chapter 5, namely that amusement distracts one from serious matters. In Plato's case, amusement is a distraction from the serious business of a lifelong commitment to philosophy. Yet, in *Gorgias*, Plato considers an objection that philosophy itself is a sort of trivial amusement distracting one from more serious issues in life. Part of Plato's *Republic* can be looked at as a response to this worry. Still, in *Theaetetus* philosophy does appear to be amusing. Maksymchuk reflects on these dialogues to develop an account of amusement and the activity of doing philosophy.

In chapter 11, Carl Helsing turns to the *Zhuangzi*, a Daoist philosophical text from ancient China. As Helsing notes, no account of amusement or humor is presented explicitly in the text. Instead, Helsing constructs a theory of amusement from the text, particularly its playful use of humor. Part of the point of humor, on this view, is to play with and challenge the limitations of language (and the limitations in thought they engender). If correct, this theory would rightly elevate the pun as more than just some antics and verbal punishment, but an elevated form of communication and thought.

Lastly, in chapter 12, Guy Axtell draws inspiration from the root of amusement, namely the Muses, to consider the relationship between amusement and inspiration. He draws from Hesiod, Homer, and Aristophanes, as well as more contemporary thinkers like Dewey and James. Amusements, Axtell argues, involve rememberings, forgettings, and imaginings.

AMUSEMENT AS EMOTION

As stated above, this volume proceeds on the assumption that amusement is an emotion. Most of the authors do not directly address challenges to this view, though they do exist. Here in this introduction, I will briefly respond to those challenges to justify this assumption for the rest of the authors.

Morreall (1983, 2015) outright denies that amusement is an emotion. Roberts (1988) expresses an "intuitive hesitation" (269) to call amusement an emotion. Sharpe (1975) strongly endorses the view. It is worth pointing out that Morreall and Roberts are strongly in the minority and have the burden of proof. As Morreall notes, Plato, Aristotle, and Hobbes all appear to regard amusement as an emotion. Still, Morreall and Roberts have arguments and should be responded to.

First of all, the arguments offered by both Roberts and Morreall are based on the incongruity theory of humor, which Morreall (1983) calls "the standard view" (299). This is no longer the standard view, especially in psychology where several new theories have arisen to contend with the incongruity theory and better explain the phenomena. Chief among these is the Benign Violation Theory (McGraw and Warren 2010; McGraw et al. 2012; Warren and McGraw 2015) that is holding up well to empirical testing and becoming increasingly popular in psychology of humor (Martin and Ford 2018).

Second, both Morreall and Roberts argue that amusement is not an emotion because amusement does not meet the criteria for an emotion, as compared to standard emotions like anger or love. The psychology and philosophy of emotion is an increasingly complex and vibrant field, and their arguments engage in almost none of it. What constitutes an emotion is a complicated question, not something intuitively obvious based on a cursory analysis of a few "standard" emotions. More nuanced accounts of emotions can account for amusement, as Shargel demonstrates in chapter 1.

Third, both Morreall and Roberts assert psychological views that are woefully uninformed by contemporary psychology or other empirical fields. Morreall (1983), for example, claims without supporting literature that chimpanzees are not amused by a model chimpanzee head and then concludes that therefore chimpanzees cannot experience amusement (which they should be able to if amusement were an emotion). Without evidence, this is a dubious claim about chimpanzee behavior. Even if true, the conclusion would far outstrip the evidence. It would only show that chimpanzees are not amused by model chimpanzee heads, not that they cannot be amused.

Fourth, the arguments against the status of amusement as an emotion are all based on supposing something is lacking from amusement that is a necessary component of any emotion: a pro or con attitude, an intentional object, a motivational component, a proprioceptive component. I do not here have the space to respond to each of these assertions, though I find each argument they produce to be dubious. They do, however, appear to be generally based on some conceptual confusion. To give one example, Morreall (1983, 298) argues that amusement lacks a pro or con attitude based on the following example. After seeing a near unending series of boring, cookie-cutter houses, I see one brightly painted with windows shaped like animals; I am amused by the house but do not have a pro or con attitude toward the house. (For the sake of this response, I will follow Morreall in assuming incongruity theory—the theory that perceiving some inconsistency produces amusement.) The mistake here is in the object of the amusement. It is not the house itself that amuses me. Rather it is the house's incongruity with all those around it. Had the rest the neighborhood had a similar facade, I would not have been as amused at *this* house. The object of my amusement is the incongruity, to which I have a pro attitude. Given how boring all the other houses were, I am pleased and in favor of one having broken the monotony. The rest of the arguments about what is lacking from amusement are based on similar conceptual mix ups, which I cannot here detail.

For now, I will merely note two things. First, these arguments are entirely based on the intuitions of Morreall or Roberts, and these intuitions are not universally shared. Moral psychology, as it progresses, has increasingly moved beyond intuition mongering to clear argument and empirical investigation. This volume aims to move the moral psychology of amusement in this same direction. Second, many of the chapters in this volume address many of these arguments. For example, in chapter 8, Rosenberg Larsen and Sackris propose new ways to test whether news satire motivates young viewers to participate in political processes. In other words, the supposed lack of a motivational component to amusement can be measured (instead of assumed), and they offer suggestion on how to better test this claim.

With that concern out of the way, I now turn matters over to the wonderful authors who have contributed to this volume. I hope you find their work as enlightening and amusing as I did.

REFERENCES

Carroll, Noël. 2014a. "Ethics and comic amusement," *British Journal of Aesthetics* 54 (2): 241–253.
Carroll, Noël. 2014b. *Humour: A Very Short Introduction*. Oxford: OUP.
Clark, Michael. 1970. "Humour and Incongruity." *Philosophy* 171 (45): 20–32.
John Morreall, "Humor and Emotion," *American Philosophical Quarterly*, vol. 20 (1983), pp. 297–304.
Jordan, Andrew and Patridge, Stephanie. 2017. "Fitting Attitude Theory and the Normativity of Jokes." *Erkenntnis*, 83 (6): 1303–1320.

Martin, Rod A. 2003. "Sense of Humor." In *Positive Psychological Assessment: A Handbook of Models and Measures*, edited by Shane J. Lopez and C. R. Snyder, 313–326 . Washington, DC: American Psychological Association.

Martin, R. A., & Ford, T. E. (2018). *The psychology of humor: An integrative approach*. Second edition. London: Academic Press.

McGraw, A. P., & Warren, C. (2010). Benign violations: Making immoral behavior funny. *Psychological Science*, 21 (8): 1141–1149.

McGraw, A. P., Warren, C., Williams, L. E., & Leonard, B. (2012). Too close for comfort, or too far to care? Finding humor in distant tragedies and close mishaps. *Psychological Science*, 23 (10): 1215–1223.

Prinz, Jesse J. 2006. "The Emotional Basis of Moral Judgments." *Philosophical Explorations* 9 (1): 29–43.

Prinz, Jesse J. 2007. *The Emotional Construction of Morals*. New York: Oxford University Press.

Prinz, Jesse J. 2015. "Is the Moral Brain Ever Dispassionate?" In *The Moral Brain: A Multidisciplinary Perspective*, edited by J. Decety and T. Wheatley, 51–67. Cambridge, MA: MIT Press.

Prinz, Jesse J. 2016. "Sentimentalism and the Moral Brain." In *Moral Brains: the Neuroscience of Morality*, edited by Matthew Liao, 45–73. New York: Oxford University Press.

Shute, Nancy. 2001. "Mel Brooks: His humor brings down Hitler, and the house." *U.S. News and World Report*, August 12, 2001.

Warren, C., & McGraw, A. P. (2015). Opinion: What makes things humorous. *Proceedings of the National Academy of Sciences*, 112 (23): 7105–7106.

Part I

AMUSEMENT AND MORAL JUDGMENTS

Chapter 1

LOL

What We Can Learn from Forced Laughter

Dan Shargel

The topic of this chapter is forced laughter, by which I mean any laughter that does not occur as a spontaneous expression of amusement. Forced laughter, as I use the term, might be deliberate or automatic, and it might occur in a pleasant social situation or under duress. These expressions tend to be overlooked in the humor literature because they are not necessarily responses to humor, and also in the emotion literature, because they do not actually express amusement. I will argue that attending to forced laughter helps us refine our theories of humor, and applies pressure to conventional theories of emotion. The phenomenon is especially puzzling in cases where we laugh despite it being perfectly clear that nothing was funny. I'll argue that an enactive approach to emotion gives us the best tools for making sense of these cases. Emotions in general change what we can do, and laughter, even in the absence of amusement, changes the affordances of our social environment.

My method is to draw connections between theories of humor and theories of emotion, and jointly apply these theories to cases of forced laughter. I'll start in section 1 by describing two recent theories of humor that I will appeal to throughout the rest of the chapter. Next, in section 2, I'll describe several cases of forced laughter, and connect them to theories of humor. Forced laughter is too diverse to discuss every variety, but I have chosen a diverse set of cases to serve as the explananda throughout the rest of the chapter. In section 3, I will return to these cases, but this time through the lens of conventional theories of emotion. Conventional theories, as I use the term, are those that take emotions to have representational contents with a mind-to-world direction of fit. These theories predominate in both philosophy and psychology, and I will argue that they have difficulty explaining some of the cases of forced laughter. In sections 4 and 5, I will present a brief summary of the enactive theory of emotion from Shargel and Prinz (2017). In section 6, I will apply that theory to the case of amusement, and connect it with the theories of humor introduced in section 1. Finally, in section 7, I will describe how the enactive theory of emotion, applied to amusement, allows for a satisfying explanation of even the most puzzling cases of forced laughter.

1. THEORIES OF HUMOR AND AMUSEMENT

McGraw and Warren's (2010) benign violations theory of humor draws inspiration in part from primates, who laugh when tickling each other or play fighting. Their proposal is clear from the name: that amusement arises when we are aware of some sort of violation, but the violation is benign. This fits the nonhuman primate cases, since during play the primates are under attack, but the attack is not truly threatening. The view makes intuitive sense when applied to human amusement as well. Humor often, perhaps always, involves something gone wrong. Curb Your Enthusiasm would not be funny if Larry David responded appropriately to conflicts, and Homer Simpson would not be funny if he had sound judgment. However, when something seems truly terrible to us we do not find it amusing.[1] This raises the question: when is a violation benign?

According to McGraw and Warren (2010), "a violation can seem benign if (a) a salient norm suggests that something is wrong but another salient norm suggests that it is acceptable, (b) one is only weakly committed to the violated norm, or (c) the violation is psychologically distant" (p. 1142). The authors performed experiments to test these conditions where they posed variants of the same scenario in different conditions and observed whether participants were amused. They tested the conflicting norms condition by posing a scenario where a man rubs a kitten on his genitals (p. 1143). Participants are amused if the kitten enjoys the contact, but not if the kitten does not. In the former case, there are conflicting norms, because sexual contact with a cat is a purity violation, but it seems as though no harm is done. They tested norm commitment by posing a scenario where a church raffles off a hummer to gain new members (p. 1145). Only nonchurchgoers, who presumably are less committed to the integrity of church activities, find the scenario amusing. Finally, to test psychological distance, they primed participants with either a short or long distance on a Cartesian plane before posing a scenario where someone has sexual contact with a chicken carcass (1146–7). The participants primed with the greater distance were more amused.[2] Notably, the participants in all three of those studies reported disgust with the scenarios, even those who found them amusing.

Noel Carroll's (2013) incongruity theory is quite similar to the benign violation theory, even though the theorists work in different disciplines, and do not discuss each others' work. Carroll (2013) presents several conditions for someone to enter what he calls comic amusement, "(1) the object of her mental state is a perceived incongruity (2) which she regards as neither seriously threatening to herself nor anyone she cares about, nor does she regard it as otherwise anxiety producing, (3) which she does not find annoying, (4) which she does not approach with a genuine, puzzle-solving attitude, but (5) which she enjoys" (p. 84). I will not discuss all of those conditions in depth, but two features stand out about them taken as a whole. First, Carroll's incongruities sound a lot like McGraw and Warren's violations. Carroll points out that amusing incongruities may violate norms of logic, manners, language, and good sense, among others (p. 80). I will take "violation" to be roughly equivalent to "incongruity" for present purposes.

Second, Carroll's conditions 2–3 essentially state that the violation must be benign. This is another similarity with the benign violations view, and it takes on greater significance if we take amusement to be an emotional state, as Carroll does. On the face of it, it seems odd that we should have a psychological system that picks out benign violations, or nonthreatening incongruities. These appear to be arbitrary combinations of features. However, it seems that some types of emotional episodes can coexist more easily than others. For example, an occurrent state of anger seems to often coexist with disgust, but not with calm. It is difficult, while angry, to become calm, but not to become disgusted. Becoming calm will reduce your level of occurrent anger, but becoming disgusted will not. With this in mind, perhaps violations are sufficient for eliciting amusement. The other conditions in both theories are only relevant because violations often also elicit other emotions, such as anxiety, fear, and anger, that are incompatible with amusement. Amusement is elicited by violations as long as those violations do not produce a negative emotion that undermines the amusement.

The benign violations and incongruity theories complement each other and explain a wide range of things that we find amusing. Will they be useful in explaining cases where we are not actually amused? In the next section, I will survey a range of cases of forced laughter, using these theories of amusement to provide a first pass of explanation.

2. FORCED LAUGHTER

Forced laughter is often a form of cooperation: cooperation by the audience with a person who intended to make a humorous comment.[3] Humor plays many different social roles, and cooperation with humor producers can take many different forms. I will present a few cases in this section that will set the agenda for the rest of the chapter.

First, humor is often a source of entertainment. The producer of humor may aim to entertain, but it is difficult to be funny at will. Some people are funnier than others, and nobody is always successful when aiming to be funny. Fortunately, laughter is contagious (Provine 1992). By amplifying your laughter, or even forcing laughter entirely, you increase the impact of genuinely funny comments, and salvage some amusement from comments that would otherwise fall flat. You are essentially creating a laugh track for your conversation. Imagine by contrast someone who only laughs when something is so amusing that they cannot help it. That person fails to cooperate with producers of humor and fails to pull their affective weight in their social group.

Second, humor can strengthen social ties. Treger et al. (2013) show that humor and liking have a reciprocal relationship. People are humorous with those they like, and when people are humorous with you, it tends to make you like them. So we sometimes produce humor with the aim of demonstrating affection or friendliness. The problem, again, is that attempts to be humorous are not always successful. If you only laughed when a comment was genuinely amusing, you might appear to reject friendly overtures, and you would sometimes allow your friends to bomb. By laughing, even if you are not amused, you demonstrate that you appreciate the humorous overture, even if it was not actually funny, and you save the joke-teller from embarrassment. These first two functions of forced laughter can be combined. You might laugh both to make a conversation more entertaining and to express appreciation to the joke-teller.

Third, humor can be used to put other people down. McGraw and Warren say that one condition for a violation being seen as benign is if you do not consider the norm violation to be very serious. This can be the case with many different kinds of humor, such as racist or sexist humor, humor used to bully a socially isolated individual, and satirical humor aimed at a social or political opponent. In all of these cases, the humor producer lacks concern for the target of the humor, and therefore, is not constrained by norms that restrict aggression. This kind of humor has at least two roles. First, for those who lack concern for specific groups or individuals, jokes at their expense are amusing and therefore also entertaining. Second, the fact that the aggressor finds it amusing to put down a group or individual implies a lack of moral concern, so producing derogatory humor can be used to express that lack of concern. Insults are not only hurtful because of the content of the insult but also because of the implied attitude.

That said, insulting humor is not always abusive, and does not always express a malign attitude. Recall the case of two primates playfully fighting. An insult is a sort of attack, but if it is made in a genuinely playful manner there is no need to be offended. Nobody would agree to be roasted on television if they expected the insults to be malicious. McGraw and Warren's appeal to psychological distance applies to these cases. An insult is benign if everyone understands that it is not intended to do harm. Part of the appeal of offensive humor is to push the boundaries of psychological distance, to use the conventions of joke-telling to laugh at taboo subjects. At the same time, a dangerous feature of offensive humor is that bullies and trolls can take advantage of this ambiguity. They can make jokes that express true lack of concern while pretending that it is all just a joke.

With all that said, what is the role of forced laughter in response to insulting humor? We can distinguish two different cases. If you sympathize with the target of the humor, or are worried that the joke-teller has gone too far, you may pretend that it really was an innocent, harmless joke. This allows everyone to save face and avoid confrontation. However, another possibility is that you do not sympathize with the target. In that case, by laughing along you cooperate with the person who is making the joke. The aim of the joke-teller is to insult some target, so by forcing laughter you signal that you agree that the target of the insult is an appropriate target of abuse. Sending this signal is itself an aggressive act toward that target. I will explore this scenario in more detail in section 3.

I will raise one more category of forced laughter: laughter in the absence of humor. Provine (1993) carried out an ethological study of laughter and its relationship to speech. Several of his findings are striking: speakers laugh more often than their audiences. Laughter almost never interrupts an utterance—instead it serves as a sort of punctuation. There are a number of gender effects: male speakers elicit more audience laughter, and male speakers rarely laugh when speaking to a female audience. Perhaps the most puzzling observation is that only 10–20 percent of laughter followed remotely humorous comments (pp. 294–5). Typical examples of comments that elicit laughter included, "I'll see you guys later" and "It was nice meeting you too" (p. 294). Provine concludes that "There is only a partial correlation between the behavioral fact of laughter and the abstract and subjective category of humor. The focus on humor deflects consideration of broader and deeper roots of laughter in human vocal communication and social interaction" (p. 296).

If Provine is right then my attempt to explain forced laughter through the lens of humor is misguided, or at least severely limited. His data does certainly provide a challenge to my approach. However, divorcing laughter from humor does not resolve the issue. Why do we use laughter, of all things, to punctuate so many nonhumorous speech acts? It is hard to see how theories of humor apply to those cases, but it is also hard to explain the role of laughter in these cases without reference to humor. I will present my own explanation of these cases, based on my enactive theory of emotions, in section 7.

3. EMOTIONAL CONTENT, EXPRESSION, AND DECEPTION

Ideally a theory of amusement would mesh with a theory of the social functions of humor, both of those theories would mesh with a theory of forced laughter, and all of those theories would mesh with a general theory of emotions. So far, I have drawn connections between amusement, the social function of humor, and forced laughter. They do seem to mesh together so far, with the exception of Provine's cases. The next step is to integrate this mass of theories with theories of emotion. In this section, I will present some challenges for conventional emotion theories, before turning to my enactive theory in the remainder of the chapter.

On almost all theories of emotion, such as cognitivist and perceptual theories in philosophy and appraisal theories in psychology, emotions have some sort of representational content. Emotions represent some feature of the world as being a certain way for you: dangerous in the case of fear, beneficial in the case of joy, and so on. These theories differ in how they characterize these representations, but a wide range of theories take emotions to have representational content with a mind-to-world direction of fit. In fact, almost all prominent theories count as conventional by these standards. While they differ in many significant ways, almost all emotion theorists agree that fear of heights represents proximity to a steep descent as dangerous, and my fear is rational only if that is true.

These theories fit with either the benign violation theory or incongruity theory in a straightforward manner: the emotion of amusement represents its object as being a violation or incongruity, and the object does not elicit any emotions that are incompatible with amusement. The next question is how well those theories of emotion handle cases of forced laughter. I'll begin with the easiest cases, and move on to progressively greater challenges.

First, sometimes forced laughter is intended to deceive others about whether you are amused. You might pretend to laugh in order to reciprocate a friendly overture. If the humor producer believes you are amused they will be pleased and will have greater confidence in your social bond. If someone makes a joke that is insulting toward its target, you could either laugh to pretend that the joke was harmless, or to cooperate with the harmful intent of the joke-teller. All of these cases are perfectly compatible with conventional representational theories of emotion, because on these theories emotional expressions such as laughter are reliable, though not infallible, social signals. Through false laughter you pretend to have an emotional response that you do not in fact have.

Contagious laughter provides a moderate challenge. On conventional theories it is only rational to enter an emotional state under certain epistemic conditions. You should only be afraid when you have evidence of danger, or angry when you have evidence that you were wronged. This makes all cases of emotion-induction through physiological changes, such as manipulation of facial expression or emotion perception, problematic (Strack et al. 1988). Perhaps one could argue that perceiving someone else's fear expression is evidence for forming the corresponding judgment. When we perceive fear in others we have evidence of danger, and therefore rationally should enter a state of fear. However, this would be a very weak form of evidence, so these cases are hard to square with conventional theories. James (1922) and Lange (1922) long since observed that these cases are widespread, and it is familiar that a wide range of emotional expressions, not just laughter, are contagious. So the fact that forced laughter plays the role of inducing laughter in others is, if considered in isolation, problematic for conventional emotion theories. However, it is only one instance of a large, very familiar set of cases, so the marginal problem that contagious laughter presents is small.

The most challenging cases for conventional emotion theories are the ones where forced laughter plays a social role, but where deception or emotional contagion is not essential to that role. I'll discuss two examples, one featuring mockery, and the other featuring laughter punctuation. Conventional theories have a plausible explanation for the former, but not for the latter.

First, imagine that a bully, Brianna, is mocking her target, Taylor. Brianna's comment is insulting, but it is not amusing, even to Brianna and her friends. Brianna's ally Abigail forces laughter in response to Brianna's joke. Her laughter fools absolutely no one, as she knew it would, but it is a successful social move nonetheless. Brianna feels supported, and Taylor can tell that Brianna and Abigail are ganging up on her.

On conventional theories of emotion, laughter is an expression of amusement. Combined with the benign violation view, laughter expresses the view that the object of amusement is a benign violation. In this case, Abigail's laughter is obviously forced, and therefore everyone can tell that it is not actually an expression of amusement. However, by forcing laughter she endorses the joke. This sends the message she considers Brianna's mockery of Taylor to be benign, because she considers Taylor to be an appropriate target for aggression. If she had actually laughed spontaneously it would have expressed her judgment that the joke was a benign violation. Abigail uses forced laughter to deliberately send the message that spontaneous laughter would have expressed. Therefore, conventional theories of emotion can handle this sort of case.

In the second case, a few college students are chatting while waiting in line at a campus snack bar. They get their drinks and snacks, and then one says, "I'll see you guys later, ha ha." I'll use the term "laughter punctuation" for laughter that punctuates totally nonhumorous utterances, utterances that are not even intended to be amusing. Provine (1993) observed that this is a very common sort of laughter.

This case is challenging because there is not even a failed attempt at humor. In the mockery case I proposed that forced laughter deliberately sends the same message that spontaneous laughter would have expressed. This allows conventional theories of emotion to be relevant, since on those views laughter expresses amusement, and amusement has representational content. However, spontaneous laughter in this case would not have made sense. Therefore, a view of laughter as expressing some content does not shed any light on this case.

Provine (1993) suggests that we need an account of laughter that does not appeal to humor at all. Emotion theorists might ultimately need to bite that bullet. However, it would be preferable to integrate even these cases into a theory of humor which is itself integrated into a theory of emotion. It would be strange if the explanations of spontaneous amused laughter and forced laughter had nothing in common. In the remainder of the chapter, I will show that an enactive theory of emotion allows us to provide a unified explanation.

4. MOTORIC ENACTION

In the next two sections, I will introduce the enactive theory of emotions from Shargel and Prinz (2017). We did not apply our theory to amusement in that chapter, but I will go on to show that it is well suited to explaining both spontaneous amusement and various cases of forced laughter.

Imagine that you are swimming in the ocean, and you find yourself a little farther from shore than you intended. The undertow is a little stronger than you anticipated, and you are not sure you are a strong enough swimmer to make it to shore. What are the things you can do to make it back safely? How can you make that stretch of water more traversable? It would help if you could become a better swimmer by improving your technique. Unfortunately, it is a little late for that now. It would make a huge difference if you could acquire some equipment, like a flotation device, or maybe scuba gear. Unfortunately, none of that is available. You might survive if you were more fit, with bigger muscles and greater endurance, but you are stuck with your body as it is.

The only thing left to do is create a temporary change in your physiology that will make the water more traversable. You enter a state of fear. This is an enactive process that creates or modifies affordances. The affordance in this case is the traversability of that stretch of water. The physiological change that you undergo as part of that fear episode modifies that affordance. It modifies the traversability for you of that stretch of water.

We can think of an affordance as determined by three different sets of properties: the properties of the object itself that has the affordance, and the physiological and cognitive properties of the agent for whom it has the affordance.[4] My glass has the right structure and form to afford transferring water to my mouth, but for a baby it does not have that affordance. His fingers are too small, and muscles too weak, to manipulate an object so large and heavy. Transferring water to a smaller, lighter cup would not help, because he also lacks the perceptual and motoric properties that constitute the skill of drinking from a cup. Affordances require the concurrence of all three types of properties.

Successful action is sometimes opportunistic: we discover objects with affordances that further our goals. Hiking in the forest, I might find a fallen branch to use as a walking stick. However, many useful affordances need to be created, and we create affordances by manipulating properties that fall into the three sets mentioned above. First, we may acquire or create objects with the right properties. If I am cooking soup, I need to buy the ingredients, bring them home to my conveniently arranged kitchen, and wash and chop them before adding them to the pot. Second, I may need to develop my skills to create the right affordances. As I learn to cook, I gain theoretical knowledge about culinary techniques, and I also acquire the motoric abilities to apply them. A knife that once afforded uneven chopping may now afford precise dicing.

Third, and most important for this chapter, I may modify my body to create new affordances. These modifications come in two forms: I can create lasting changes in affordances by improving my conditioning or flexibility, or create temporary changes by initiating a specific autonomic or somatic state. Both lasting and temporary bodily changes often alter affordances by degrees. After a few months of working out, you may be able to pick up a box that previously would have been very difficult or even dangerous for you. You have increased the liftability of the box. Similarly, you can make a box more liftable through an autonomic or somatic change that deploys bodily resources appropriately. Merely deploying those resources expends energy. However, we save energy by (ideally) deploying just enough of our resources to create adequate affordances for the task at hand, and only for long enough to complete that task.

These temporary autonomic and somatic changes are, of course, features of emotional episodes, and the systems that deploy them operate largely outside of our conscious control. During an episode of fear our heart rate, and blood pressure all enter a modified state that facilitates great cardiac, respiratory, and muscular exertion (Kriebig 2010). If you are swimming in the ocean and feel a strong undertow, these bodily changes increase the waves' affordances for swimming back to shore. There are other ways to control those affordances. However, when you are already swimming far from shore and you feel a dangerously strong undertow, it is too late for those measures. You will make due with the affordances that you find, or an involuntary fear response will improve those affordances through a temporary bodily change.

We also undergo generic changes in our motivations that are integrated with these physiological changes, and that are appropriate and compatible with these changes (Shargel 2017). When we are angry, we are physiologically prepared to take aggressive action, and we are also motivationally prepared to do so. We are motivated to do just what we are physiologically prepared to do, because we can temporarily do them more effectively and efficiently than usual. This explains why physiological manipulation can create or modify an emotional state. It is inefficient for our motivations to fall out of step with our physiological action-readiness, so changes in our physiological action-readiness need to influence our motivations. Our physiology creates and modifies affordances, and generic motivations help us capitalize on them.

5. SOCIAL ENACTION

My analysis in the preceding section focused on somatic and autonomic changes that directly influence the efficacy and efficiency of action, as well as compatible motivations. This leaves out some of the most conspicuous features of emotional embodiment: facial expression, vocal inflection, and body language.

Our approach to the publicly observable features of emotional embodiment builds on Paul Griffiths and Andrea Scarantino's (2009) situated theory of emotions. They cite a wide range of empirical evidence that contradicts conventional representational models of emotion. For example, we do not smile in response to beneficial events—we smile in response to publicly observed beneficial events (Fernandez-Dols and Ruiz-Belda 1997). Birds often display anger before fleeing, rather than attacking (Hinde 1985). These cases would be puzzling if emotional displays were merely effects or adjuncts of representational states. Why do we not always smile when we are happy? Why display anger if you are on the brink of retreat? Griffiths and Scarantino (2005) conclude that "Emotional content has a fundamentally pragmatic dimension, in the sense that the environment is represented in terms of what it affords to the emoter in the way of skillful engagement with it" (p. 8).

The skillful engagement that they have in mind is engagement in social transactions. A victorious smile engages others in our success, encouraging them to see us as an appealing partner in future projects. An angry glare (human or avian) deters others from crossing us, or demands that others address our concerns. Misdirected or ill-timed smiles and glares can lead to trouble—hence, the need for skillful engagement.

Given the examples they discuss, it is puzzling that Griffiths and Scarantino say that emotions represent affordances. Skillful emotional displays advance social transactions in beneficial directions. In doing so, they create or modify, rather than represent, social affordances. An effective smile turns a bystander into an ally; an effective glare turns a threat into a bystander. Emotional displays, like autonomic or somatic states, create affordances, but the affordances that they create are grounded in complex features of social reality.

Earlier in this chapter, I identified three kinds of properties that determine affordances: the properties of an external object, and the physiological structure and skills of an agent. Emotions alter motoric affordances by temporarily changing one's physiological structure. We can treat external social structures as the external object with regard to social enaction. Different social structures afford different types of social moves, and those moves will depend on our resources and skills. However, it is a familiar feature of game theory that the decisions of one agent are determined in part by the anticipated choices of other agents. It follows that an agent can alter social structures and create social affordances, by credibly indicating a disposition to act in a certain way.

I have already discussed how features of anger such as autonomic arousal improve affordances for addressing offenses. In addition, the social displays characteristic of anger send a visible and audible sign to other agents that one has improved affordances in this way. Our motivations change in sync with our affordances, so other agents also have reason to believe that the angry individual has a greater motivation to act aggressively. This public display will serve as a warning to others to avoid confronting the angry individual, and may lead others to make concessive moves. Anger may, of course, have the opposite effect and motivate greater opposition. However, there is a clear mechanism for social displays, operating in harmony with the bodily systems responsible for motoric enaction, to produce social enaction.

6. NORMATIVE DISARMAMENT

I have presented an abbreviated account of an enactive theory of emotions, including the enaction of social affordances. How might this account apply to humor and amusement? My view is that amusement induces a state of normative disarmament. Strohminger et al. (2011) provide evidence that mirth (their term for amusement) increases our tolerance for violation of deontological rules. When we are in a state of amusement, we're temporarily disposed not to take things so seriously. We're not inclined to take our own problems seriously, or to take other people's violations of mild social norms seriously.

If someone does something mildly inappropriate when we are in a state of amusement, we are less likely to be offended and more likely to be amused.

It makes sense that amusement would have this motivational effect, since it is equivalent to the motivational features of other types of emotional episodes. During an episode of fear, we are disposed to see ambiguous objects as dangerous, during episodes of disgust we are disposed to see them as revolting, and so on. In general, occurrent emotions bias us to respond to ambiguous objects in a way that accords with that emotion, rather than in a way that accords with incompatible emotions. Norm violations can be amusing, but they can also be threatening or offensive. During an occurrent episode of amusement, we tend to perceive norm violations as amusing rather than the alternatives.[5]

It follows that amusement will modify social affordances. Expressions of amusement display to others that we are in a state of normative disarmament. We're not currently prepared to retaliate against mild norm violations, because we will find them pleasing rather than threatening or offensive. That is an invitation for others to violate minor norms, to be a little bit silly, since we are currently disposed to reward silly behavior.

Why should we ever enter a state of normative disarmament? First, policing social norms in a rigorous way is important, but it can also be difficult, dangerous, and expensive. It is not always necessary to take a rigorous approach, since we often spend time with people that we trust, who we don't expect to violate serious norms. It makes sense, under appropriate conditions, to enter an episode where we can give each other permission to be a little bit less proper and take mild violations of norms less seriously.

It is best to police norms cooperatively rather than individually, since, again, policing norms can be difficult, dangerous, and expensive. Normative disarmament among individuals, just like military disarmament among states, is best undertaken in a coordinated way. When others we trust enter a state of normative disarmament, it makes sense to do likewise. Contagious laughter is a mechanism that coordinates our normative disarmament.

Second, normative disarmament allows for exploration of the boundaries of norms. This is particularly useful for children. Small children need to learn about the rules that govern their society. By learning what is silly under safe conditions, they learn what is normally forbidden or discouraged. Potty humor becomes very amusing as small children take greater responsibility for their personal hygiene, and insulting humor takes hold as they are expected to participate in more cooperative and prosocial behavior.

Third, it is also possible for a group to use the license derived from collective amusement to attack outsiders. Trust allows us to let down our guard and be amused together, because we trust each other not to abuse the license granted by normative disarmament. However, that trust does not extend to the protection of those beyond the group, particularly those whose interests are beyond the concern of the members of the group. In fact, under normative disarmament the group may take pleasure in doing harm to unprotected outsiders, since group members are amused by violations of the relatively weak norms that restrict harm to outsiders. This can take the form of bullying marginalized groups and individuals, but it is also the mechanism underlying satire, which can be used to unite opposition to the powerful.

To summarize, emotions modify social affordances by credibly displaying to others what we are currently prepared to do. During an episode of amusement, we are prepared to welcome benign violations rather than punish them. Credibly displaying that we are in this mode encourages others to join us in our normative disarmament. The affordances produced by this shared normative disarmament allow for friendly recreation, for playful exploration, and even for coordinating a group against outsiders.

It may seem contradictory that the social enaction account of amusement appeals to the benign violations theory. After all, according to the enactive theory of emotion, emotions do not have representational content (Shargel and Prinz 2017). Their content is strictly enactive, constituted by the creation of affordances. The benign violations theory says that emotions represent benign violations. How can one make use of the benign violations theory without accepting a conventional theory of emotion?

A full response to this challenge can be found in Shargel (2017) and Shargel and Prinz (2017). In brief, an enactive theory of emotion can accept that representations of benign violations are one possible method for eliciting amusement, just as representations of loss are one possible method for eliciting sadness. However, the fact that representations can play that role does not mean that the emotions that they elicit have representational content. In fact, in the context of this chapter, it is not important to argue that emotions lack representational content. The thesis is that in order to explain the full range of forced laughter, we need to accept that emotions do have enactive content. I will make that argument in the next section.

7. ENACTIVE FORCED LAUGHTER

In section 3, I described a range of cases of forced laughter and discussed how conventional emotion theories might address them. I'll now return to the same cases and argue that my enactive account is able to illuminate even the most challenging cases.

In the first class of cases, forced laughter deceives its audience into thinking that the laughter is spontaneous. These cases include responding encouragingly to a not-so-funny joke made by a friend and cooperating with the mockery of an outsider. Conventional theories had no trouble explaining these cases, and the enactive theory does not either. Spontaneous laughter is a sign of amusement, which in my view implies normative disarmament. Displaying that you are in a state of normative disarmament creates social affordances in the ways described in section 6. Deceptive forced laughter creates all of the same social affordances, so it can be an effective way to manipulate your social environment.

The second class of cases is those that rely on emotional contagion. This phenomenon is difficult to explain within a conventional emotion theory because conventional theories take emotions to essentially feature judgments or perceptions, and it is irrational to adopt whatever judgments your peers express. The enactive theory has an elegant explanation of these cases which I briefly discussed in section 6. Emotions prepare us to act by creating useful affordances. Cooperative action is generally more effective, so it is rational to coordinate action-preparation with your peers. Contagious laughter fits within this general account of emotion contagion. Amusement specifically is a state of normative disarmament. There are significant benefits to disarming among those we trust when they do likewise. Therefore, it makes sense to enter a state of amusement when others are amused too. Through forced laughter we help create normative disarmament in others even when we are not amused ourselves, or when we are amused but not enough to laugh spontaneously.

Finally, I'll turn to the most challenging cases. These are the cases where laughter is not contagious, and nobody is deceived about whether it expresses amusement. In the first of these cases, Brianna is bullying Taylor, and Abigail laughs at her unfunny joke. In the second, a friend punctuates an ordinary, entirely nonhumorous utterance with forced laughter.

The enactive theory can appeal to the role that normative disarmament plays in uniting a group against an outsider. When we are amused, we may tolerate or even welcome the violation of weakly held norms, such as the norms that protect strangers and outsiders. Brianna takes advantage of this effect to mock Taylor. When Abigail forces laughter it signals that she wishes to maintain normative disarmament, which is the basis of Brianna's mockery, even if the joke itself was not funny. If Abigail instead defended Taylor, it would undermine their cooperative normative disarmament. It would imply that the norms defending outsiders like Taylor should be enforced.

Turning to the second case, it helps to recall again that we more often would like to say something funny than we actually have something funny to say. The enactive account of emotions, combined with the normative disarmament theory of humor, explain why it is so often valuable to be amusing. Of course, we enjoy being amused, but there are also more subtle social benefits. When we are spending time with friends it is helpful to enter a social dynamic where each individual would tolerate and even welcome mild norm violations, and where everyone knows that everyone else would do so as well. This helps us enjoy our time together and become more intimate.

The question then becomes: how can we coordinate this mutual normative disarmament? One strategy is to be really funny, frequently provoking amusement and perhaps even spontaneous laughter. That is a perfectly good strategy to pursue, but it cannot be the only strategy, because most of us are not funny enough. An alternative strategy is to punctuate your speech with a signal that the group should normatively disarm. Forced laughter is that signal. This does not work as well as being funny, because the signal will not itself cause others to disarm. However, it can still be effective if others understand your signal and wish to cooperate.

One might object that this strategy should not work. After all, according to the enactive theory I presented, emotional expressions create social affordances because they are reliably integrated with episodic changes in motivational and physiological action-readiness. Spontaneous laughter is integrated with one's own normative disarmament, so it induces normative disarmament in others too. Forced laughter is not integrated in that way, so it should not be able to create the same social affordances. Emotional enaction does not work when there is no emotion involved.

However, expressing an emotion is not the only thing that can create social affordances. Any communicative act can do so. Any form of communication potentially creates a social affordance. The problem is not explaining how forced laughter could create affordances. The problem is explaining what exactly forced laughter communicates, and how this relates to the enactive qualities of spontaneous laughter.

There is something strange about using forced laughter in a nonhumorous context. The speaker said something that was not funny at all, and then laughed for (apparently) no good reason. If the audience responds with stony silence then the speaker really does look ridiculous. However, the speaker is not trying to trick anyone with this forced laughter. She is just inviting the audience to cooperate in changing the rules of their normative engagement. Specifically, the speaker is suggesting that they deliberately adopt the normative mode that is automatically produced through shared amusement. Given this message it is natural that forced laughter would serve as the signal.

We can now see how the enactive account of amusement informs the explanation of laughter punctuation. This sort of forced laughter, which clearly does not express amusement, may seem entirely unrelated to humor. However, according to the enactive account, humor has the effect of inducing a state of normative disarmament, and spontaneous laughter helps coordinate normative disarmament through its contagious effects. We often wish to enter a state of mutual normative disarmament, even when nobody is amused. We wish to create just those affordances that humor has the power to create.

Forced laughter serves as an invitation to join the laugher in deliberately creating those affordances.

I'll raise one more objection to this view: does this interpretation imply that the folk already understand and endorse the enactive view of humor? After all, I claim that laughter punctuation is an invitation to cooperate in creating a set of social affordances. Approximately no one has the necessary concepts to either make or accept that invitation. Does that mean that forced laughter cannot serve that role?

Fortunately, there is a less technical, and functionally equivalent, way to analyze laughter punctuation. The speaker laughs, inviting the audience to play along. Playing along means acting as if you were amused, even if you are not. By playing along you are creating a state of mutual normative disarmament, even if you lack the concept "normative disarmament." The enactive theory of humor provides an explanation of what playing along amounts to in this sort of case, and why it is valuable.

I have argued that forced laughter complicates our understanding of amusement in a productive way. If you approach amusement from the perspective of conventional theories of emotion it is natural to think of amusement as an emotional state with representational content, and laughter as a public expression of that content. However, forced laughter is pervasive and diverse, and it demands explanation. In particular, forced laughter frequently occurs in the absence of anything humorous, and those cases resist assimilation into conventional theories of emotion and emotional expression. In all of these cases, why do we laugh? Why not cough, blink, say "um," or do nothing at all? The enactive theory of emotion provides us with a unified account of amusement that is well suited to explain even the most challenging cases of forced laughter.

NOTES

1. Deliberately offensive humor may seem to contradict this claim. However, the notion of psychological distance, which I introduce below, helps explain how offensive jokes seem benign to those who find them amusing.

2. In this case psychological distance is achieved by priming for physical distance, but elsewhere the authors propose that hypothetical events would also seem distant. This does raise the question of whether psychological distance is sufficiently well defined.

3. This view does not fit as neatly with cases where someone forces laughter after their own remark. In section 7, I will present a more detailed view which applies to these cases.

4. The concept of affordances in the enactive theory of emotions deviates from Gibson's (1979) original usage. For a comparison see Shargel and Prinz (2017).

5. That may sound like an endorsement of a perceptual theory of emotion. It is in fact a feature of our enactive theory that emotions bias perceptions. However, that is because emotions are identified with integrated physiological states, generic motivational states, and social displays, and the generic motivational states bias perception.

REFERENCES

Carroll, N. (2013). Comic amusement, emotion, and cognition. In J. Deigh (Ed.), *On emotions: Philosophical essays* (pp. 76–98). New York: Oxford University Press.

Fernandez- Dols, J. M., & Ruiz- Belda, M. A. (1997). Spontaneous facial behavior during intense emotional episodes: Artistic truth and optical truth. In J. A. Russell & J. M. Fernandez- Dols (Eds.), *The psychology of facial expression* (pp. 255–274). New York: Cambridge University Press.

Gibson, J. J. (1979). *The ecological approach to visual perception.* Boston: Houghton Mifflin.

Griffiths, P. E., & Scarantino, A. (2009). Emotions in the wild: The situated perspective on emotion. In P. Robbins & M. Aydede (Eds.), *Cambridge handbook of situated cognition* (pp. 437–453). New York: Cambridge University Press.

Hinde, R. A. (1985). Expression and Negotiation. In G. Zivin (Ed.), *The Development of Expressive Behavior* (pp. 103–116). New York: Academic Press.

James, W. (1922). What is an emotion? In K. Dunlap (Ed.), *The Emotions* (pp. 11–30). Baltimore: Waverly Press.

Kreibig, S. D. (2010). Autonomic nervous system activity in emotion: A review. *Biological psychology, 84*(3), 394–421.

Lange, C. G. (1922). The emotions. In K. Dunlap (Ed.), *The Emotions* (pp. 33–90). Baltimore: Waverly Press.

McGraw, A. P., & Warren, C. (2010). Benign violations: Making immoral behavior funny. *Psychological Science, 21*(8), 1141–1149.

Provine, R. R. (1992). Contagious laughter: Laughter is a sufficient stimulus for laughs and smiles. *Bulletin of the Psychonomic Society, 30*(1), 1–4.

Provine, R. R. (1993). Laughter punctuates speech: Linguistic, social and gender contexts of laughter. *Ethology, 95*(4), 291–298.

Shargel, D. (2017). Appraisals, emotions, and inherited intentional objects. *Emotion Review 9*(1), 46–54.

Shargel, D., & Prinz, J. (2017). An enactivist theory of emotional content. In H. Naar & F. Teroni (Eds.), *The ontology of emotions* (pp. 110–129), Cambridge: Cambridge University Press.

Strack, F., Martin, L.L., & Stepper, S. (1988). Inhibiting and facilitating conditions of the human smile: A nonobtrusive test of the facial feedback hypothesis. *Journal of Personality and Social Psychology, 54*(5), 768–777.

Strohminger, N., Lewis, R. L., & Meyer, D. E. (2011). Divergent effects of different positive emotions on moral judgment. *Cognition, 119*(2), 295–300.

Treger, S., Sprecher, S., & Erber, R. (2013). Laughing and liking: Exploring the interpersonal effects of humor use in initial social interactions. *European Journal of Social Psychology, 43*(6), 532–543.

Chapter 2

An Interactional Sociolinguist Engages the Moral Psychology of Amusement

Catherine Evans Davies

This chapter offers an interactional sociolinguist's perspective on the moral psychology of amusement, which means that I am considering the topic as a scholar whose research is based in ethnography. As a linguist, I don't typically think of my work in terms of philosophy, although I am aware of potential implications from various perspectives. In particular, sociolinguists use ethical guidelines when we do our research, and our theorizing has to take into account the moral judgments that speakers make about dialects (e.g., "good English"). In terms of psychology, I am concerned with identity, and in this chapter, I use a psychological framework for analyzing the sense of humor as a dimension of enacted identity. I am intentionally sidestepping what I consider an annoying debate in the study of humor concerning whether there is some core moral or ethical orientation attaching to humor as a human interactional phenomenon. I hope to offer something of interest to the study of the moral psychology of amusement with an unusual and unorthodox kind of empirical data that attempts to track how an individual sense of humor is enacted. This is the core of the chapter. The individual sense of humor is located both within a personal ethical stance and also within a psychological framework that uses the terms "mal/adaptive" with a clear moral orientation. This ethnographic analysis, which considers the ethically informed psychology of an individual in relationship to others, is then expanded to consider metadiscoursal manipulation of the joking frame, that is, how speakers can maneuver ambiguously to avoid responsibility for a statement by claiming that it was "just joking." I then expand further to a broader sociocultural perspective on changing social norms for what is considered suitable for amusement, and reactions to those norms, which are often framed in both psychological and philosophical terms. Drawing back to the personal in a situated psychological and ethical context, I conclude with a consideration of the dilemmas of response when an individual is confronted with violations of current social norms, and finally with a linguist's reflection on the etymology of the word "amusement." I hope that the sections of the chapter create a logical progression for the reader.

AN INDIVIDUAL SENSE OF HUMOR

I begin in a very personal way, with a brief sketch of the moral psychology of my own sense of humor, based on a recent autoethnographic study. To read the entire study, please see C. E. Davies (2019); for this chapter, I attempted to draw out the most relevant points in relation to moral psychology. Previous empirical data on the sense of humor has been drawn from a range of approaches, including humor appreciation measures (e.g., rating perceived funniness of jokes, cartoons, or other humorous material in a laboratory setting), ability tests (e.g., creating humorous monologues or cartoon punch-lines, which are then rated by trained judges for the degree of funniness), behavioral observation techniques (e.g., using trained observers well acquainted with an individual's behavior patterns to sort statements concerning humor-related everyday behaviors into nine piles from least to most characteristic) and self-report scales (e.g., assessing brief descriptions of situations in terms of potential for humorous response, or characterizing oneself in terms of a range of humorous behaviors) (Ruch 1998, Martin 2003). Sociolinguists have traditionally been cautious about self-report data because people may orient to norms and often honestly don't realize what they actually say (Dollinger 2012). There have been a few diary studies (e.g., Kambouropoulou 1926, in which college students were asked to make notes on when they laughed with a brief description of the circumstances), but nothing that attempted to document the enactment of a sense of humor with interpretation by the individual involved. The emerging approach known as "autoethnography" (Chang 2007, Ellis et al 2011) seemed to offer an opportunity to try this. My extensive experience as an interactional sociolinguist doing discourse analysis involving playback techniques (in which speakers are recorded in interaction and then asked to listen/watch and reflect on their intentions and interpretations) (e.g., C. E. Davies 2005, 2015, 2018) prepared me to attempt to study my own behavior. Ethical considerations of recording my everyday life, to say nothing of the impossibility of sorting out IRB complexities (e.g., how in the world would I get informed consent to audio record from a grocery clerk before I went through her line?), dictated that I would have to keep a notebook with me at all times and make immediate notes on interactions with my intents and interpretations. This was very challenging because auditory memory is typically quite short; the circumstances of my life during the span of months when I gathered the data fortunately helped with this, because almost all of the data were from brief interactions. In one case, a long weekend with some female friends, I was able to get informed consent in advance. This allowed me to make a lengthy audio recording that included more extensive humorous interaction with which we amused ourselves. I was focused on my own sense of humor, so I was not investigating what others intended in interacting with me, but rather with my own intentions in initiating humor and my own interpretations of what others intended in their initiations or responses. I realize that this is a fraught area, because I may be unaware of certain aspects of my own motivations and also may tend to interpret what I do through the lens of my own ethical and psychological self-image.

I began the study with a general idea about my sense of humor, an idea that had a strong ethical component, but I was prepared to discover that I was wrong, based on the data that I could collect. As I was growing up, humor (as joking directed at me and also in the form of humorous stories with a point) was used as criticism of me and others. I grew up without any brothers, so I never learned how to do the typically male "ritual insult joking" that can build solidarity if you know the rules (e.g., Labov 1972). In reading the scholarly literature on this form of joking, I learned that each player has to know the other joker well enough to know what is acceptable as an insult and what is out of bounds because it is actually hurtful. Since learning about the practice, I have actually tried to do it and quickly realized that it's too risky for me. Because I didn't know how to play the ritual insult game, I experienced "teasing" as a form of joking that was hurtful. I suspect that these experiences shaped my ethical stance that I would never knowingly use humor to hurt another person. This was my idea about the ethical dimension of my own sense of humor as I embarked on the project.

Referring to Ruch's (1998) historical overview of conceptualization of sense of humor, Martin (2003) notes that the earlier formulation in terms of psychological well-being has been obscured during the past century as the term "humor" has been expanded to cover both adaptive and maladaptive forms. He has returned to the link between particular humor styles and healthy psychological functioning as part of a trend in the field framed as "positive psychology." Martin proposes four main dimensions of humor expression. The two adaptive or healthy ones are (1) affiliative, defined as amusing others and promoting social cohesion, and (2) self-enhancing, defined as "perspective-taking" and using humor to cope with difficult circumstances. The two maladaptive or unhealthy ones are (3) aggressive, defined as the use of sarcasm and the general attempt to ridicule or manipulate others, and (4) self-defeating, defined as avoidance, denial, or excessive self-disparagement. One of Martin's key points is that psychological health is contingent on not only the presence of the healthy styles but also the absence of the unhealthy ones. There is a clear moral dimension here, in terms of good psychological health (which inevitably also has a cultural dimension).

Given my assumptions about my sense of humor, I expected to find that my data revealed exclusively "adaptive" strategies. That is, in fact, what I found, as the following examples of "affiliative" and "self-enhancing" humor expression will show.

Affiliative (defined as amusing others and promoting social cohesion)

I was waiting to check out at a local grocery store and I heard the female checker talking about an accident that had just occurred with a pickle jar. She was clearly upset and I interpreted her behavior as indicating that she was feeling as if she had failed to live up to her high standards of performance in the job, even though it sounded as if it was a faulty jar rather than anything that she had done wrong.

1. Me: Did a jar break?
2. Female Checker: Yes. It was a pickle jar. I picked it up to scan it and it broke in my hand. That's never happened to me before. We had pickle juice all over the scanner.
3. Me: (deadpan, with exaggerated muscle-man gesture of my arms) Well, obviously you just don't know your own strength.
4. Female Checker: (some indication of laughter) Yeah, I've GOT to stop working out so much.

In terms of my perspective as the joker, I think that I might not have entered into interaction if it hadn't been clear to me that the checker was upset about the incident and was interpreting the event as somehow a blot on her performance in her job as checker. Thus, it was clear to me that this was about her sense of identity as a good checker (and that's something that I can admire and identify with, that is, taking pride in good performance even in a job that is low on the status hierarchy). I asked for more detail about the event because it would have felt uncaring to not engage her about something that seemed important to her as she was turning to my set of items to check. My question to her intentionally used the verb "break" in a way that removed her as agent; it was the jar that broke. I realize that this could seem unbelievable, as too self-reflective in the moment. On the other hand, I'm a linguist and I engage my students on ways that language can be used strategically to remove responsibility, such as the passive voice. I also use "break" as an example of a verb that can be used in transitive (I broke the jar) and intransitive ways (The jar broke). Given my conscious motivation in the moment, it seems reasonable to me that I intuitively used that construction, based on my interactional intention. On the other hand, the moment I wrote it down and reflected on it, my analytical awareness also entered in.

In the checker's response in 2, she affirmed the proposition of my question and then elaborated in a way that repeated the intransitive use of the verb "broke." Then she supplied additional information that included the agentless verb "happen" with herself ("to me") as the victim, in a sense, given the negative affect surrounding the event. This choice of verb extends the linguistic framing that the breakage was not her fault. Then she described the result of the breakage, again with a linguistic construction "We had . . . " that did not ascribe responsibility, in contrast with something like "I got pickle juice all over the scanner." This was clearly a serious nuisance for a checker, which had to be cleaned up before she could get on with her job.

Once she had answered my question, I felt that I needed to respond in some way. I could have chosen an expression of sympathy, like "What a hassle," or "I'm sorry that you had to deal with that." In the moment, however, it felt as if that sort of response wouldn't address the identity issue in a way that felt acceptable to me. I should note that I was not consciously aware at the time whether her gender was a factor; it might have been important that she was a fellow woman, but I can imagine myself responding similarly to a man acting in this way. What I decided to do was to joke in a very obvious deadpan that would reframe the situation to recast her identity in a positive way, that is, as a strong and fit woman who doesn't even realize how strong she is. I did not smile when I produced utterance 3, but I made an exaggerated and very stereotypically masculine gesture of flexing my biceps. My use of "obviously" in utterance 3 was part of the deadpan in that I was trying to claim this reframing as the natural interpretation of the event, but with a woman checker. I was also playing with gender stereotypes, assuming that she would know that I believed that even if women work out with weights, they are not trying to build big biceps. What I was trying to do was to lighten up the situation for her and reframe it in a positive way that probably wouldn't have occurred to her. The concept of "not knowing one's own strength" is a potentially positive aspect of identity, implying that one has hidden strengths, whether muscular or in terms of character.

I took her response in 4 as a clear indication that she (1) appreciated the humor by means of the laugh particles, (2) affirmed that she understood the reframing, potentially by means of uttering the 'yeah' affirmation, and (3) further conveyed that she understood what I was doing by playing within the new frame that I had offered. She took on the identity of a woman who works out so much that she doesn't even know her own strength, and jokingly commiserated with me about her situation in 4. It has been pointed out to me that her final utterance could also be interpreted as a sardonic comment on her own professional identity, as her job might not have allowed her the time or flexibility to "work out." This seems like a reasonable interpretation to me, but it didn't occur to me in the moment or upon reflection. Many people belong to fitness centers, and those fitness centers are open for extended hours.

I came away from this joking interaction feeling proud of myself for having been able to respond in that way, and feeling happy that the checker had understood and joined me in the humorous identity reframing.

Self-enhancing (defined as "perspective-taking" and using humor to cope with difficult circumstances)

This second example is drawn from my private humor expression. When I began this autoethnographic project in the form of a diary study, it did not occur to me that individual sense of humor could also be enacted privately or perhaps "intrapersonally." My interactional sociolinguistic orientation predisposed me to see identity as enacted and coconstructed in discourse, and of course, this was the kind of joking interaction that I had studied in the past. As I paid close attention to what I experienced as my sense of humor in my life in an ongoing way, I began to notice a range of private experiences. I have since learned that psychology refers to this phenomenon as "intrapsychic" (Pieper and Pieper 1990). One area where I found lots of examples was my daily written journal. I have spent some time in the early morning each day keeping a journal as a mental health exercise for most of my life, in which I reflect on events, work through issues, set priorities, and at a very mundane level plan my day. As part of the autoethnography I noticed that I was finding humor in my own thoughts about myself in the world as I wrote this journal. When I realized that I was writing "HAHA," I used the Word search function to find examples within the time period of the diary study.

I was writing about the skin cancer surgery on my nose (the "good" kind of skin cancer that is unlikely to spread) and the wound care afterward that I was finding very difficult to handle. The background to this entry was that I had had to wear a large bandage for the first two weeks that covered my whole nose. "I just changed the bandage on my nose and I THINK that it looks like it's healing nicely. More 'ooze' on Thursday, just a tiny bit today. I'm getting better at this, I think. HAHA." The dark humor here had to do with the frightening idea of skin cancer, especially on such a visible part of my identity as my nose. I was also playing with the idea that I was supposed to make medical judgments, in the identity as patient, without any expertise. This can be seen in the capitalized THINK and in the reference to the colloquial term "ooze" that is actually quoted (from the doctor/nurse). But the humor was focused on the final sentence before the "HAHA," in which I was pitifully trying to affirm my identity as capable nurse to myself on my own wounds, something in which I definitely did not want to develop expertise. The identity that I was concerned with here was the frightened but brave patient who was doing her best at something that she did not want to do now and did not want to have to do ever again. This was the strongest example in my data of what Freud (1928) was talking about with his designation of humor as a healthy defense mechanism (in his terms, in which the superego speaks words of comfort to the frightened ego).

In addition to my own enactment of humor, I also find amusement in humor that is different from my own style. This is where I enjoy "maladaptive" humor, in the form of satire and jokes directed at political figures with whom I disagree. I don't produce this humor myself, however, or even typically repeat such jokes. The humor is maladaptive in that it is directed in a critical way at another person, but it could be argued that it is "adaptive" for me in terms of my own mental health. It seems to be a way of working against a feeling of powerlessness as a citizen. As expected, I did not find any maladaptive humor in my data (although there was one interaction that was not intended as maladaptive, but may have had some sort of maladaptive consequence; I refer you to the complete study for a description and analysis). I was actually surprised that my notes didn't include my amusement at political humor, but in retrospect I realize that the data-gathering was done during a time when I was comfortable with the political administration, and when there was a hiatus of satirical political programs that I typically enjoy.

METADISCOURSAL MANIPULATION USING "I WAS JUST JOKING"

Every individual of course operates in a social world and thus is forced to deal with a range of styles of sense of humor and material presented as "amusing." This situation inevitably poses both ethical and moral dilemmas. The humor frame itself can be manipulated to create ambiguity and confusion in terms of the message. In particular, the claim that "I was just joking" can be used to both enact and then deny messages conveyed through the maladaptive, unhealthy "aggressive" style, defined as the use of sarcasm and the general attempt to ridicule or manipulate others.

In terms of a theoretical perspective on the "just/only joking" strategy, we start with Bateson (1972, 177–193) and the metacommunicative function of what Bateson identified as the message "This is play" in his classic study of the otters in the San Francisco Zoo. In other words, the message that appears to be conveyed (i.e., "I am fighting with you" in the case of the otters) is vitiated by the metamessage that "this is play." For human communicators, there is the verbal utterance and a nonverbal metamessage signaling that the utterance is not to be taken seriously. If all goes as the speaker intended, the interlocutor will respond immediately with laughter or other typical uptake.

If all does not go well, however, a possible next move is for the speaker to claim that he/she was joking or "only joking." In American English, this is a classic interpersonal move for plausible deniability, including a mimimizer, either "only" or the nicely alliterative "just." A synonymous, but perhaps slightly more informal version of the expression is "just/only kidding," Skalicky, Berger, and Bell (2015, 23) found that "the most common function of 'just kidding' (in American English) was to inoculate the speaker against any negative reaction that they anticipate following humor that might be seen as unfunny, inappropriate, or offensive." I think it is important here to note that this is what the speaker "anticipates," which allows for even less timelag between the utterance and the disclaimer. In the prototypical face-to-face situation, the speaker is closely monitoring the response and can act immediately with the joking response if the interlocutor isn't responding as expected.

The most benign situation here would be one in which the joker is trying to engage in ritual insult joking (as discussed above) and suddenly realizes either that the utterance was inappropriate or that the addressee wasn't playing the game. The least benign situation is one in which the speaker is intentionally using an aggressive style, knowing that responsibility for the hurtful message can be shirked. The "just joking" move confronts the addressee with an ethical dilemma having to do with interpersonal expectations and a sense of identity. At the most basic level, not accepting the move puts the addressee in the awkward position of the participant who disrupts the flow of interaction. Appearing to be amused and go along with the joke, even if the utterance was hurtful, allows the addressee to claim the identity of "a good sport," an identity that is highly prized in American society. At the same time, however, the utterance has introduced the hurtful idea into the discourse; going along with the "just joking" move appears to accept it, with implications for identity and self-esteem. On the other hand, refusing to accept the move and showing offense not only reveals sensitivities but also displays oneself as "somebody who can't take a joke," an undesirable persona in American society. It also matters how many people are present for the interaction; if more than two people are present (beyond the joker and the addressee), then the potential interpretations of the wider audience may be relevant to either or both the joker and the addressee. Sinkeviciute (2017) found that in the Australian/British reactions to such joking there was the notion of the "preferred reaction" in a particular cultural context, and that interviewees made different judgments in relation to public and private perspectives. In other words, they might react as a "good sport" in the public moment when they actually felt hurt or offended. For an analysis of the "just joking" strategy used in American political discourse to convey different messages simultaneously to supporters and opponents, see C. E. Davies 2020.

CHANGING NORMS ON WHAT IS SUITABLE FOR AMUSEMENT

The social world also confronts the individual with ethical and moral challenges concerning the basis for "amusement." Just as we no longer find public executions to be a form of entertainment (although we may accept the fictional equivalent in movies), norms have changed concerning the targets of humor. J. C. H. (Christie) Davies (1982) offered a macrosociological analysis of the content and targets of ethnic jokes in democratic Western industrial societies such as the United States, where waves of immigrants have arrived and become part of the structure. New arrivals are often at the bottom of the social hierarchy if they lack the linguistic and job skills to compete for desirable jobs. The lack of particular expertise, along with the inability to speak English, is often misinterpreted (especially by monolingual English speakers) as a lack of intelligence. In a society with an ideology of upward mobility for anyone who tries hard enough, it becomes easy to target the new arrivals. Davies found that characters in the jokes that were popular among the middle class tended to be "stupid" or "canny" (clever, crafty, calculating, stingy). His analysis was that middle-class people, who had been successful within the social organization, used jokes to project their negative stereotypes and prejudices either toward groups that were lower on the social hierarchy or toward groups that were "Other" but had somehow managed to succeed in the society. The "stupid" groups (e.g., in the United States Polish jokes that dated back to large Polish immigration of unskilled workers) were thus characterized as deserving of nothing more than the lower social status that they had achieved; the "crafty" groups were presented as having achieved their success illegitimately through trickery by being "too smart." There are undoubtedly updated versions of those jokes for current immigrants, but most Americans have become aware that such jokes are no longer acceptable, from an ethical or moral point of view, as part of public discourse. The same applies to racist and sexist jokes, as effects of the civil rights movement and the Women's Movement, and to homophobic jokes, as an effect of the Gay Rights Movement. From the point of view of those who welcome greater inclusion of groups who have historically been marginalized and denied access in various systemic ways, it is important to scrutinize the ways that we talk about (and find amusement in jokes about) these groups. The basic premise here is that language both reflects and potentially shapes social attitudes and thus behavior. Those who want to change society toward more inclusion believe that it is extremely important to influence how people talk, and thus think, about certain groups. Attempts to raise awareness have focused on how people might feel if they are referred to, or joked about, in particular ways. One example for me, having to do with people with disabilities, were the "little moron" jokes that I remember from my childhood. I suddenly realized that it had never occurred to me that I was making people with intellectual handicaps the butt of jokes. Another example for me as I was growing up, of course, were sexist jokes, about which I felt angry but powerless.

REACTIONARY REVOLT AGAINST SO-CALLED "POLITICAL CORRECTNESS"

Social changes inevitably have reactions. Racism, sexism, and homophobia have deep roots in American society. The term "political correctness" came to be used to condemn attempts to change racist, sexist, and homophobic uses of language, especially for humor. It is richly ironic that it was apparently originally a part of left-wing discourse, but has been appropriated by the right wing, currently, to condemn those they perceive to be more "liberal." Trying to make people change their jokes and sources of amusement is highly problematic because it is linked to identity. Being expected to change a lifetime of behavior, especially if the pressure is perceived to come from "outsiders," can inspire resistance. People may perceive amusement that is objectively racist, sexist, or homophobic as detached from their own personal characteristics; thus they may claim that they enjoy a racist joke because it's "funny" but disclaim any racism in themselves. One effect has been to banish such "amusement" from public spaces, while retaining it in private spaces. If we assume that the absence of such public discourse is a positive thing because it removes legitimization, we have to also acknowledge that pushing it underground does not remove it from circulation, and in the worst case, gives it a kind of outlaw caché. An interesting, and particularly American, dimension of the reactionary revolt against so-called political correctness is that it is framed in terms of the First Amendment right to free speech. Anybody who tries to censor amusement based in racism, sexism, or homophobia is violating the right to speak freely. A corollary is that by producing such humor, people are just saying what everybody thinks anyway but are afraid to express in this social climate.

ETHICAL DILEMMAS OF RESPONSE IN SITUATIONS WHERE PEOPLE VIOLATE CHANGING NORMS

Finally, we shift back to the interpersonal and interactional sociolinguistic, enlarging the "I was just joking" discussion concerning personal maladaptive humor, to consider ethical dilemmas of response in situations where people violate changing norms. One can take an ethical stance never to repeat jokes or engage in joking behavior that creates amusement based in racism, sexism, or homophobia. But how should one react if someone produces such humor for amusement in one's presence? Does one assume that the joker assumes a set of shared assumptions and attitudes? If so, then failing to indicate otherwise in some way allows the joker's assumption to persist; thus a failure to act potentially constitutes an act of silent assent. How does one take the context into account? Is it a one-on-one conversation or is it a larger group where there would be an audience for one's response? Does one take a moral stance on the behavior and condemn it? If so, how? Does labelling the joke as racist inevitably imply to the teller that s/he is racist? Is it possible to condemn the behavior without making the joker feel rejected, for example by saying "I know you and I know that you're not racist, so I'm puzzled by this joke that seems racist to me"? Is it possible to respond in a way that will make the joker see things in a new way and perhaps change in future? Such a response might involve an ethical appeal: "In our diverse society that I know you value, I'm concerned that jokes like the one you just told perpetuate attitudes that I'm confident you wouldn't want to promote." What about beloved, older family members who are drawing on lifelong racist, sexist, or homophobic habits concerning sources of amusement and are unlikely to change? What about situations where the joker is in a higher status position with considerable power? Among dilemmas described to me is also the situation where the joke is experienced as simply so "good" (considering form and not content) that it elicits an involuntary laugh response even as the recipient's brain is condemning the content.

CONCLUSION

In writing this chapter, I have become aware of the interesting and important complexities of the moral psychology of amusement. As a linguist, I need to close with some observations about the word "amuse" itself. I was intrigued to learn that we acquired it from Old French as "to cause to stare stupidly"; in the sense of "confound, distract, bewilder, puzzle." The usual sense in the seventeenth and eighteenth centuries was "to divert the attention of any one from the facts at issue; to beguile, delude, cheat, deceive." In military tactics, it was "to divert the attention of the enemy from one's real designs." Over time, usage has changed so that it is now used to refer to benign diversions associated with joviality. I wonder, however, if there isn't still an unacknowledged element of distraction from important matters, as captured in Postman's (1985) arresting title, "Amusing Ourselves to Death." This may be an important moral issue for the moral psychology of amusement.

REFERENCES

Bateson, Gregory. 1972. *Steps to an Ecology of Mind*. New York: Ballantine Books.

Chang, Heewon, 2007. "Autoethnography: Raising Cultural Consciousness of Self and Others." In *Methodological Developments in Ethnography* Vol 12, edited by Geoffrey Walford, 207–221. Somerville, MA: Emerald Group Publishing Limited.

Davies, Catherine Evans. 2005. "Learning the Discourse of Friendship." In *Language in Use: Cognitive and Discourse Perspectives on Language and Language Learning*, edited by Andrea E. Tyler, Mari Takada, Yiyoung Kim, and Diana Marinova, 85–99. Washington, DC: Georgetown University Press (Georgetown University Round Table on Languages and Linguistics).

Davies, Catherine Evans. 2015. "Humor in Intercultural Interaction as Both Content and Process in the Classroom." *HUMOR: International Journal of Humor Research* 28 (3): 375–395.

Davies, Catherine Evans. 2018. "Culture, Gender, Ethnicity, Identity in Discourse: Exploring Crosscultural Communicative Competence in American University Contexts." In *Language Learning, Discourse and Cognition: Studies in the Tradition of Andrea Tyler*, edited by Vyv Evans and Lucy Pickering, 11–36. Amsterdam and New York: John Benjamins (Human Cognitive Processing Series).

Davies, Catherine Evans. 2019. "An Autoethnographic Approach to Understanding Identity Construction through the Enactment of Sense of Humor as Embodied Practice." *Journal of Pragmatics* 152: 200–215.

Davies, Catherine Evans. 2020. "Interpretive Challenges with American Presidential Discourse Described as Joking." To be published in Russian in a special issue of the *New Literary Observer* on parody and humor, edited by Sergey Troitsky. English version available on request from cdavies@ua.edu

Davies, J. C. H. (Christie). 1982. "Ethnic Jokes, Moral Values and Social Boundaries." *The British Journal of Sociology* 33(3): 383–403.

Dollinger, Stefan. 2012. "The Written Questionnaire as a Sociolinguistic Data Gathering Tool: Testing its Validity." *Journal of English Linguistics* 40(1): 74-110.

Ellis, Carolyn, Tony E. Adams, and Arthur P. Bochner. 2011. "Autoethnography: An Overview." *Historical Social Research* 36 (4): 273–290.

Freud, Sigmund. 1928. "Humour." *International Journal of Psychoanalysis* 9: 1–6.

Kambouropoulou, Polyxenie. 1926. "Individual Differences in the Sense of Humor." *American Journal of Psychology* 37 (2): 268–278.

Labov, William. 1972. "Rules for Ritual Insults." In *Language in the Inner City: Studies in the Black English Vernacular*, edited by William Labov, 297–353. Philadelphia: University of Pennsylvania Press.

Martin, Rod A. 2003. "Sense of Humor." In *Positive Psychological Assessment: A Handbook of Models and Measures*, edited by Shane J. Lopez and C. R. Snyder, 313–326. Washington, DC: American Psychological Association.

Oxford English Dictionary. Accessed online through the library of the University of Alabama.

Pieper, Martha Heineman, and William Joseph Pieper. 1990. *Intrapsychic Humanism: An Introduction to a Comprehensive Psychology and Philosophy of Mind*. Chicago: Falcon II Press.

Postman, Neil. 1985. *Amusing Ourselves to Death: Public Discourse in the Age of Show Business*. New York: Viking Penguin.

Ruch, Willibald, ed. 1998. *The Sense of Humor: Explorations of a Personality Characteristic*. Berlin, Germany: De Gruyter.

Sinkeviciute, Valeria. 2017. "Funniness and 'the Preferred Reaction' to Jocularity in Australian and British English: An Analysis of Interviewees' Metapragmatic Comments." *Language & Communication* 55: 41–54.

Skalicky, Stephen, Cynthia M. Berger, and Nancy D. Bell. 2015. "The Functions of 'Just Kidding' in American English." *Journal of Pragmatics* 85: 18–31.

Chapter 3

It's All Fun and Games until Someone Gets Hurt

Amusement's Negative Influence on Moral Judgment

Nathan Stout

What influence do our judgments of right and wrong have on our experience of amusement? This is a common question asked by philosophers interested in exploring the nature of humor, and, unsurprisingly, it has been given a wide variety of answers. On one view, a judgment of immorality can be seen as enhancing amusement. On such a view, if a joke, say, is judged to be immoral, then that judgment of immorality serves to make the joke funnier. One paradigmatic example here is the oft-told Aristocrats joke. Traditionally, the comedic value of the joke is taken to be a function of just how filthy and immoral the teller is able to make the joke's setup.[1] Following Aaron Smuts (2009), call this view—that moral flaws enhance amusement—"comic immoralism."

In opposition to this view, however, is "comic moralism," or the view which says that a judgment of immorality detracts from the comedic value of a joke or situation. On this view, if we sincerely judge the content of a joke to be immoral, then we will not find the joke amusing, or we will at least find it less amusing—with our amusement lessening in proportion with the severity of our judgment that the joke is immoral. So, on this view, when one hears a racist or sexist joke and judges the attitudes expressed by its content to be immoral, then one will not find the joke amusing. This is the position that Smuts defends, and, more recently, Noël Carroll (2019) has offered this type of view as well, arguing that since jokes are necessarily performative, moral flaws in the performer's attitudes or intentions can detract from the amusement that one may appropriately feel.[2]

Each of these views posits some effect that moral judgments have on amusement (either on our tendency to experience it or the appropriateness of doing so). However, in this chapter, I want to explore the converse relationship, about which relatively little has been said. To what extent does the experience of amusement affect our moral judgments? When we're amused are we apt to make better or worse moral decisions?

In what follows, I argue that there are two ways in which amusement may influence our moral judgments, one benign and the other pernicious. First, it may be the case that amusement affects moral judgments dispositionally. To the extent that amusement is a case of positive affect, it likely serves in some instances to dispose us to prosocial behavior. Anecdotally, this seems to be confirmed by common experience (i.e., one is more likely to be beneficent and agreeable when one is in a good mood, and amusement is an effective means of heightening one's mood), and the empirical evidence bears this out as well. This discussion occupies part I of this chapter.

In part II, I address the more pernicious influence of amusement on moral judgment, which results from the fact that amusement is inherently a form of distraction. As an example, the case of a cruel joke is instructive here. When one makes (or participates in) a cruel joke, one's attention is diverted from the reasons one has not to act cruelly and is instead focused on the amusing features of the joke itself. I argue that this is significant for moral judgment insofar as amusement may, in many cases, serve to divert our attention from important moral reasons and direct it toward whatever else we may find pleasant or humorous about a given situation.

The chapter closes, in part III, with a discussion of the broader implications of these effects on moral judgment for our understanding of the nature of amusement and for how we should treat it for the purposes of moral education.

PART I: AMUSEMENT'S POSITIVE INFLUENCE

That amusement can have positive influences on moral judgment is suggested by experiences that many of us have likely had since we were young of the ways in which positive affect can bring about prosocial behavior. Perhaps you recall a time in your childhood when you had a special request to make of a parent—a request for that toy that you wanted so badly or for permission to stay at a friend's house for the weekend, say. When making such requests, you likely said to yourself, at one point or another, "I'm going to wait until mom is in a really good mood, and then I'll ask her." The reason, of course, is that even then you knew that your request would be heard more favorably if the requestee was positively disposed at the time.

Not surprisingly, there is an abundance of empirical evidence suggesting that your childhood self was correct. Since the early 1970s a multitude of studies have demonstrated that there is a strong correlation between positive mood and prosocial behavior.[3] In short, positive mood and positive affect seem to cause us to be more beneficent, more charitable, more helpful, and more willing to benefit others at some cost to ourselves. Insofar as prosocial behavior is strongly associated with good moral judgment, this would seem to suggest that positive affect or mood may serve to improve moral judgment.[4] This is relevant to the case of amusement, of course, because amusement, as a type of positive affect (more on this below), enhances mood in a positive way. Thus, amusement might indirectly improve moral judgment by creating positive mood and disposing us toward prosocial behavior.

It is important to note, however, that the influence of positive mood on moral judgment is limited. For example, Kayser et al. (2010) sought to test the effects of positive (and negative) mood on help-giving behavior in both low- and high-cost situations. Consistent with other studies (e.g., Berkowitz 1987), they found that positive mood enhanced help-giving behavior in situations that involved small sacrifices on the part of subjects. However, their results also showed that it had no effect in situations requiring what they call "moral courage"—situations in which providing help would involve danger or substantial cost to the subject. So while amusement might indirectly improve moral judgment by improving one's mood, its contribution only goes so far. It may lead us to offer help and support, but it is unlikely to cause us to do so at great sacrifice to ourselves.

Other evidence that may point toward amusement's positive role in moral judgment can be found in Barbara Frederickson's "broaden and build" theory of positive emotions. "This theory states," she says, "that certain discrete positive emotions . . . although phenomenologically distinct, all share the ability to broaden people's momentary thought-action repertoires and build their enduring personal resources, ranging from physical and intellectual resources to social and psychological resources" (Frederickson 2001, 219). The central idea here is that positive emotions are adaptive insofar as they create a particular sort of action tendency. To see this, it is helpful to consider them in contrast to negative emotions such as fear. When one is afraid one's attention narrows and focuses on the threat that is the source of one's fear. Additionally, one's immediate action tendency in response to the fearful object is to recoil or retreat—to avoid the threat. Frederickson's claim is that positive emotions have the opposite effect. When one is in the throes of some positive emotion one's attention and manner of thinking broaden, and one begins to build resources from engaging with the source of the positive emotion.

Consider, for example, Frederickson's comments on joy—which I take to be closely related to (and perhaps necessarily includes) amusement. "Joy," she says, "broadens by creating the urge to play, push the limits, and be creative. These urges are evident not only in social and physical behavior, but also in intellectual and artistic behavior" (2001, 220). Thus, to the extent that amusement and joy are phenomenologically similar, we should expect the same to be true of amusement. In a later study, Frederickson and Branigan (2005) found that this was indeed the case. In a pair of experiments designed to test the effect of positive emotions on the scope of cognition and attention they found that participants who were experiencing amusement displayed a global information processing bias (indicating a wider scope of attention) and were able to articulate a greater number and variety of activities that they wished to engage in as a result of reflecting on the situation eliciting their amusement (indicating a larger thought-action repertoire). Thus, we have evidence in support of the broaden and build hypothesis with respect to amusement in particular.

So, how, if at all, is this evidence relevant to amusement's effect on moral judgment? If amusement results in a broadening of patterns of thought and action and helps to build resources by way of social, intellectual, and creative engagement, this quite likely disposes the person experiencing it to engage in prosocial ways with others. This outcome would be consistent with other accounts of amusement's action tendency as well. As Griskevicius et al. put it, "Amusement is the positive emotion experience during social or cognitive play, including humor . . . [P]lay behavior and the experience of humor are both associated with a distinctive 'drop-jaw' smile, laughter, or both . . . , expressions that promote social bonding by letting down one's guard and signaling social support" (2010, 193). These theoretical considerations, bolstered by the evidence in support of the broaden and build theory, provide further evidence for the claim that the experience of amusement may create a positive dispositional influence for moral judgment. To the extent that amusement creates conditions conducive to engaging in social play, it creates a disposition toward positive, prosocial attitudes which, as I have suggested, promote certain moral judgments.

Thus, we have a case for a positive influence of amusement on moral judgment in some circumstances. However, as I will argue in the next section, this is not the whole story. We have seen that amusement may have some indirect positive effects on moral judgment. However, these effects are limited, and in many cases, amusement serves to impair, rather than enhance, such judgments, or so I will argue.

PART II: AMUSEMENT'S NEGATIVE INFLUENCE

To begin this discussion of amusement's negative influence, it may be helpful to explore the origin of the term itself. Etymologically, the term "amuse" originates from the Old French *amuser* and was used to mean "to divert the attention, beguile, or delude." Literally, it means "to cause to muse." Early uses of the term had a decidedly negative connotation and typically implied deception of some sort. At some point during the seventeenth century, that usage shifted to take on a more positive meaning, though it retained the crucial implication of distraction. Thus, the term "amusement" came to be used to refer to "anything which pleasantly diverts the attention."[5]

So the element of distraction is built into our concept of amusement. Given this, there could be no more apt a name than "amusement park" for places like Disneyland or Six Flags. Such places are intended to function as worlds all their own, and when one enters them one is distracted from the actual world outside their gates. While there is some controversy over whether the feeling one has when one is amused is properly understood to be an emotion,[6] I will understand it as such here. Moreover, while my remarks in the introduction to this chapter focused on amusement in the context of humor, it is not limited to that context. One need not be laughing at a joke or finding humor in something in order to be amused. Returning to the word's etymology, we also find that it has been used since the 1600s not only to mean "to divert from serious business" but also "to tickle the fancy of," and it's this meaning that I prefer when considering what it's like to be amused. I won't try to specify with any precision exactly what it's like to have one's fancy tickled. Instead, I'll simply trust that readers have some acquaintance with that particular phenomenon.

So what's the point of this etymological digression? The point is that seeing amusement as conceptually tied to distraction has important implications for its potential influence on moral judgment. If morality is "serious business," and amusement diverts us from it, then amusement may well impede our ability to make sound moral judgments. To my knowledge, there have been no systematic studies on the negative influence of amusement on moral judgment. However, other empirical work may help to point us in the right direction. My focus here will be on work which suggests that (1) positive emotions seem to reduce our ability to process persuasive messages, and (2) positively valenced music seems to increase acceptance of immoral conduct. Together, I'll argue, these studies make a speculative case for the negative influence of amusement on moral judgment. I'll then offer a theoretical framework in support of this speculative conclusion.

To begin, many studies have shown that individuals who are experiencing positive affect are more likely to rely on heuristic information processing when presented with a persuasive message as opposed to a deeper, more systematic cognitive strategy (e.g., Mackie & Worth 1989). In summarizing this research, Griskevicius et al. note that "people in a good mood tend to be relatively persuaded regardless of whether the arguments themselves are strong or weak, as long as there are enough arguments" (2010, 191). So heightening a person's mood makes them less likely to scrutinize the message they are receiving, which may explain why every comedy club has a two-drink minimum or why the Catholic church serves wine at every service.

Of course, having a heightened mood is not identical to feeling amusement, so more needs to be said here in order to draw out a connection between cognitive processing of persuasive messages and amusement in particular. Fortunately, Griskevicius et al. do just that. In two separate experiments designed to show the effect of particular positive emotions on persuasion processing, the authors found that amusement was strongly correlated with a tendency to engage in heuristic processing and, as a result, a higher likelihood of being persuaded by weak argumentation. This result was seen most dramatically in the results from the first of their two experiments. In that study, six test groups of college students were given tasks aimed at eliciting a distinct positive emotions (as well as a neutral control task). They were then presented with an essay containing arguments in favor of instituting comprehensive exams at their university. One essay presented strong arguments in favor of doing so while the other presented a number of relatively weak arguments for the proposal. Participants who were primed with the amusement task were significantly more likely to be swayed by the weak arguments than were participants in the neutral control group, and this effect was stronger than that observed for any of the other emotions tested. Thus, when coupled with the expansive literature on the effect of positive affect on persuasion processing, this study offers compelling evidence that the experience of amusement in particular increases the tendency of individuals to scrutinize persuasive messages.

It is not immediately clear, however, that amusement's having an effect on persuasion processing implies anything about its effect on moral judgment. To claim as much requires further evidence. That additional evidence, I think, can be found by looking at the literature on the effect of music in similar domains. Marketing and advertising professionals have long known that music plays a role in how consumers perceive the products that they advertise. A number of explanations for this have been proposed. For example, some (e.g., Kenealy 1988) have argued that positively valenced music conditions us to associate the positive feeling created by the music with the product being advertised. Others (e.g., Kellaris, Cox, & Cox 1993) have claimed that music activates prior knowledge and evokes associations based on familiarity which, when fitting the product being advertised, cause us to react positively to it. Still others (e.g., Petty & Cacioppo 1986) have argued that music increases the cognitive load of an advertisement and, as a result, distracts from the overall content of the ad in such a way as to decrease critical scrutiny of it.[7] Whatever theoretical model we endorse, what is clear is that music plays a role in consumer psychology.

Ziv et al. (2011) attempted to extend this research on music's role in advertising to determine whether it may have detrimental effects on moral judgment. In three separate experiments, they sought to determine whether music had an effect on individuals' perceptions regarding products that promote immoral behavior. In two of these studies, participants were shown an advertisement which promoted an unethical product (an ad for a service that would falsify documentation in order to increase the amount received in a retirement pension and an ad for a service in which students could pay others to write term papers for them which they could submit and claim as their own). In each of these experiments, the test group viewed an ad which contained background music intended to induce positive mood while the control group viewed the same ad without any background music, and in the second study, a third group viewed the ad with background music intended to induce negative mood. The results were striking. In the first study, participants who viewed the ad with music were significantly more likely to describe the cheating as advantageous and significantly less likely to describe it as disadvantageous. While a judgment that these products are advantageous is not, strictly speaking, a moral judgment (it's unclear whether Ziv et al. take this judgment to be moral or merely prudential), it is clear that such judgments were implicated in the participants' responses. Most notably, this can be seen in the fact that of those who viewed the ad with music 87.5 percent of them said they would recommend the product to others compared to 13.3 percent of those who viewed the ad without music. The participants' endorsement of the product—their making the normative claim, "you ought to use this"—is undoubtedly a sign of their moral judgments about the products in the study.

In the second study, participants who viewed the ad with positively valenced music were significantly more likely to judge the cheating behaviors advertised to be morally acceptable than were those who viewed the ad with negatively valenced music and were also significantly more likely to recommend the product to others (83.9% versus 28.6% in the negative music group). It is also important to note that when asked to recall details of the advertisement, participants who viewed the ad with positively valenced music were able to recall significantly fewer details than were those who viewed the ad without music or those who viewed it with negatively valenced music. Thus, it seems that positively valenced music both increases the likelihood of viewers to endorse an immoral product and decreases their ability to retain information about the product in question.

So the evidence presented so far shows: (1) positive affect, in general, and amusement, in particular, decrease an individual's ability to process persuasive messages and make them more likely to employ a heuristic reasoning process that involves less scrutiny of the message in question, and (2) positively valenced music causes individuals to be significantly less likely to discern immoral qualities in a persuasive message and more likely to endorse the immoral behavior being recommended by distracting them from the content of the message and by inducing positive affect in the person hearing it. Discerning readers, however, will be quick to point out that this doesn't tell us anything explicitly about the relationship between amusement and moral judgment (and undiscerning readers were likely just too amused by the chapter thus far). This point is well taken, but it seems to me that the above evidence can offer a speculative account of that relationship, at least.

An intuitive way of constructing this speculative account may go as follows:

1. Amusement inhibits an individual's ability (or tendency) to carefully process persuasive information.
    a. Processing persuasive information involves the same, or similar, mechanisms as processing moral information
2. Positively valenced music inhibits an individual's ability (or tendency) to respond appropriately to immoral messages.
    a. Positively valenced music induces amusement, or something sufficiently similar to it, in the person hearing it.
3. Therefore, the data from the above studies, when taken in conjunction with one another, offer strong support for the view that amusement inhibits us from making sound moral judgments.

Of course, whether we accept this speculative conclusion will depend in large part on whether we have good reason to think that (1a) and (2a) are true. I think that we do, and I'll begin with a first pass as to why that is. First, with respect to (1a), given that moral judgment is normative by definition, it is similar to persuasive reasoning insofar as persuasion involves normative reasoning (persuasion aims at getting the person to agree that she *ought to* behave in some manner or believe some proposition). So it does not seem unreasonable to think that persuasion processing and moral judgment draw on some of the same psychological mechanisms. Second, with respect to (2a), it seems to me that we can draw on the common experience of listening to positively valenced music as evidence here. Anyone who has listened to "up-beat" or "happy" music will, I think, agree that in at least some cases they feel amused when doing so. Moreover, the studies from Ziv et al. discussed above show that participants viewing the ads with positive music were less able to recall details from those ads, which indicates that the positively valenced music distracted them in a way that the negatively valenced music did not. Given that distraction is conceptually tied to amusement, this would suggest amusement is implicated in the experience of those hearing the positive music. So it seems to me that there are grounds for accepting the speculative conclusion above given what has been said so far. However, the claim that amusement negatively affects moral judgment will be on even stronger footing if we can provide it some theoretical support as well. That theoretical support can be found in recent work on dual process theories of moral judgment in the moral psychology literature and in philosophical work on moral perception.

Over the past two decades, considerable research on moral judgment has shown that our moral decisions tend to involve separate processes depending on the conditions under which they are made. For example, Jonathan Haidt's (2001) influential Social Intuitionist Model of moral judgment holds that our moral judgments are primarily driven by an affective response which is then subjected to rational scrutiny in a post hoc manner. More recently, Joshua Greene (2008) has endorsed a dual process view which posits that deontological moral judgments are furnished by a quick emotional response, whereas consequentialist judgments stem from a process of rational reflection. Each of these views proposes that some of, or some aspect of, our moral judgments stem from emotional processes while others arise out of a rational process, and this emotion/reason distinction has become common in dual process theories of moral judgment.

However, a more recent view, defended by Fiery Cushman (2013; 2015) among others (see also Crockett 2013; Dolan & Dayan 2013), takes a different approach which is, I think, instructive for our purposes here. On this view, moral judgment does indeed proceed along two distinct routes, but rather than appealing to distinct emotional and rational processes, this view distinguishes between model-based and model-free judgments. Model-based judgments occur when a decision is made by constructing a mental model. In model-based judgments, the individual decides according a decision tree, of sorts, which models the potential outcomes of the decision along with any intermediary decisions or variables that may be needed. These judgments are slow, relatively speaking, and, according to Cushman, they tend to result in consequentialist judgments (we decide based on the outcome of the model). Model-free judgments on the other hand are quick and habitual. When we receive positive feedback for a particular decision-type, we habituate that decision into a decision rule which we can draw on in the future. Thus, model-free judgments are quick, and they tend to take the form of deontological moral judgments. Cushman characterizes the distinction as follows:

> Goal-directed actions require a working model of the world. You pick a desirable outcome, and then form a plan to bring it about. Thus, they correspond to the class of model-based reinforcement learning algorithms. In contrast, habits are reactive stimulus-response pairings that are strengthened when followed

by reward. Executing a habit does not require planning toward a valued outcome, and thus corresponds to the alternative class of model-free algorithms. (Cushman 2015, 59)

Another way to put it is that model-based judgments are, to a certain degree, reflective while model-free judgments are heuristic.

Providing a full account of the debate over dual process models of moral judgment is beyond the scope of this chapter. I'll simply say that I find the model-based/model-free distinction compelling, and I will be relying on it here without further defense.[8] The reason that it is useful for understanding amusement's influence on moral judgment is that, as we have seen, in the context of persuasion processing, amusement causes us to employ heuristic cognitive strategies and, consequently, to fail to scrutinize the persuasive message in the appropriate way. Given this, it seems likely that amusement would cause us to fall back on heuristic strategies in the moral context as well, and the model-based/model-free account is well equipped to explain the detrimental effects that this would have for moral judgment. In short, a tendency to rely solely on heuristic judgments would inhibit our ability to construct decision models and would thereby preclude certain reflective avenues to moral judgment. While this might not always result in poor moral judgment (our deontological moral judgments are often correct, after all), it would surely do so in many cases—specifically cases that are novel to us and for which we don't have a readily available model-free solution. In such cases, even if amusement positively disposes an individual to prosocial behavior, the unavailability of slow, reflective processing may result in worse moral judgment. Imagine, for example, a group of friends at a bar. They're joking around and ribbing each other with what seem like innocent jabs. At a certain point, we can imagine one of the friends feeling as though the ribbing has gone too far. He stops laughing at the jokes. His face takes on an uncomfortable expression. A slow, reflective processing of information might result in the others reading these social clues and letting up or apologizing. However, the jocular nature of the interaction and the shared amusement of the friends often lends itself to the quick, heuristic approach of continuing to make jokes even to the point of hurting a friend.

Thus, we have an explanation for how, given the data regarding persuasion processing, amusement may have similar negative impacts in the moral domain, and as a result, we have some theoretical meat on the bones of our speculative conclusion. To add further support, it will be useful to see how philosophical work on moral perception may play an explanatory role as well. The simple thought here is that amusement may also negatively impact moral judgment by inhibiting our ability to perceive the moral features of our situation.

The notion of moral perception has a long history in the virtue ethics tradition. The basic claim of moral perception is that the virtuous person simply *sees* the right thing to do in a given situation. This view can be found in Aristotle, and many virtue theorists have endorsed some version of it.[9] John McDowell, for example, writes, "Occasion by occasion, one knows what to do, if one does, not by applying universal principles but by being a certain kind of person: one who sees situations in a certain distinctive way" (1998, quoted in Jacobson 2005, 388). There is a good deal of controversy among ethicists regarding the status of moral perception (McBrayer 2010) as well as how best to characterize it. McDowell uses "moral perception" metaphorically to refer to a special type of susceptibility to reasons, and he sets his view apart from an intuitionist model which advocates for a special faculty of moral perception over and above our other perceptual modalities. Regardless of how it is characterized, the significant point here is that virtue requires that we be able to apprehend the morally significant features of any given situation. A virtuous person is one who is properly attuned to the requirements of virtue in their daily life.

If this is true, and in a general sense, it must be,[10] then we have another means by which we might explain amusement's negative influence on moral judgment. Recall that we began with the conceptual point that amusement, by definition, involves being distracted—having one's attention pleasantly diverted from serious business. This seems to be borne out in the Ziv et al. studies in which participants who were listening to positively valenced music were less able to recall details of the ad they were viewing and were more likely to endorse the immoral product being advertised. The positive mood induced by the music can plausibly be understood as diverting the attention of participants from the content and causing them to be less able to appreciate the moral features of the ad in question.

What is the nature of the distraction? It can't be the mere presence of music, as the same effect was not observed when negatively valenced music was played. The more likely explanation is one that goes back to Frederickson's work in support of the broaden and build a theory of positive emotions. In the case of amusement, individuals tend to display a global processing bias—they miss the trees for the forest. The fact that amusement is generally experienced in the context of play is likely to exacerbate things here as well. As Griskevicius et al. note, "Theories of play emphasize that these behaviors allow one to practice risky or high-investment skills ... under safe circumstances, without real time pressure or risk of harm" (2010, 193). Thus, the experience of amusement is likely to signal that the stakes are low and that there is no significant risk of harm. Given this contextual signal and the inattention to detail in favor of "big-picture" processing that amusement generates, it seems highly likely that it would inhibit moral perception. That is, experiencing amusement likely makes one less able to appreciate the moral features of a situation, and, thereby, less able to make sound moral judgments.

All of this suggests, rather convincingly, that despite its potential to dispose us toward good, prosocial behavior, amusement also stands to impair moral judgment in serious ways. The argument in this section is simultaneously simple and complex. The simple thought is this: if you're too busy joking around, you're likely to miss morally significant features of your surroundings and you're unlikely to employ moral reasoning to the best of your ability. The complex part is spelling out just why that is. There exists, to my knowledge, no direct empirical evidence for the connection between amusement and moral judgment. As a result, I have drawn on related research and attempted to make a speculative argument to this effect while providing a theoretical backdrop which can give it some explanatory force. In the next section, I will offer some thoughts on the implications of what I've said so far.

PART III: IMPLICATIONS

To this point, I have argued that the available evidence suggests that amusement may, in some cases, enhance moral judgment by disposing an individual positively toward others. However, this effect is limited, and, as I have tried to show, in many cases amusement is likely to impair our moral judgment by limiting our moral reasoning and distracting us from morally significant aspects of our circumstances. These observations about amusement's negative influence on moral judgment are a novel contribution to the literature on the moral psychology of amusement, but it is worth considering what, if anything, follows from this.

The most obvious implication of what I've said here is just that more empirical work on the connection between amusement and moral judgment is necessary. Such work would not be difficult to conduct as all of the necessary methods and materials that would be required have already been developed and validated. A simple protocol in which participants are induced to experience amusement and then given standard moral judgment vignettes and their associated questionnaires would go a long way toward confirming or disconfirming what I have proposed here.

That empirical work *could* be conducted to this end, of course, doesn't entail that it would be worthwhile to do so. In order to show that, I'd need to offer some reason to believe that learning more about the connection between amusement and moral judgment stands to teach us something important. Dear reader, you are in luck, as it seems to me that understanding this relationship better has demonstrable theoretical and practical upside.

I'll start with the theoretical. One important upshot of the discussion in this chapter is that it seems to make amusement theoretically unique insofar as it sets it apart from other positive emotions. Are there any other positive emotions that are fundamentally a form of distraction? It is not obvious to me that there are. Many other positive emotions may result in our being distracted or in monopolizing our attention—hope or enthusiasm come to mind here. However, these surely are not constituted by their distracting qualities, and it seems unlikely that they have the same negative effects on moral judgment that have been discussed here. Whether they are so constituted, or have said effects, is an empirical question which may be falsified by testing, to be sure, but if I am correct, then amusement seems a strange phenomenon—a state that disposes us to behave prosocially but which makes us poor judges of what we ought to do. From the perspective of emotion theorists, this feature is worth exploring further.

From the perspective of moral theory, amusement's connection to attention is also significant. Much recent work in moral responsibility has focused on the psychological features that underwrite responsible agency.[11] In theorizing about responsible agency, virtually everyone will agree that certain baseline executive functions are required in order for an individual to be responsible for her conduct. Arguably, attentional capacities are among those baseline executive capacities that must be present in order to underwrite moral agency. If amusement truly does impair moral judgment, and it does so by overriding one of the executive functions necessary for responsible agency, then it would seem, at first blush, that we should be less likely to hold someone responsible for the things they do while there are amused. This would be a startling outcome and one that requires more general theoretical attention. One could find other areas within ethical theory, no doubt, where similar attentional deficits become theoretically significant.

As to the practical upside of discovering more about the relationship between amusement and moral judgment, I think there are two important points to make. The first has to do with the role of amusement in moral education and character development. Pedagogical theory has long held that humor and laughter are important teaching tools. This is unsurprising given what was said above regarding the importance of play in learning and the role of amusement in play contexts. However, if it's true that amusement can in fact undermine moral judgment, then it may behoove us to rethink the effectiveness of humor in teaching overtly moral lessons. At the risk of sounding like a killjoy moralist (which is just to say, a moral philosopher), it may be more effective to leave humor a relatively small role in moral development. The other side of this, of course, is that an overdeveloped sense of humor may, in some cases, impede the development of moral character if, in the course, of development that sense of humor obscures the moral lessons being taught. This is not to say, by any means, that a well-developed sense of humor is a morally bad thing or that moral education must be uniformly somber. Rather, it is to say that a sensitivity to amusement's potential dampening effect on moral judgment should lead us to temper amusement by, for example, a continual focus on empathy and other attention-demanding skills that will counterbalance amusement's distracting tendency.

A second practical upshot of recognizing amusement's negative impact on moral judgment is that it may help to sensitize us to cases in which humor is, and is not, an appropriate response to social issues. Humor is clearly an effective way to bring attention to injustice. Satire plays an important role in social issues insofar as it is an effective means of shedding light on oppression and other institutional harms. That said, if what I have offered above is correct, then we must be careful not to allow humor and amusement to play the opposite role—to distract us from the moral consequences of our social institutions or to truncate our ability to think carefully on moral issues. Sadly, many forms of amusement serve precisely this end, and we would do well to identify them and to better understand their moral implications. Perhaps it is the case certain varieties of humor or ways of inducing amusement produce different moral responses—some better and some worse. It would certainly be worthwhile to investigate this possibility, as doing so may help us to better understand how to use amusement to our moral advantage.[12]

CONCLUSION

The ordinary approach to the question of amusement's relation to moral judgment is to ask how judgments of immorality affect our experience of amusement. In this chapter, I have tried to explore the relationship from the opposite direction by asking how the experience of amusement affects moral judgment. It turns out, not surprisingly, that this question is difficult to answer. It may be that, in some cases, amusement enhances moral judgment by making us prone to prosocial attitudes and behaviors. Interestingly, however, I've tried to show that in many cases, amusement impairs our moral judgment. Its distracting influence and its tendency to preclude goal-directed, model-based moral reasoning make us significantly worse moral judges, and I've briefly pointed to some of the theoretical and practical implications of this fact. Amusement plays an important role in our everyday lives and contributes significantly to our well-being, but in the context of moral judgment, it's all fun and games until someone gets hurt.

NOTES

1. To see this, compare Gilbert Gottfried's telling of the joke with Dwight Schrute's version in NBC's "The Office."
2. It is worth noting that these two views are not exhaustive. Others have argued that whether a joke is moral or immoral is entirely irrelevant to the question of whether or not the joke is funny. Justin D'Arms and Daniel Jacobson (2000) take this view, as does David Shoemaker (2017). According to them, while there may be good moral reasons for us not to laugh at, say, racist jokes, these are not reasons to think that the joke is not funny. On their views, whether a joke is funny is entirely a function of whether it is fitting for one to be amused by it. Amusement tracks "the funny," and a joke may well merit amusement even if it would be wrong for one to express that amusement. In other words, to appeal to moral reasons in order to explain whether something is humorous is to appeal to the wrong kind of reason.
3. See Carlson et al. (1988) for a review of some of these as well as an evaluation of a number of the hypotheses for this connection.
4. I'm using "judgment" rather expansively, here, and do not mean to limit it to judgments that are made consciously or reflectively.
5. See the entries for "Amuse" and "Amusement" in the Online Etymology Dictionary, http://www.etymonline.com
6. See Roberts (1988)
7. See Ziv et al. (2011) for a discussion of these various models.
8. I have discussed its implications in other areas of moral psychology in previous work. (Stout 2016a; 2016b)
9. See Jacobson (2005) for a helpful discussion.
10. Even apart from virtue theory, any moral theory must have some requirement that an individual be able to grasp the moral features of a given situation. If a Kantian, for example, doesn't notice that she's dealing with a rational, autonomous human, then she can't reflect on whether she is treating him as an end in himself.
11. See, for example, Shoemaker (2015); Doris (2015). I discuss a number of these issues in Stout (2016b); (2017); (2019).
12. I'm grateful to Brian Robinson for suggesting this point.

REFERENCES

"Amuse." *Online Etymology Dictionary*. https://www.etymonline.com/word/amuse

"Amusement." *Online Etymology Dictionary*. https://www.etymonline.com/word/amusement

Berkowitz, Leonard. (1987) "Mood, Self-awareness, and Willingness to Help." *Journal of Personality and Social Psychology*. 52: 721–729.

Carlson, Michael, Ventura Charlin, and Norman Miller. (1988). "Positive Mood and Helping Behavior: A Test of Six Hypotheses." *Journal of Personality and Social Psychology*. 55(2): 211–219.

Carroll, Noël. (2019) "When Is Someone 'Just Joking'?" *New Statesman America*. June 4, accessed at https://www.newstatesman.com/2019/06/when-someone-just-joking

Crockett, Molly. (2013) "Models of Morality." *Trends in Cognitive Sciences*. 17(8): 363–366.

Cushman, Fiery. (2013) "Action, Outcome, and Value: A Dual-System Framework for Morality." *Personality and Social Psychology Review*. 17(3): 273–292.

Cushman, Fiery. (2015) "From Moral Concern to Moral Constraint." *Current Opinion in Behavioral Sciences*. 3: 58–62.

D'Arms, Justin and Daniel Jacobson. (2000). "The Moralistic Fallacy: On the 'Appropriateness' of the Emotions." *Philosophy and Phenomenological Research*. 61: 65–90.

Dolan, Ray and Peter Dayan. (2013) "Goals and Habits in the Brain." *Neuron*. 80: 312–325.

Doris, John. (2015) *Talking to Ourselves: Reflection, Ignorance, and Agency*. Oxford: Oxford University Press.

Frederickson, Barbara and Christine Branigan. (2005) "Positive emotions broaden the scope of attention and though-action repertoires." *Cognition and Emotion*. 19(3): 313–332.

Frederickson, Barbara. (2001). "The Role of Positive Emotions in Positive Psychology: The Broaden-and-Build Theory of Positive Emotions." *American Psychologist*. 56(3): 218–226.

Green, Joshua. (2008) "The Secret Joke of Kant's Soul." In *Moral Psychology Volume 3. The Neuroscience of Morality: Emotion, Brain Disorders, and Development*. 35–79. Edited by Walter Sinnott-Armstrong. Cambridge, MA: MIT Press.

Griskevicius, Vladas, Michelle N. Shiota, and Samantha L. Neufeld. (2010) "Influence of Different Positive Emotions of Persuasion Processing: A Functional Evolutionary Approach." *Emotion*. 10(2): 190–206.

Haidt, Jonathan. (2001) "The Emotional Dog and Its Rational Tail: A Social-Intuitionist Approach to Moral Judgment." *Psychological Review*. 108(4): 814–834.

Jacobson, Daniel. (2005) "Seeing by Feeling: Virtues, Skills, and Moral Perception." *Ethical Theory and Moral Practice*. 8: 387–409.

Kellaris, James, Anthony Cox, and Dena Cox. "The Effect of Background Music on Ad Processing: A Contingency Explanation. *Journal of Marketing*. 57: 114–125.

Kenealy, Pamela. (1988) "Validation of a Music Mood Induction Procedure: Some Preliminary Findings." *Cognition and Emotion*. 2(1): 41–48.

Mackie, Diane M. and Leila T. Worth. (1989) "Processing Deficits and the Mediation of Positive Affect in Persuasion." *Journal of Personality and Social Psychology*. 57(1): 27–40.

McBrayer, Justin P. (2010) "A Limited Defense of Moral Perception." *Philosophical Studies*. 149: 305–320.

McDowell, John. (1998) *Mind, Value, and Reality*. Cambridge: Harvard University Press.

Morreall, John. (2016) "Philosophy of Humor," *The Stanford Encyclopedia of Philosophy* Edward N. Zalta (ed.), URL = <https://plato.stanford.edu/archives/win2016/entries/humor/>.

Niesta Kayser, Daniela, Tobias Greitemeyer, Peter Fischer, and Dieter Frey. (2010). "Why Mood Affects Help Giving, but Not Moral Courage: Comparing Two Types of Prosocial Behavior." *European Journal of Social Psychology*. 40: 1136–1157.

Petty, Richard and John Cacioppo. (1986) "The Elaboration Likelihood Model of Persuasion." *Advances in Experimental Social Psychology*. 19: 123–205.

Roberts, Robert C. (1988) "Is Amusement an Emotion?" *Philosophical Quarterly*. 25(3): 269–274.

Shoemaker, David. (2015) *Responsibility from the Margins*. Oxford: Oxford University Press.

Shoemaker, David. (2017) "Response-Dependent Responsibility, or A Funny Thing Happened on the Way to Blame." *Philosophical Review*. 126 (4): 481–527.

Smuts, Aaron. (2009) "Do Moral Flaws Enhance Amusement?" *American Philosophical Quarterly*. 46 (2): 151–162.

Stout, Nathan. (2016a) "Conversation, Responsibility, and Autism Spectrum Disorder." *Philosophical Psychology*. 29(7): 1015–1028.

Stout, Nathan. (2016b) "Reasons-Responsiveness and Moral Responsibility: the Case of Autism." *The Journal of Ethics*. 20(4): 401–418.

Stout, Nathan. (2017) "Autism, Meta-Cognition, and the Deep Self." *Journal of the American Philosophical Association*. 3(4): 446–464.

Stout, Nathan. (2019) "Emotional Awareness and Responsible Agency." *Review of Philosophy and Psychology*. 10(2): 337–362.

Ziv, Naomi, Moran Hoftman, and Mor Geyer. (2011) "Music and Moral Judgment: The effect of Background Music on the Evaluation of Ads Promoting Unethical Behavior." *Psychology of Music*. 40(6): 738–760.

Part II

MORAL JUDGMENTS OF AMUSEMENT

Chapter 4

Beyond a Joke
A Defence of Comic Moralism
Alan Roberts

Humor is a source of moral concern because some jokes contain both elements of immorality and funniness. Consider the following from Ronald de Sousa (1990, 290):

> M. visits the hockey team. When she emerges she complains that she has been gang-raped. Wishful thinking.

In this joke "M" referred to the wife of a former prime minister of Canada, rumoured to be sexually hyperactive. Clearly, then the joke employs sexist stereotypes about female promiscuity, and hence plausibly contains an element of immorality. But, also clearly, the joke employs a form of deliberate misdirection employed by other jokes, and hence also contains an element of funniness. This raises the question of whether jokes can be funny despite moral flaws and, more generally, how immorality affects funniness.

There are three broad answers to the question of how immorality affects funniness:

Comic amoralism: Immorality does not affect funniness.[1]
Comic immoralism: Immorality positively affects funniness.
Comic moralism: Immorality negatively affects funniness.

The two key terms in these three positions are "immorality" and "funniness"—immorality merits moral disapproval, whereas funniness merits amusement.[2] Hence, one way to examine the three positions is to examine how moral disapproval affects amusement. If moral disapproval does not affect amusement, then comic amoralism is the right position; if moral disapproval positively affects amusement, then comic immoralism is the right position; and, if moral disapproval negatively affects amusement, then comic moralism is the right position.[3]

In this chapter, I defend the "merited-response" argument for comic moralism from a criticism given by Noël Carroll (2014a; 2014b). Specifically, I argue that Carroll's criticism has appeal only because the concept of amusement has been philosophically and empirically under-researched. A more detailed conceptual analysis of amusement reveals that the criticism is flawed. Moreover, since comic amoralism, comic immoralism, and comic moralism are mutually exclusive positions, a positive argument for one position is also a negative argument against the other two. Hence, my defence of a positive argument for comic moralism also doubles as support for a negative argument against comic amoralism and comic immoralism.[4]

In section 1, I outline the merited-response argument for comic moralism and Carroll's criticism. In section 2, I argue for a benign-appraisal condition for amusement. Finally, in section 3, I conclude how a benign-appraisal condition for amusement defends the merited-response argument from Carroll's criticism.

1. THE MERITED-RESPONSE ARGUMENT

Berys Gaut (2007) first formulated his merited-response argument during a wider debate about art and morality, specifically to support the view that immoral elements in an artwork negatively affect the aesthetic success of the artwork. Roughly, the argument holds that if an artwork prescribes certain responses, then the aesthetic success of the artwork depends on whether those responses are merited, and that whether those responses are merited partly depends on whether they are ethical. Gaut's merited-response argument can be more narrowly applied to support comic moralism as follows[5]:

Premise 1: x is funny if and only if x merits amusement.
Premise 2: Immoral elements in x negatively affect whether x merits amusement.
Conclusion: Immoral elements in x negatively affect whether x is funny.

Clearly, the merited-response argument is a defence of comic moralism because the conclusion is equivalent to comic moralism.

However, Noël Carroll (2014a, 247) has criticized the merited-response argument by claiming that the comic moralist "has begged the question by including moral appropriateness as a necessary condition for comic appropriateness."[6] His claim is that premise 1 seems true only if the term "merits" means "comically merits," whereas premise 2 seems true only if "merits" means "morally merits." But the conclusion follows from premise 1 and premise 2 only if "merits" has the same meaning in both premise 1 and premise 2. So according to Carroll, the merited-response argument seems sound only if we conflate comic merit with moral merit. Carroll's (2014a, 246) criticism is that such a conflation is illegitimate because "a *comically* appropriate response—finding something funny—does not in everyday parlance require moral appropriateness."

Carroll (2014a, 246) continues his criticism of the merited-response argument by claiming that the main defence open to the comic moralist is flawed:

> In response, the comic [moralist] may put his cards on the table and say outright that it is not our ordinary concept of comic amusement that is at stake, but one in which the appropriateness of an amused response requires that the response be morally appropriate. Yet this seems to beg the question, for, then, moral appropriateness appears to be built into the very criteria of comic amusement.

In short then, Carroll's criticism of the comic moralist is that they should be proving that comic merit includes moral merit rather than simply assuming it. Aaron Smuts (2010, 342) similarly argues as follows:

> [The comic moralist] needs to give us some reason to think that this is how we use the term "humor" and not just stipulate a new use, since whether or not the ethical dimensions of a joke do affect its humorousness is exactly what is at issue.

Carroll's criticism depends upon the claim that it is illegitimate to conflate comic merit with moral merit. He (2014a, 246) gives a full characterization in the following:

> Critics of [comic moralists] complain about the legitimacy of [their] conception of comic amusement. Certainly it does seem to be at odds with our ordinary concept of comic amusement, which, roughly speaking, seems to be thought of as a matter of enjoying certain perceived incongruities (including moral ones). But the comic [moralist], in addition, requires, as a criterion of appropriateness for an amused response, that the humour not be morally defective despite the fact that a comically appropriate response—finding something funny—does not in everyday parlance require moral appropriateness.

So, in formulating his criticism, Carroll says that the ordinary concept of amusement roughly seems to be the enjoyment of perceived incongruity. Under this conception, something merits amusement if and only if it is an enjoyable incongruity. But, since being an enjoyable incongruity does not imply moral rectitude, Carroll (2014a, 246) then criticizes the comic moralist for claiming that comic merit includes moral merit:

> Whether, for instance, a joke-candidate merits comic amusement, it can be argued, depends upon whether, with reference to the prototypical case, it engenders pleasure through its manifestation of certain perceived incongruities—which, of course, may extend to moral incongruities.

Carroll's criticism implies that the comic moralist commits what Justin D'Arms and Daniel Jacobson (2000, 65–90) previously termed the "moralistic fallacy." To commit the moralistic fallacy is to infer from the fact that it would be immoral to have a particular attitudinal response toward a particular object and that object does not have the evaluative property associated with that attitudinal response. One of the examples D'Arms and Jacobson give is inferring from the fact that it would be immoral to be amused toward a particular joke that that joke is not funny. They maintain that "a joke can be funny even though it is wrong to be amused by it" (D'Arms and Jacobson 2000, 80). Contra D'Arms and Jacobsen, Gaut (2007, 237–241) argues that there is no conflation in the merited-response argument and so it does not commit the moralistic fallacy.[7] Specifically, Gaut (2007, 239) says that there is no conflation because "the point appealed to is that the response prescribed does not correspond to the evaluative properties of the object—it is the cognitive–evaluative aspect of rationality that in each case is impugned by its immorality."

However, in defense of comic moralism, I argue that Carroll's criticism has appeal only because the concept of amusement has been philosophically and empirically under-researched. That is why it seems plausible that amusement consists merely of the enjoyment of perceived incongruity. But, once a fuller conceptual analysis is started, this idea loses its plausibility.

2. A BENIGN-APPRAISAL CONDITION

An often-proposed condition for amusement is that in order for a perceived incongruity to elicit amusement and not anxiety, the incongruity must be appraised to be benign. For example, play fighting with a child will elicit anxiety from them as opposed to amusement if they appraise one's incongruous behavior to be malign as opposed to benign.

This benign-appraisal condition is often extended beyond personal threat to include threat to others. Carroll himself (2014b, 30) gives the following example:

> When someone is killed in a joke—as so many lawyers are—we are not treated to the gruesome details of their demise. Thus, when the lawyer in the outhouse

in *Jurassic Park* is stomped to death by the T. Rex, the audience howls with glee. Had they been treated to a view of his broken body, accompanied by sobs of pain, their laughter probably would have been silenced.

In general, if a comedic character is depicted as suffering, then this suffering is rendered nonthreatening in order to not impinge on a benign appraisal. There are a number of ways in which this can occur. When one dislikes the comedic character, such as in Carroll's lawyer example, often the suffering is not dwelt upon or is represented as deserved. When one likes the comedic character, such as the scene in *Modern Times* when Charlie Chaplin passes through the gears of a factory machine, often they are depicted as a clown-figure who can withstand the suffering inflicted upon them. So, in general, there are a number of ways used to render suffering as nonthreatening in order to not impinge on a benign appraisal applied to others.

One kind of counterexample to a benign-appraisal condition would be cases of amusement in a threatened state. One potential counterexample is black humor since, rather than not dwell upon suffering, black humor positively relishes it. For example, consider the following black joke:

> An orphan is diagnosed with cancer. They ask, "How much time do I have left, doctor?" "Ten," answers the doctor. "Years or months?" " . . . Nine. Eight . . . "

Clearly, this joke depicts suffering but, rather than not dwell upon it, the joke positively relishes it. No reason is given to dislike the orphan so the suffering is not represented as deserved. Moreover, the orphan is not depicted as a clown-figure who can withstand the suffering. Such jokes are then a potential counterexample to a benign-appraisal condition because it may be argued that black humor is both threatening and amusing.

However, I argue that this potential counterexample misunderstands the nature of black humor, which is based on a distinction between representation and reality. The suffering depicted in black humor serves to increase amusement only because one bears in mind that the suffering depicted is merely a representation and not reality. There are many people who would be amused by the above orphan joke but would, of course, be mortified if they encountered the depicted scene in reality.

So, in black humor, all amusing suffering is represented suffering and it is because the suffering is represented as opposed to real that allows it to be rendered nonthreatening. Hence, black humor is not amusement in a threatened state because, in black humor, suffering is represented as opposed to real and is thereby rendered not threatening. Then there is gallows humor, such as Sigmund Freud's (1928, 1) example of a criminal who, while being led to their execution on a Monday, remarks "Well, this is a good beginning to the week." Here even when the suffering is real it is being admirably overcome and rendered nonthreatening, which is why Freud praised such humor as an exalted character trait.

Of course, when representations of suffering are particularly gratuitous, black humor can "cross the line." But even these cases are not counterexamples to a benign-appraisal condition. This is because, once black humor "crosses the line," it becomes threatening but is no longer amusing. Conversely, before black humor "crosses the line," it is amusing but not threatening. Exactly where "the line" lies will depend on the subject's dispositions. But whatever the subject's dispositions, once black humor "crosses the line," they will switch from pleasant amusement to unpleasant anxiety. This explanation certainly agrees with cases of black humor which start off amusing, then "cross the line" and become unamusing as a result. Thus, black humor is not a counterexample to a benign-appraisal condition after all.

Furthermore, a benign-appraisal condition is a commonly proposed claim across many disciplines: Evolutionary biologists, Matthew Gervais and David Wilson (2005, 414) state that proto-humor among primates, such as wrestling and tickling, would have "inherently indicated that a situation was safe and conducive to positive emotion and social play." Likewise, neuroscientist Vilayanur Ramachandran (1998) proposed a "false-alarm" theory in which amusement consists of a gradual build-up of expectation followed by a sudden violation, but only as long as the updated expectation is nonthreatening. In their benign violation theory, behavior scientists Peter McGraw and Caleb Warren (2014, 75–6) similarly specify that "for a violation to produce humor, it also needs to seem OK, safe, acceptable, or, in other words, benign." Psychologist Mary Rothbart (1977) also states that in order for something to be amusing, it must be processed as "safe" and psychologist Michael Apter (1991, 14) proposes that amusement only occurs when we "create a small and manageable private world . . . into which the outside world of real problems cannot properly impinge."

Moreover, Carroll (2014b, 49–50) himself states the following as provisional necessary and sufficient conditions for amusement:

(i) The object of one's mental state is a perceived incongruity which (ii) one regards as non-threatening or otherwise anxiety producing, and (iii) not annoying and (iv) towards which one does not enlist genuine problem-solving attitudes (v) but which gives rise to enjoyment of precisely the pertinent incongruity and (vi) to an experience of levity.

It is Carroll's acceptance of a benign-appraisal condition, like (ii), which means that, even on Carroll's own analysis, an absence of moral disapproval is necessary for amusement and thereby that comic merit includes moral merit. I will now elaborate on this claim in the next section.

3. DEFENDING FROM CARROLL'S CRITICISM

If benign appraisal is a necessary condition for amusement, then moral disapproval is incompatible with amusement, because if immoral elements merit responses that are incompatible with a benign appraisal, then they cannot be appraised to be benign. Accepting a benign-appraisal condition like (ii) means that immoral elements negatively affect the meritedness of amusement.

That immoral elements merit responses which are incompatible with a benign appraisal is an idea that is even suggested by Carroll (2014b, 29, 32, 113) in his discussion of (ii):

> Cases of found humour, then, require that the situations that comically amuse us not be ones in which we feel personal threat . . . nor will we be comically amused if we perceive the situation as in some other way dangerous, for example as threatening harm to others; for that will produce anxiety.
>
> In fact, invented humour generally trades in fictional worlds that are devoid of sustained acknowledgements of pain in such a way that our normal empathetic and moral responses remain in abeyance, thereby divesting the situation of the potential to provoke anxiety.
>
> Where the perceptible evil of [humour] is itself a predictable source of anxiety, it seems reasonable to conjecture that the immorality in question can contribute to the alienation of comic amusement.

According to Carroll, humor which threatens harm or conveys pain to oneself or others will merit anxiety and so infringe on a benign-appraisal condition, like (ii). Hence Carroll's (2014b, 32) suggestion that anxiety is detrimental to amusement becomes the suggestion that empathy and moral responses are detrimental to amusement. If immoral elements merit responses that are incompatible with a benign appraisal, then they cannot be appraised to be benign. So, to the extent that humor contains immoral elements, amusement toward it is unmerited (qua amusement). Then immoral elements negatively affect the meritedness of amusement. Therefore, even Carroll's own conceptual analysis of amusement indicates that comic merit includes moral merit. This may be consistent with Carroll's own view of moderate comic moralism, which states that immorality can negatively affect funniness but does not always, but it also undermines his criticism of the merited-response argument.

Furthermore, acceptance of a benign-appraisal condition, like (ii), would also allow the comic moralist to answer another criticism Carroll (2014a, 247) makes of the merited-response argument, as characterized in the following:

> It grades humour as comically defective if it is morally defective, but it does not find humour funnier if it is morally inspiring. Wouldn't the Merited Response Argument predict that more morality should make a joke more merited in terms of comic amusement, if less morality makes it less funny? Unfortunately, the [comic moralist] never explains this asymmetry between the satanic and angelic potentials of humour, though surely it is worthy of comment.[8]

Accepting a benign-appraisal condition allows the comic moralist to explain this asymmetry of comic merit. Immoral elements in humor merit responses that, according to a benign-appraisal condition, negatively affect its funniness. However, moral elements in humor may not merit these responses, but this does not then mean that they merit other responses that positively affect funniness. A benign-appraisal condition is proscriptive but not prescriptive: it specifies only what negatively affects funniness and not what positively affects it; so it makes sense for comic merit to be asymmetrical. Hence, accepting a benign-appraisal condition, like (ii), does not only allow the comic moralist to avoid Carroll's criticism of the merited-response argument, it also has the additional value of being able to answer another substantial criticism Carroll makes of the comic moralist position as a whole.

In conclusion, Carroll's criticism has appeal only before a richer conceptual analysis of amusement and the addition of a benign-appraisal condition. The addition of this condition implies, contra Carroll, that comic merit includes moral merit. Carroll's criticism of the merited-response argument is then unsuccessful and the merited-response argument is a sound argument for comic moralism.[9] Therefore, immorality negatively affects funniness.

However, note that the merited-response argument for comic moralism cannot easily be extrapolated from amusement to aesthetic appreciation. Such an extrapolation would conveniently solve a long running dispute in the philosophy of art about the relationship between aesthetics and morality (Jacobson 1997; D'Arms & Jacobson 2000; Gaut 2007; Carroll 2000). However, this extrapolation cannot be easily made because there are good reasons to believe that benign appraisal is a precondition for amusement, but no parallel reasons for believing that benign appraisal is also a precondition for aesthetic appreciation. Hence, to extrapolate the merited-response argument for comic moralism from amusement to aesthetic appreciation would yield a far more dubious argument.

NOTES

1. Note that this position is different to that which Noël Carroll (2014a; 2014b) labels "comic amoralism." What Carroll labels comic amoralism amounts to the claim that humor cannot be moral or immoral—a claim which Berys Gaut (2007, 245) calls "comic autonomism."

2. That immorality merits moral disapproval is widely accepted since, even though different theories of normative ethics disagree on the definition of "immorality," they generally agree that immorality merits moral disapproval. Whether immorality is defined in terms of breaching principles, negative consequences or manifesting vices, the merited response to immorality is moral disapproval.

3. Which of these three positions is right will be of relevance to the relationship between immorality and aesthetic value in general. For example, the more general analogue of comic immoralism is aesthetic immoralism—the position that the immorality of an artwork positively affects its aesthetic value. Daniel Jacobson (1997) even argues for aesthetic immoralism by way of analogy to comic immoralism.

4. Positive arguments for comic immoralism are given by Daniel Jacobson (1997), Scott Woodcock (2015), and Ted Nannicelli (2014).

5. Berys Gaut (1998, 51–68; 2007, 227–252) gives a version of this merited-response argument in defence of his special brand of comic moralism, called "comic ethicism." Comic ethicism is the position that each immoral element will negatively affect funniness and if their cumulative effect is sufficient, then funniness is eliminated. This is not necessarily to claim that any immoral element in humor will eliminate funniness. Hence, comic ethicism can grant that some humor with immoral elements is still funny, because the cumulative negative effect of those immoral elements is not suffcient to completely eliminate funniness. Nonetheless, to the extent that any humor contains immoral elements, it is not funny. Hence, comic ethicism can also grant that some humor is so immoral that it is not funny at all.

6. Note that Carroll presents the criticism as made by critics of comic ethicism but, for stylistic ease, I refer to the criticism as Carroll's and to Carroll himself as a critic of comic moralism. The criticism is similar to that raised by Daniel Jacobson (1997).

7. Also contra D'Arms and Jacobsen, Andrew Jordan and Stephanie Patridge (2012) argue that moral considerations can be relevant for ascribing funniness. On their view, a joke is funny only if an appropriate subject takes themselves to have a contributory reason to be amused, and sometimes the absence of such a reason is best explained in terms of moral considerations.

8. Contra Carroll, Berys Gaut (1998, 65–66) does argue that moral elements can positively affect funniness, provided that there is already some humor to make funnier.

9. This conclusion has consequences for D'Arms and Jacobson's (2000, 65–90) exposition of the moralistic fallacy. Recall that to commit the moralistic fallacy is to infer from the fact that it would be immoral to have a particular attitudinal response toward a particular object that that object does not have the evaluative property associated with that attitudinal response. One of the supposed examples D'Arms and Jacobson (2000, 80) give is how "a joke can be funny even though it is wrong to be amused by

it." However, the failure of Carroll's criticism means that it does not necessarily amount to committing the moralistic fallacy to infer from the fact that it would be immoral to be amused toward a particular joke that that joke is not funny. This does not mean that D'Arms and Jacobson cannot claim that the moralistic fallacy exists and is committed in other inferences. Merely, it means that they cannot use funniness as an example to illustrate the moralistic fallacy in their exposition of it.

REFERENCES

Apter, Michael. J. 1991. "A Structural-Phenomenology of Play." In *Adult Play: A Reversal Theory Approach*, edited by John H. Kerr, Michael J. Apter, (13–29). Amsterdam: Garland Science.

Carroll, Noël. 2000. "Art and Ethical Criticism: An Overview of Recent Directions of Research," *Ethics*, 110 (2): 350–387.

Carroll, Noël. 2014a. "Ethics and Comic Amusement," *British Journal of Aesthetics* 54(2): 241–253.

Carroll, Noël. 2014b. *Humour: A Very Short Introduction.* Oxford: OUP.

D'Arms, Justin and Daniel Jacobson. 2000. "The Moralistic Fallacy: On the 'Appropriateness' of Emotions," *Philosophy and Phenomenological Research*, 61 (1): 65–90.

Freud, Sigmund. 1928. "Humour." *The International Journal of Psychoanalysis* 9 (1): 1–6.

Gaut, Berys Nigel. 1998. "Just Joking: The Ethics and Aesthetics of Humor," *Philosophy and Literature* 22(1): 51–68.

Gaut, Berys Nigel. 2007. *Art, Emotion and Ethics,* Oxford: OUP.

Gervais, Matthew. and David Sloan Wilson. 2005. "The Evolution and Functions of Laughter and Humor: A Synthetic Approach." *The Quarterly Review of Biology* 80(4): 395–430.

Jacobson, Daniel. 1997. "In Praise of Immoral Art," *Philosophical Topics*, 25 (1): 155–199.

Jordan, Andrew and Stephanie Patridge. 2012. "Against the moralistic fallacy: A modest defense of a modest sentimentalism about humor," *Ethical Theory and Moral Practice*, 15 (1): 83–94.

McGraw, A Peter and Caleb Warren. 2010. "Benign violations: Making immoral behavior funny." *Psychological Science* 21 (8): 1141–1149.

Nannicelli, Ted. 2014. "Moderate Comic Immoralism and the Genetic Approach to the ethical Criticism of Art," *Journal of Aesthetics and Art Criticism* 72 (2): 169–179.

Ramachandran, V. S. 1998. "The Neurology and Evolution of Humor, Laughter, and Smiling: The False Alarm Theory." *Medical Hypotheses* 51: 351–354..

Rothbart, M. 1976. "Psychological Approaches to the Study of Humour." In *It's a Funny Thing, Humour* 1st edition, edited by Antony J. Chapman and Hugh C. Foot. Oxford: Pergamon.

Smuts, Aaron. 2010. "The Ethics of Humor: Can Your Sense of Humor be Wrong?" *Ethical Theory and Moral Practice*, 13 (3): 333–347.

de Sousa, Ronald. 1990. *The Rationality of Emotion.* Cambridge, MA: MIT Press.

Woodcock, Scott. 2015. "Comic Immoralism and Relatively Funny Jokes," *Journal of Applied Philosophy*, 32 (2): 203–216.

Chapter 5

This Isn't Funny

It's Serious

Brian Mondy

1. INTRODUCTION

The contrast of humor with taking something seriously is a common form of criticism of both those who produce humor and those who consume it. For instance, in *Nanette*, comedian Hannah Gadsby (2018) relates the following "advice" she received at the beginning of her comedy career. "Back then, lesbian wasn't about sexuality, a lesbian was just any woman not laughing at a man. 'Why aren't you laughing? What are you? Some kind of lesbian?' Classic. 'Go on. You gotta laugh. Lighten up. Stop taking everything so seriously!'" Humor is more often criticized for not taking a serious subject seriously enough. In his documentary series *Larry Charles' Dangerous World of Comedy*, Charles (2019, Ep. 4) comments on the prevalence of comedy about rape in Nigeria: "In a patriarchal religious and political environment . . . [in which] violence against women is common, rape is more than tolerated. It's not taken seriously. It's a joke." Though it is a common criticism of humor, it has mostly been overlooked in the philosophical literature. In this chapter, I provide a framework for understanding and evaluating these kinds of criticisms.

In §2, I argue that by intending to produce amusement, producers of humor can express or encourage serious or unserious attitudes about the subject of their humor. Similarly, an audience member's response to humor can express and encourage serious or unserious attitudes toward the subject. I give an account of what it means to take a subject seriously in terms of serious and unserious intellectual, practical, and emotional attitudes, and relate these attitudes to humor and amusement. In §3, I use the account to explain some common criticisms of humor. In §4, I go beyond explaining criticisms of humor as failing to take something seriously, and show how my account can be used to evaluate these criticisms as correct or incorrect. Finally, in §5, I show how the framework can account for contextual features about the producer, audience, and environment in which a bit occurs, and use these features of the framework to show what is mistaken about both views that prohibit humor about a subject like rape altogether, and views that take the fact that a statement was made in jest as exculpatory.

Before proceeding, I'd like to make a few points about method. First, I think that to really understand humor and moral criticism, we have to go beyond the philosophical literature and look at what comedians and critics have to say, so I draw on a variety of sources. Second, the view I defend is meant to apply broadly to all forms of humor, so I use examples from stand-up comedy, online memes, practical jokes, satire and parody, and comedic television and movies. As such, I use the broader term "bit" to refer to instances of humor or comedy. Third, I think that the contrast of humor with seriousness applies to a broad spectrum of kinds of criticism of humor including that it is racist or sexist, and that humor about a particular subject like suicide bombings is immoral. The breadth of kinds of sources, humor, and criticism I will consider should make clear the need for an account like mine, but it means that I won't be able to address all of the relevant philosophical literature or provide the precision and detail that might be possible with a narrower focus.

2. HUMOR, AMUSEMENT, AND SERIOUS ATTITUDES

In this section, I will argue that producers of humor intend to produce amusement, and that in doing so, they can express or encourage unserious attitudes. I'll then explain three kinds of unserious attitudes and how they relate to humor. To begin, attitudes are something we have, so my view applies in the first place to those who produce and respond to humor, not to jokes as abstract forms or types. In the usual case, humor involves both producers and respondents. However, sometimes the producer and respondent are the same person, such as when you laugh at a joke to yourself without telling it. We are also sometimes amused by features of the world that are not produced as instances of humor, such as animal behavior, a poorly designed house, or an oddly shaped cloud.[1] However, there is a producer of humor who can be criticized if these things are pointed out by another person such as on the blog *McMansion Hell* (mcmansionhell.com).

My concern is with the attitudes we express and encourage in producing and responding to humor, and amusement is the attitude most associated with humor. Let's begin with producers of humor. In the normal case, the producer finds the bit amusing regardless of the kind of bit it is.[2] In presenting the bit as a bit, they are acknowledging that they find it amusing. Beyond their own attitudes, we can also think about the attitudes producers of humor bring about in others. I defend the following view:

(A) producers of bits intend to produce amusement in at least *some* respondents.

Before defending (A), two points about it should be clarified. First, a bit need not actually amuse anyone—since it just might not be funny—but what is relevant is that it is intended to amuse. Second, a bit need only be intended to amuse some, not all, respondents.

In support of (A), consider a case where we are unsure whether the action was meant humorously or not, such as someone posting the video meme of a woman spinning wildly on a backboard underneath a helicopter during a rescue (Know Your Meme, n.d.). Suppose someone posts it with no comment, or just the comment, "Holy crap." Is this a bit? It seems to me that it depends on what they intended. If I'm unsure, I might ask what they intended. If they respond that they were interested in figuring out how this physically happens, then it was not a bit; if they posted it either because they were amused or they thought it would amuse others, then it was a bit.

Though nearly all philosophers of humor have connected humor with amusement, Gimbel (2018) is perhaps unique in the contemporary literature in holding the view that humor has nothing to do with amusement or the intended response to it. He contends, "The fundamental flaw that plagues the contemporary discussion in the philosophy of humor is the claim—implicit or explicit—that humor is essentially connected to laughter, mirth, or amusement" (1). As I've already noted, he is right that humor need not actually amuse. Though I don't have space to consider all of his arguments, one way that Gimbel argues that humor need not even be intended to amuse is by rightly pointing out that humor can be put to many purposes besides amusement: "we tell jokes to cut someone else down to size," "to humanize ourselves in the eyes of others," "to break the ice," "to cut the tension when there is conflict," "to create conflict," "to express embarrassment," or "to apologize" (2–3). Though humor can be put to further purposes, I don't think any of these examples show that humor can be separated from its essential purpose of producing amusement. In fact, some of these cases seem like examples where amusement actually explains how the further purpose is achieved. Why is someone cut down to size by a joke in a way that he wouldn't be by a mere insult? Because he is now an object of amusement for others. Moreover, his being the object of amusement might raise tension and create conflict. Why would we try to humanize ourselves, break the ice, or ease tension with humor? Because we are trying to produce a positive feeling of amusement in the other that will make them feel positively toward us (see Morreall 2009, Chap. 4 for further explanation of similar examples). Intentional acts of humor, the object of Gimbel's analysis, can be characterized by the response they *intend*. There are other ways to cut someone down to size, or to break the ice; what makes a particular way of doing it a humorous way is that it is intended to cause amusement.

So we should accept (A), but what is amusement, and how does amusement relate to (lacking) seriousness? There is an ongoing debate about whether or not amusement is an emotion, but one feature of amusement that is accepted by those on both sides is that amusement can block other attitudes. Morreall (1983, 221–3; 2009, Chap. 4) argues that amusement is not an emotion in part because it can prevent us from feeling other emotions like anger or fear, and from acting, which he argues is uncharacteristic of other emotions. He further argues that this feature of amusement can serve to explain the morality of humor. Put briefly, in Morreall (2009) he argues that humor involves adopting a playful attitude, and "the practical and cognitive disengagement in humor can have harmful effects (102)," since it can: promote irresponsibility, such as when we laugh off a problem that we shouldn't; block compassion resulting in harm; and promote prejudice, since we are more receptive to prejudice in the playful contexts of humor. In contrast to Morreall, Palencik (2007) argues that amusement is an emotion, but he also believes that amusement can block other emotions. Palencik just argues that it is common for a stronger emotion to block a weaker one.

Similar to Morreall, I think the way that humor, in intending to produce amusement, can limit or discourage other attitudes can serve as a basis for moral criticism of humor and explain what is going on when a bit is criticized as failing to take a subject, person, or group seriously. However, my view differs from Morreall's in three important respects. Morreall claims that an attitude of disengagement is involved in all humor, and can serve as the basis for a general consequentialist ethic of humor. First, though I think my account of what it means to take something seriously figures in much moral criticism of humor, I don't think it is comprehensive. This is related to the second point: I don't think that all humor blocks seriousness or involves an attitude of disengagement. Third, while my view considers consequences, it is not solely or even primarily concerned with consequences. Bits are morally criticized not just for what they cause but also for the attitudes they express, and the attitudes they encourage even if no one takes up those attitudes. A racially insensitive joke might be criticized even if no one in the audience agrees with it (Anderson 2015).

As argued by Morreall and Palencik, amusement can conflict with other attitudes, and I've suggested that moral criticism of humor often looks at how humor can express or encourage a lack of seriousness. What does it mean to take a subject seriously? Perhaps unsurprisingly given the previous discussion, the OED (*Oxford English Dictionary* 2013) defines "serious" in part in opposition to terms related to humor such as "joking," "comic," or "intended simply to amuse."[3] It defines "serious" generally as "weighty, grave, important," a "serious person" as "having a grave or solemn disposition"; and a "serious action" as "requiring earnest thought," and "careful consideration." Though the dictionary can serve as a tool, I want to look at serious attitudes paying particular attention to their relation to humor and amusement. On my view, taking something seriously can be characterized in terms of the (a) intellectual, (b) practical, and (c) emotional attitudes one has toward it. Thus, to claim that someone is not taking something seriously is to imply that they lack (or are deficient in) one or more of these attitudes. In the remainder of this section, I'll explain each of these kinds of serious attitudes, what it means to lack them, and how they can figure in criticisms of humor.

In terms of intellectual attitudes, if one views a subject as "important" and requiring "earnest thought," then one has an interest in understanding it. In the ideal case, someone who takes a subject seriously understands it, but a student can be serious about a subject without yet fully understanding it. At a minimum, taking a subject intellectually seriously requires being interested in understanding and learning about it, filling in gaps in one's understanding, and engaging in further inquiry if necessary.[4] Seriousness can come in degrees, so a more serious attitude corresponds to a greater understanding or a greater interest in improving one's understanding. Therefore, in the intellectual sense, failing to take something seriously (or as seriously as it should be) is failing to understand it, and failing to have much (or any) interest in learning more about it.[5]

In relation to humor and its criticism, a producer of humor can express and/or encourage serious or unserious attitudes toward the subject(s) of a bit. A respondent might also express these attitudes in their response, and given the social nature of attitudes, in expressing an attitude, encourage others to adopt it. Thus, to criticize a producer or respondent for not taking a subject seriously is to imply two things. First, that they have expressed that they do not have a serious attitude toward it, and/or that they have encouraged failing to adopt a serious attitude. Second, that they ought to have the relevant serious attitude(s), or ought not to discourage them in others.

In a piece for *Vice* criticizing bits about Asians and Asian-Americans at the 2016 Oscars (#OscarsSoWhite), Asian-American author Tony Tulathimutte (2016) concluded:

> No one really believes those comedians harbor any real malice for Asians or Latinos, and surely the main reason they're reaching for this material is to deliver a little shock with their punchlines, but their intent isn't the point. The point is that there's hardly any media representation for Asians, Latinos, and

other non-black minorities *except* in the form of these insipid comic tropes; it's hard to take jokes when we're never taken seriously. (Hey, did you know more white actresses have won Oscars for playing Asian women than actual Asian women have?) Give us a few Asian Oscar nominees, and (why not?) an Asian Supreme Court Justice and an Asian president, and it'll be easier to laugh it off.

Many philosophical accounts of the morality of racial humor appeal to the racist beliefs or stereotypes that must be endorsed in producing or responding to a racist joke, for example, DeSousa (1987), LaFollette and Shanks (1993), and Bergmann (1986). However, Tulathimutte does not appear to think that endorsement of racist beliefs is the appropriate criticism of the comedians he is considering. Rather, in terms of intellectual attitudes, his primary criticism is of their ignorance or lack of understanding: for instance, most probably don't know that more white than Asian actresses have won Oscars for playing Asian women.

Unserious intellectual attitudes can also explain two further points about moral criticism of humor that are not so easy to explain on belief-based accounts. First, Anderson (2015) rightly notes that criticism of humor can come in degrees, and in his discussion of racial humor he distinguishes "racist" from "racially insensitive" humor. Interest and understanding also come in degrees and allow for a range of more or less serious attitudes, and a range of criticisms of humor producers and respondents. Moreover, failing to understand an issue can capture why some humor is insensitive without the producer endorsing racist views (Lengbeyer [2005] makes a similar point).

Second, as Bicknell (2007, 459) suggests, there seems to be a difference between asserting racist (or sexist, homophobic, transphobic, etc.) views and stereotypes and joking about them.[6] Bicknell (2007), Cohen (1999), and Morreall (2009) appeal to the fictional nature of jokes to draw this distinction, but not all humor involves participation in a fiction. Much modern stand-up comedy involves telling stories about things that actually happened to the comic, and videos of actual events shared as humorous memes are not fictions but could involve stereotypes. Serious and unserious intellectual attitudes can be used to explain the difference between asserting a stereotype and joking about it. A comic might tell true stories in a way that indicates a lack of understanding without outright asserting a racist, sexist, or transphobic stereotype.[7]

The second kind of serious attitudes are practical. Seriousness about most issues involves both an interest in understanding and an interest in doing something about it. Thus, the OED notes that a serious person is "responsible," and serious acts require "careful consideration." Practical attitudes concern one's actions and plans, and taking a subject seriously in the practical sense means incorporating it into one's planning for contexts in which it is relevant, including thinking about the consequences of one's actions for those issues. For example, there have been many calls to take Covid-19 seriously by taking appropriate actions to protect oneself and others (see, e.g., Noor 2020).

Contrarily, one fails to take something seriously in the practical sense if one fails to incorporate it (at all or sufficiently) into one's planning or to consider the consequences of one's actions for it. While they are not the same, intellectual seriousness and practical seriousness are related in that if one fails to understand a subject, then one is unlikely to be concerned about it practically. For example, if a person fails to understand that Covid-19 is real and dangerous, then they are unlikely to consider it in their planning, or seriously consider the consequences of their actions on the pandemic (Penrod 2020).

In making something a subject of humor, we can express that we are not particularly concerned about acting to do anything about the issue, and we might encourage apathy on the part of others, or even cause them harm. Sometimes the way the expression of amusement prevents practical seriousness is obvious. For example, in Stanley Kubrick's *Full Metal Jacket*, Private Leonard Lawrence begins to smile at Drill Sergeant Hartman's aggressive, sometimes comedic (not to mention racist and homophobic), introduction to boot camp. The physical manifestation of his amusement thwarts his practical aim of avoiding punishment.[8] Expressing or encouraging unserious practical attitudes can also serve as a basis of criticism of humor. For instance, it is clear that Tulathimutte's criticism of the Oscars bits is not merely about intellectual attitudes; he'd like to see practical action taken for better representation of Asians and Asian-Americans and sees humor about the subject as standing in the way.

The third kind of serious and unserious attitudes is emotional. According to the OED, a serious person has a "solemn disposition." It's difficult to be specific about what constitutes a serious emotional attitude without knowing more about context. Serious emotional responses are probably the most easily blocked by amusement, so we might understand serious emotional attitudes by their contrast with amusement. Morreall (2009, 103–4) notes that humor can "[block] compassion for those who need help (103)," and "promote insensitivity, callousness, and cruelty (104)," and Lengbeyer (2005, 314) states that in some contexts "a laughing response bespeaks a deficient degree of humanity." Thus, at least when considering someone's pain or experience, serious attitudes seem to include compassion, sensitivity, and empathy. If the context is a ritual, then serious emotional attitudes might include contemplativeness, solidarity, and solemnity.

Since emotional attitudes are less directly under our control, the development of the right habits of emotional response can be a goal of education, and humor can discourage the proper habits and resulting emotional responses.

For example, to deal with the difficulty and awkwardness of the task, medical students used to be counseled to take a comical approach to working with cadavers in anatomy labs such that they would give bodies humorous names or use the body to play pranks on other students (Allen 2015). More recently the humorous approach has been called into question, not because students weren't learning the relevant material, nor because they were making mistakes in practical matters of dissection, but because of the emotional habits it encourages. One criticism is that amusement discourages or blocks the appropriate gratitude and respect due to someone who has virtuously donated their body to science and education. A second criticism holds that a humorous approach to cadavers in the lab could encourage a callous lack of empathy for future patients. In order to inculcate more serious emotional responses, many medical schools now have students meet with the family of the donor prior to the term and participate in a solemn ceremony at the end of the term.

To sum up, seriousness can be characterized in terms of intellectual, practical, and emotional attitudes, and both producers of and respondents to humor can express or encourage unserious attitudes about the subject(s). However, we should not assume that all humor expresses some form of unserious attitude. In fact, some humor clearly expresses and encourages taking a subject seriously. For instance, on the comedic news program *Last Week Tonight*, John Oliver discusses issues in a way that is generally well-researched, often encourages practical action, and shows genuine concern and righteous anger. Thus, Morreall (2009, 101) is wrong when he asserts, "When we want to invoke anger or outrage about some problem, we don't present it in a humorous way precisely because of the practical disengagement of humor." I think many people are stirred to anger or outrage by comedic news programs; I certainly have been.

3. EXPLAINING CRITICISM OF HUMOR AS LACKING SERIOUSNESS

In this section, I will show how the account explains the meaning of some criticisms of humor, and further, illustrate the prevalence of this sort of criticism.

In 1995, Weird Al's hit "Amish Paradise" parodied Coolio's even bigger hit, "Gangsta's Paradise," and at the time Coolio did not approve. When asked about "Amish Paradise" in an interview, he said, "I ain't with that. I think that my song was too serious. I really don't appreciate him desecrating the song like that" (McKeon 2011). In some sense, Coolio is right that his song was desecrated. As a white suburban teen at the time, I sang along enthusiastically to both songs, the sacred and the profane, and now the lyrics to both songs are mixed up in my mind. What were the serious themes in Coolio's song? It seems that Coolio meant the song to be about how many young black men were forced into living a fantasy gang life that led to their own deaths. That's serious. Waking up and churning butter has nothing to do with it. If Coolio had hoped that his song would raise intellectual understanding and awareness about the plight of young black men that might actually lead to practical change, then it seems clear that Weird Al's silly parody could undercut and discourage the serious attitudes Coolio was hoping to encourage. None of this necessarily shows that Weird Al's parody was immoral, nor that Weird Al or anyone else had these unserious attitudes (though it seems clear that at least some kids like me did), but it does allow us to understand Coolio's criticism.[9]

Lack of seriousness as a criticism of humor is not unique to English-speaking countries. In 2010, the privately owned Iraqi channel Al Baghdadia aired the hidden camera prank show *Put Him in Bucca*, spurring a national and international debate about the morality of the humor in the show.[10] "Bucca" refers to the formerly U.S.-run high-security prison in Iraq that is well-known to Iraqis (Ghazi 2010; Al Jazeera English 2010).[11] On the show, Iraqi celebrities were invited to the studios of Al Baghdadia for a meeting, but while driving to the meeting, they would be stopped at a fake security checkpoint. While the car was searched by actual Iraqi soldiers who were part of the prank, a fake bomb would be found, leading to accusations that the celebrity is a terrorist who will be incarcerated or executed. The celebrities respond with the expected surprise, outrage, fear, and indignation before the producers let them know it was all a prank. Many Iraqis criticized the show on Al Baghdadia's website, in complaints to newspapers, and in a petition calling for the show to be canceled (Ghazi 2010; Charles 2019). Saleh Mahdi Saleh, an Iraqi psychologist interviewed on the street by Al Jazeera (2010), said, "It's inappropriate humor that belittles a serious issue. Also, television has a direct effect on the audience who tend to imitate what they watch. People may start staging similar pranks at school and work, and that can't be a good thing."

Most accounts of the morality of humor have been either belief-based, like the accounts of racial humor discussed in the previous section, or harm-based (Bicknell 2007 provides a useful division of accounts into these categories. I discussed belief-based account in §1. For harm-based accounts, see Benatar 1999; Gimbel 2018; Morreall 2009; Philips 1984). *Put him in Bucca* didn't cause any actual harm, even if potential harm explains Saleh's concern about the possibility of copycat pranks. The show also doesn't really express any immoral beliefs or stereotypes. Still, the criticism that it failed to take its subjects seriously is meaningful. Serious issues that are the subject of the show include the constant danger that Iraqi citizens faced, the presence of fake

Al-Qaeda checkpoints, the prevalence of just the sort of suicide bombings of which the celebrities were falsely accused, and the real harms that were done in Bucca prison. Other critics also noted that the show was intentionally aired during the holy holiday of Ramadan when families, including children, would be home together watching. These critics can be taken as saying that the show expressed and encouraged flippant emotional attitudes toward serious issues during the solemn holiday of Ramadan.

The criticisms of humor we've examined so far appeal explicitly to concerns about taking things seriously, but my account might also help to explain other criticisms of humor as well. For instance, statements like "This is no laughing matter," "That's not funny," or "This is no joke" seem to trade on the contrast of humor with serious matters, and might be thought to lend weight to positions in debates over comic moralism: whether and to what extent the immorality of a joke affects its funniness. However, my view provides a way that these phrases can be made sense of without taking them literally as relating funniness to morality.[12] Rather, we can take them as admonishing either producers, respondents, or any other listeners to take the subject seriously intellectually, practically, and/or emotionally. This allows that the phrases can be apt insofar as the subject morally ought to be taken seriously, and the producers or respondents are failing to do so. This interpretation often fits better with the use of these phrases in context. It seems unlikely that typical respondents want to weigh in on the esoteric debate of whether there is some objective property of funniness that is affected by morality. Rather, critics generally want people to think, feel, or act differently. Tony Tulathimutte wants people to understand the experience of Asian Americans, and for Asian Americans to be cast in more roles. Writers to Iraqi newspapers wanted *Put Him in Bucca* off the air. It would be surprising if the correctness of these prescriptions depended on whether the bits were in fact less funny as a result of their immorality. On the other hand, it is relevant whether or not the bits are actually failing to take the subjects seriously and encouraging similar attitudes, and whether those subjects actually should be taken seriously. While it is still possible that some instances of phrases like "That's not funny" are meant literally, and are approximately correct as the comic moralist holds, the fact that what seem like the important public debates can still be had without settling questions concerning comic moralism should serve to weaken some of the appeal of arguing over comic moralism.

4. EVALUATING CRITICISMS OF HUMOR

In the previous section, I looked at how the account of seriousness and its relation to humor could be used to understand some common criticisms of humor. In this section, I want to examine how criticisms of humor along these lines can be evaluated as correct or incorrect. I've contended that to criticize a producer or respondent for not taking a subject seriously is to imply (1) that they have expressed and/or encouraged one or more of the unserious attitudes, and (2) that they ought to have or encourage the relevant serious attitude(s). Accurate criticism of humor as unserious requires that both features be met, so criticisms of humor as unserious can be mistaken in two ways, and debates can occur around each sort of mistake.

The first sort of mistake, corresponding to implication (1), occurs when the critic mistakenly takes the producer of a bit as expressing an unserious attitude toward the subject, and/or mistakenly takes the producer to be encouraging unserious attitudes in the respondents. This could occur because the critic (1a) mistakes the attitudes of the producer, or (1b) mistakes the subject or target of the humor. Debate about the Iraqi show *Put Him in Bucca* can serve as an example of each kind of mistake and debate. In an example of debate over (1a), critics argued that the pranks in the show did not take seriously the serious subject of fake checkpoints and the threat of death that Iraqis faced on a daily basis. However, the creators of the show argued that they did take fake checkpoints and death seriously. Ali al-Khalidi, the host of the show, said that they were aware of fake checkpoints, and that the show was aimed at "exposing" fake checkpoints to the public (Charles 2019). Thus, he can be seen as arguing that he takes the issue intellectually seriously and sees his comedy as a way of making people aware of a very real threat.

Whether or not he takes the issue seriously *enough* is open for debate, but the important point is that there is room for mistakes and debate about whether and to what extent a producer is taking an issue seriously. My account allows for an explanation and assessment of this sort of criticism. It seems clear that the producers of *Put Him in Bucca* intellectually understood the subject of their humor and that they were at least trying to do something practical to improve the situation. One debate concerns the nature of this practical approach and whether it was sufficiently serious. For instance, Saleh, the psychologist quoted previously, suggests that further practical ramifications might not have been considered and taken seriously, such as copycat pranks that are not as safe or carefully orchestrated.[13] Defenders of the show might argue that those risks are justified, since a popular TV show is more likely to raise awareness than simple PSAs.

Debate about the emotional seriousness of the show seems to have been at least as significant as debate about its intellectual or practical seriousness. The show aired during Ramadan as a show to be watched and enjoyed by families. Ramadan is a holiday calling for serious contemplation that might be a poor fit with the comedy of "Bucca," and there is certainly reason to think that children might not grasp the serious issues addressed in the show, and be more likely to walk away with different emotional attitudes than the producers intended. As a result, the producers might be criticized for encouraging or teaching flippant emotional attitudes, even if they didn't intend to.

The producers' responses to criticism also suggested that some critics might be making a mistake as to (1b) the target of the humor in claiming that the show was "mocking, especially to Iraqis (An Iraqi commenter quoted in Ghazi 2010)." The producer of the show Najm al-Rubaie explained the aim of the show as follows: "Most importantly, we wanted to undermine these scary weapons of Al Qaeda: car bombs and suicide vests.... The joke's on Al Qaeda not the Iraqi people" (Al-Jazeera English 2010). As with al-Khalidi's defense, this assertion can be challenged. It seems obvious that the joke was also on the celebrities who were pranked on the show. Part of the humor depends on these being pranks and not a scripted show, and on the subjects of the pranks being celebrities. In a complicated bit, it is often common for there to be more than one subject of the bit, so the fact that one subject is being taken seriously might not preclude that another subject is not. However, as above, I want to point out that my view allows for mistakes to be made about the subject of a bit and provides a framework for legitimate debate.

We can also be mistaken about (2) whether a subject actually should be taken seriously or seriously in the way that the critic thinks it should. Tyrants might believe that everyone should take a serious and respectful attitude toward them, but that does not mean they are correct. The tyrant ought to be taken seriously in understanding how he will behave, and in practically planning accordingly, but he need not be taken seriously in the way he would like: as a leader who should be revered, respected, or loved. The tyrant is too sensitive, or sensitive about the wrong things. Thus, offense is not the measure of morality. Rather, critical moral judgments of the sort under consideration are accurate insofar as there are good moral reasons for taking the subject seriously intellectually, practically, and/or emotionally, and the bit expresses or encourages attitudes that are not equally serious.

5. CONSIDERING CONTEXT

Thus far I've shown how the producer of a bit can express or encourage unserious attitudes, how this can explain a variety of criticisms of humor, and how those criticisms can be evaluated and debated. In this section, I want to show that my account explains how contextual features can figure in moral evaluations of producers and respondents. By looking at contextual features from within the framework I've provided, we can see the mistake in both extreme moralist views that preclude humor about some subjects altogether and extreme amoralist views that deny that humor can ever be the subject of moral evaluation.

I'll begin with an example of the moralist view. In 2012, after comedian Daniel Tosh finished a bit that included a reference to rape, an audience member shouted, "Rape jokes are never funny" (Zinoman 2012). Tosh responded to the audience member by saying, "Wouldn't it be funny if that girl got raped by like, five guys right now? Like right now? What if a bunch of guys just raped her." The exchange went viral online and stimulated a public debate about rape humor in which many male comedians defended Tosh by claiming that nothing is off-limits to comedy.

Though initial opponents and defenders of humor about rape in the debate didn't consider context, more sophisticated critics illustrate how contextual features such as facts about history, culture, the producer, and the (likely) respondents are relevant to moral criticism of humor. Lindy West commented on humor about rape and the controversy surrounding Tosh's comments in a piece for the feminist website *Jezebel*:

> Here's the problem: *everybody* is wrong. I actually agree with Daniel Tosh's sentiment in his shitty back-pedaling tweet ("The point I was making before I was heckled is there are awful things in the world but you can still make jokes about them #deadbabies"). The world *is* full of terrible things, including rape, and it *is* okay to joke about them. But the best comics use their art to call bullshit on those terrible parts of life and make them better, not worse. (West 2012)

Later in the piece she writes, "It's really easy to believe that 'nothing is sacred' when the sanctity of your body and your freedom are never legitimately threatened," before proceeding to state a number of facts about rape in the United States, including that given the Center for Disease Control statistics on the prevalence of rape it is likely that at least one woman in any comedy audience actually has been raped.

West, like other commentators such as Jennifer L. Pozner, allows that some jokes involving rape are morally permissible and funny. In fact, West (2012), Pozner (2012), and Kresinger (2012) cite and link to examples of rape jokes (Pozner even includes Tosh's joke that the audience member commented on). Pozner argues that there is a "difference between 'rape jokes' that target victims and mock their pain, and 'rape culture jokes' that dismantle the systems that protect rapists and blame women for sexual assault. . . . Feminists aren't against good comedy—they're just against lazy hacks." She also points us to George Carlin who said something quite similar in his HBO special *Doin' It Again* (1990) in a bit that involves a number of jokes involving rape: "I believe you can joke about anything. It all depends on how you construct the joke. What the exaggeration is."[14]

As West, Pozner, and Carlin make clear, trenchant, effective, and accurate moral criticism of humor considers contextual features; it doesn't make blanket statements that something cannot be the subject of humor.[15] Within the framework I've been developing, we can see that some bits about rape (e.g., most of the bits by the Nigerian comics documented in *Larry Charles' Dangerous World of Comedy*) fail to take the serious subject seriously, while other humor about rape does not express or encourage that rape should not be taken seriously. We can tell the difference by asking questions about context. Who is producing the bit? What do they know? As West points out, do they know how common rape is in America? Are they encouraging more thought on the part of the respondents or dismissal? For example, in a bit that is praised by Pozner, John Mulaney (2009) explains realizing that a woman was afraid of him, a scrawny guy, walking behind her at night. Many male listeners might be encouraged to consider the dangers women face as a result of this bit. As Carlin makes clear, criticism that considers context asks what parts of the subject is the producer targeting, making salient, or exaggerating? In terms of seriousness, public criticism tends to focus on intellectual seriousness like listening, learning, and raising awareness, but this should ideally lead to taking something practically seriously by acting. As to emotional seriousness, we might ask, "Does this person seem like they give a damn?" Contextual questions about the producer tie in with the popular sentiment that it is wrong to "punch down." Comedians are told not to "punch down," and members of a group have license to make and laugh at jokes about that group that nonmembers do not. If we look at these criticisms in terms of expressing and/or encouraging serious or unserious attitudes, a member of a group is more likely to take matters that affect a group seriously even while laughing at them.

To determine whether a bit expresses and encourages serious or unserious attitudes, a critic (or a responsible comedian) should also consider the context of likely respondents. Dave Chappelle reported walking away from his popular show, *The Chappelle Show*, for these reasons. While taping a sketch about racial stereotypes, Chappelle noticed a white audience member laugh at a point that made Chappelle feel uncomfortable (Farley 2005). Chappelle took his comedy seriously, but in functioning as his own critic, he considered that his show aired nationally on Comedy Central. In Chappelle's case, considering context included thinking about the audience of a bit and whether the bit encouraged unserious intellectual and practical attitudes toward race matters for at least some of that audience. We can disagree with Chappelle's assessment, but not with his concern that the audience of a bit is relevant to determining what the bit actually expresses and encourages.

Just as looking at context from within the framework of serious and unserious attitudes shows that extreme moralism about the subject matter of humor is mistaken, looking at context from within the framework also shows what is mistaken about excuses like, "I was only joking. Quit taking everything so seriously." For instance, consider the defense of humor within the alt-right movement offered by Allum Bokhari and Milo Yiannopoulos (2016) in a piece on Breitbart.com:

> The alt-right openly crack jokes about the Holocaust, loudly—albeit almost entirely satirically—expresses its horror at "race-mixing," and denounces the "degeneracy" of homosexuals . . . while inviting Jewish gays [Yiannopoulos] and mixed-race Breitbart reporters [Bokhari] to their secret dinner parties. What gives?
> . . . For the meme brigade, it's just about having fun. They have no real problem with race-mixing, homosexuality, or even diverse societies: It's just fun to watch the mayhem and outrage that erupt when those secular shibboleths are openly mocked. These younger mischief-makers instinctively understand who the authoritarians are and why and how to poke fun at them.

Their defense throughout the piece is that alt-right humor is not serious, since most in the movement don't actually hold bigoted views, and the humor is mostly meant to needle what they view as overly sensitive liberals and "grandparents." However, this defense trades on an ambiguity about what it means to be serious. In one sense, "serious" means "honest" or "sincere," so it could be right to say that those who make these jokes don't seriously hold bigoted views. But, endorsing bigoted beliefs is only one kind of criticism of humor. As I've been arguing, "serious" can also mean understanding a subject, having an interest in doing something about it, and having appropriate emotional attitudes, and it seems clear that many alt-right jokes are morally objectionable because they are unserious in this sense. It is unlikely that those in the alt-right understand the history of discrimination in the United States, or the culture of white privilege. Nor do they seem to "understand who the authoritarians are" if they think grandparents condemning Holocaust jokes are authoritarians. Moreover, the piece admits that the movement who consumes these jokes includes actual bigots and white supremacists. Thus, the producers of the memes can be criticized for encouraging unserious, or worse, bigoted attitudes, and in doing so, failing to have the appropriate serious practical attitudes that consider the consequences of their actions.

Since there are three kinds of serious attitudes, and those attitudes can come in degrees, the importance of considering contextual features is important to understanding and evaluating criticisms of humor as failing to take a subject seriously. Features of the social environment, the producer of the bit, and the likely respondents are relevant to determining whether a bit expresses or encourages unserious attitudes.

6. CONCLUDING REMARKS

In this chapter, I've provided a framework for understanding and evaluating criticism of producers and respondents to humor as taking a subject too seriously or not seriously enough. As I've shown, the framework can be used for thinking about a wide variety of humor. Given that any kind of humor could express or encourage a lack of seriousness about a subject, I'm inclined to think it could be applied to all forms of humor.[16] The view also applies to a broad range of moral criticisms of humor, including that it fails to take seriously a person or their pain, an immoral act like rape, and systemic oppression like sexism or racism. Though I only addressed them in passing, I think the account can also be used to help understand the sense of humor as a virtue or vice and criticism of humor in particular situations like funerals as inappropriate or immoral.

While I think the breadth of the account is a strength, it can also be a weakness in that it results from a greater level of abstraction. Many accounts of the morality of humor admirably describe in more detail moral criticism of particular kinds of humor, most often jokes, or particular kinds of immorality like racism, sexism, or self-deprecation. I don't intend for my view to replace all of those accounts—though I indicated some cases in which it seems to perform better—nor do I think that criticism in terms of seriousness is the only form of moral evaluation that can apply to humor. In fact, it is often a weaker criticism: a racist joke that expresses racist beliefs is usually worse than a joke that merely fails to take racism seriously. In some cases, the more specific accounts can be seen as filling in details within the general framework I've provided. For example, accounts of self-deprecation can explain in more detail the ways in which immoral self-deprecating humor fails to take oneself or one's pain seriously and the ways in which self-deprecating humor can take one's pain seriously. As with explanations in general, the degree of abstraction in an explanation can make salient different features of the total picture, and being able to explain a phenomenon with varying degrees of abstraction can lead to a greater level of understanding.

NOTES

1. Gimbel (2018) draws a distinction between humor and what we find funny where humor is an intentional act. If he is right, then humor without a producer isn't humor, but it can be something we find funny, and can be something we are criticized for finding funny, for instance, somebody being seriously injured.

2. As with nearly any claim there are exceptions. For instance, a producer might have formerly found a bit amusing, which they no longer do, such as the recorded work of a comic. Or, a producer might not find a bit amusing, but knows that an audience will, such as someone entertaining children.

3. I also use the adverbial phrase "take seriously," but the definition of that phrase leads us to the definition of "serious" according to the OED: "*to take (*a person or thing*) seriously*: to treat or regard as serious, important, or in earnest."

4. I refer to understanding instead of knowledge or mere belief here deliberately, since accounts of understanding are more suited to thinking about subjects or domains than knowledge. The contemporary discussion of understanding in epistemology begins with Kvanvig (2003). He calls understanding a subject as opposed to a proposition, "objectual understanding."

5. There are interesting issues that I will leave aside for now. What exactly is understanding? How do understanding and an interest in understanding relate? For example, is a person who is interested in a subject, and falsely thinks they understand it, taking the subject seriously? What if they have no evidence that they are mistaken? What if they do have evidence that they might be mistaken?

6. This distinction might not always hold up. Some jokes do just assert the stereotypes they invoke.

7. Dave Chappelle's (2017) standup about transgender people and the #metoo movement might be criticized in this way. He attempts to speak as an ally for women and the transgender community, and to draw parallels between their struggle and the struggle of Black Americans, but his comedy indicates a lack of understanding of those groups, even if he is trying to understand.

8. For more on similar cases see Egan (2014) and Morreall (2009, 94). Both consider a case where someone laughing at seeing a person fall prevents them from helping the injured person.

9. For those concerned, Coolio and Weird Al seem to have made up (McKeon 2011).

10. I'll be focusing mostly on how Iraqis criticized the program, but at the time the show was discussed in American news, for instance, Keith Olbermann declared the producers of the show his daily "Worst Persons in the World" on his nightly MSNBC program *Countdown*, and the *New York Times* covered the controversy (Ghazi 2010). It was also covered in Europe by *Der Spiegel* (Smoltczyk 2011), and *The Telegraph* (Hough 2010). More recently the show was portrayed in the documentary Charles (2019, Ep. 1).

11. I'm not sure if it is funny, ironic, disgusting, or something else, but I can't help but point out that the United States named the prison for New York City Fire Marshall, Ronald Bucca, who died in the September 11, 2001 attacks, which had nothing to do with Iraq.

12. Walton and Tanner (1994) make a similar point that these phrases need not be taken literally. There are other ways of cashing out these phrases that don't take them literally; for instance, Egan (2014) develops a view that sees them as relative statements about the speaker's attitudes, but not statements of objective truth or values.

13. In considering the morality of pranks, Egan & Weatherson (2004) support something like Saleh's point. They argue that a world with some pranks is better than one with no pranks, but that too many pranks would be bad.

14. In a statement relevant to our discussion, Carlin goes on to say that he likes to "piss off people who take themselves too seriously."

15. In the philosophical literature, Lengbeyer (2005) makes a similar sophisticated criticism of DeSousa's (1987) position that rape jokes necessarily involve objectionable sexist attitudes. He also points out that DeSousa's mistake is in part the result of focusing on only one particular joke about rape.

16. I'm least certain about slapstick, though the view seems to work to explain what is going on in some moral criticism of slapstick. For instance, slapstick that imitates the movements of a disabled or injured person could be criticized for failing to take a serious attitude toward the difficulties faced by that individual or individuals with that disability.

REFERENCES

Al Jazeera English. 2010. Iraq comedy show under fire. Sept. 9, 2010. https://www.youtube.com/watch?v=J6UCWmeNhPI.

Allen, John Tyler. 2015. "Learning Empathy from the Dead." *The Atlantic.* July 28, 2015. https://www.theatlantic.com/health/archive/2015/07/cadaver-dissection-empathy-medical-school/398429/.

Anderson, Luvell. 2015. "Racist Humor." *Philosophy Compass* 10, no. 8 (August): 501–509. https://doi.org/10.1111/phc3.12240.

Benatar, David. 1999. "Prejudice in Wit: When Racial and Gender Humor Harms." *Public Affairs Quarterly* 13: 191–203.

Bergmann, Merrie. 1986. "How Many Feminists Does It Take to Make a Joke? Sexist Humor and What's Wrong with It." *Hypatia* 1, No. 11 (Spring): 63–82. https://doi.org/10.1111/j.1527-2001.1986.tb00522.x.

Bicknell, Jeanette. 2007. "What Is Offensive about Offensive Jokes?" *Philosophy Today* 5, No. 4 (Winter): 458–465. https://doi.org/10.5840/philtoday200751430.

Bokhari, Allum, and Milo Yiannopoulos. 2016. "An Establishment Conservative's Guide to the Alt-Right." *Breitbart.com.* Mar. 29, 2016. https://www.breitbart.com/tech/2016/03/29/an-establishment-conservatives-guide-to-the-alt-right/

Carlin, George. 1990. *Doin' It Again.* HBO Special.

Charles, Larry (Producer, Director). 2019. *Larry Charles' Dangerous World of Comedy.* Netflix.

Chappelle, Dave. 2017. *Dave Chappelle: Equanimity & The Bird Revelation.* Netflix.

Cohen, Ted. 1999. *Jokes: Philosophical Thoughts on Joking Matters.* Chicago: University of Chicago Press.

De Sousa, Ronald. 1987. "When Is It Wrong to Laugh?" In *The Philosophy of Laughter and Humor,* edited by John Morreall, 226–49. Albany: State University of New York Press.

Egan, Andy. 2014. "There's Something Funny About Comedy: A Case Study in Faultless Disagreement." *Erkenntnis* 79: 73–100. https://doi.org/10.1007/s10670-013-9446-3

Egan Andy, and Brian Weatherson. 2004. "Prankster's Ethics." *Philosophical Perspectives* 18:45-52.

Farley, Christopher John. 2005. "Dave speaks." *Time.* May 14, 2005. http://content.time.com/time/magazine/article/0,9171,1061512,00.html

Gadsby, Hannah. 2018. *Nanette.* Netflix.

Ghazi, Yasir. 2010. "Punk'd, Iraqi-style, at a checkpoint." *The New York Times.* Sept. 3, 2010. https://atwar.blogs.nytimes.com/2010/09/03/punkd-iraqi-style-at-a-checkpoint/

Gimbel, Steven. 2018. *Isn't that Clever: A Philosophical Account of Humor.* New York: Routledge.

Know Your Meme. n.d. "Helicopter Lady Rescue." Accessed July 1, 2020. https://knowyourmeme.com/memes/helicopter-lady-rescue

Hough, Andrew. 2010. "Iraqi Prank Television Show Condemned for 'Fake Bomb' Stunts." *The Telegraph.* https://www.telegraph.co.uk/news/worldnews/middleast/iraq/7988631/Iraqi-prank-television-show-condemned-for-fake-bomb-stunts.html

McKeon, Conor. 2011. "Gangsta's Parodist: Revisiting 'Weird Al' vs. Coolio." *Vulture.* Dec. 19, 2011. https://www.vulture.com/2011/12/gangstas-parodist-revisiting-weird-al-vs-coolio.html

Kresinger, Elisa. 2012. "Rape Joke Supercut: I Can't Believe You Clapped for That." *Women's Media Center.* July 13, 2012. https://www.youtube.com/watch?v=LIVmI6N6JjY

Kubrick, S. (Producer, Director, Writer). 1987. *Full Metal Jacket.* Warner Bros.

Kvanvig, Jonathan L. 2003. *The Value of Knowledge and the Pursuit of Understanding.* Cambridge: Cambridge University Press. doi:10.1017/CBO9780511498909

LaFollette, Hugh, and Niall Shanks. 1993. "Belief and the Basis of Humor." *American Philosophical Quarterly* 30, No. 4:(October): 329–39.

Lengbeyer, Lawrence. 2005. "Humor, Context, and Divided Cognition." *Social Theory and Practice* 31, No. 3 (July): 309–336. https://doi.org/10.5840/soctheorpract200531316

Morreall, John. 1983. "Humor and Emotion." *American Philosophical Quarterly* 20: 297–304.

Morreall, John. 2009. *Comic Relief: A Comprehensive Philosophy of Humor.* Malden, MA: Wiley-Blackwell.

Mulaney, John. 2009. "Comedy Central Presents: John Mulaney." *Comedy Central Presents* Season 13, Episode 23. Comedy Central. http://www.cc.com/video-clips/uykiqr/comedy-central-presents-subway-station-chase.

Noor, Poppy. 2020. "If I Get Corona, I Get Corona: the Americans Who Wish They'd Taken Covid-19 Seriously." *The Guardian.* Mar. 28, 2020. https://www.theguardian.com/lifeandstyle/2020/mar/28/americans-who-dont-take-coronavirus-seriously.

Oxford English Dictionary. 2013. "Serious." *Oxford English Dictionary* (3rd Edition). Oxford: OUP.

Palencik, Joseph T. 2007. "Amusement and the Philosophy of Emotion: A Neuroanatomical Approach." *Dialogue* 46, No. 3 (Summer): 419–434. https://doi.org/10.1017/S0012217300001992

Penrod, Emma. 2020. "How to Explain to a Skeptic That the Coronavirus Should Be Taken Seriously." *Business Insider.* April 5, 2020. https://www.businessinsider.com/how-to-convince-skeptics-to-take-the-coronavirus-seriously-2020-3

Philips, Michael. 1984. "Racist Acts and Racist Humor." *The Canadian Journal of Philosophy* 14: 75-96.

Pozner, Jennifer L. 2012. "Louis C. K. on Daniel Tosh's Rape Joke: Are Comedy and Feminism Enemies?" *The Daily Beast.* July 18, 2012. https://www.thedailybeast.com/articles/2012/07/18/daniel-tosh-rape-joke-are-comedy-and-feminism-enemies

Smoltczyk, Alexander. 2011. "Uncertainty Reigns as Baghdad Enters New Era. *Der Spiegel.* July 1, 2011. https://www.spiegel.de/international/world/life-after-the-americans-uncertainty-reigns-as-baghdad-enters-new-era-a-737791.html

Tulathimutte, Tony. 2016. "The Oscars Showed That People Think It's Still Funny to Mock Asians." *Vice.* Mar. 1, 2016. https://www.vice.com/en_us/article/mvxd5v/the-oscars-show-that-people-think-its-still-funny-to-mock-asians

Walton, Kendall L. and Michael Tanner. 1994. "Morals in Fiction and Fictional Morality." *Aristotelian Society Supplementary Volume* 68, No. 1 (July): 27–66. https://doi.org/10.1093/aristoteliansupp/68.1.27

West, Lindy. 2012. "How to Make a Rape Joke." Accessed July 1, 202.: https://jezebel.com/how-to-make-a-rape-joke-5925186

Zinoman, Jason. 2012. "Toe-to-Toe at the Edge of the Comedy Club Stage." *The New York Times,* July 17, 2012. https://www.nytimes.com/2012/07/18/arts/television/when-the-comic-and-the-heckler-both-take-offense.html.

Chapter 6

The Ethics of Humor

Tristan Nash

This chapter will explore the conflict that can exist between humor and morality. To cast this conflict, I will assume that immoral jokes can sometimes be funny and can play a part in the valued contribution that humor makes to our lives. This conflict between humor and morality regularly arises in popular discussions. For example, in 2008, comedian Russell Brand and presenter Jonathan Ross came under criticism for a radio broadcast in which they left answerphone messages for actor Andrew Sachs that included jokes about Russell Brand's sexual relationship with Andrew Sachs's granddaughter (The Guardian 2008). In 2018, Mark Meechan was convicted of an offence under the 2000 Communications Act at Airdrie Sheriff Court, Scotland (BBC 2018). He had trained his girlfriend's pug to raise its paw as if saluting when he said "Sieg Heil" and posted a video of this, along with the dog's reaction to the phrase "Gas the Jews" as the dog sat in front of footage of the Nuremberg Rallies, to YouTube. Meechan offered the fact that it was a joke that juxtaposed "an adorable animal reacting to something vulgar" as a defense for his actions (BBC 2018). In 2020, in the wake of the protests following the murder of George Floyd by police in Minneapolis, streaming services pulled comedy series that featured blackface (Marshall 2020). Even the sitcom *Friends* has faced a moral reappraisal following its inclusion on *Netflix* (Michallon 2019). This chapter will place this debate within the broader discussion of the conflict between moral, nonmoral, and immoral considerations. I will argue that morality should not play an adjudicating role when considering which jokes to tell, and, as a result, there are occasions when being humorous should take precedence over being moral. However, I will argue that there are still limits to the degree of immorality that is acceptable.

I.

Conflicts between moral considerations and other spheres of value fall into two categories. The first category, which I will refer to as the *moral/nonmoral conflict*, are those cases in which nonmoral considerations, considerations which are not immoral in themselves, and moral considerations compete for our time and resources. An example of this is the debate about the extent of our obligations to help those who are living in poverty.[1] In such cases, the moral demand to use our time and resources to help those in need conflicts with our desire to use those resources to pursue other ends, such as buying luxury goods or engaging in hobbies. The second category, which I will refer to as the *moral/immoral conflict*, covers those cases where there is a direct conflict between morality and immorality, either because the value placed on nonmoral considerations can lead to immoral acts (e.g., the value placed on financial security leading to the temptation to commit theft) or when something immoral in itself is desired (e.g., causing a person unnecessary and undeserved suffering). When conflict occurs between moral considerations and the value placed on humor, it usually falls into the second category, the *moral/immoral conflict*, for example, when a joke is cruel. However, there can also be examples of the first category of conflict, the *moral/nonmoral conflict*, if, for example, a person devotes time to cultivating a sense of humor or developing their comedic skills at the expense of pursuing moral ends.

One approach to dealing with such conflicts is to assert that moral considerations should always take priority. D. Z. Phillips captures such a view when he states, "that to care for moral considerations is to hold that they are more important than considerations of any other kind" (Phillips 1977, 150). To support this position, Phillips presents the example of a situation in which etiquette decrees that one should bow rather than shake hands. If a person unfamiliar with the etiquette that governs such occasions offers us their hand to shake, Phillips argues that the moral consideration of not upsetting them will outweigh the demands of etiquette (Phillips 1977, 149). Philippa Foot challenges this view that moral considerations should override nonmoral considerations. She presents a modification of Phillips's example in which the cost of shaking the person's hand is not just the rule of etiquette but also a considerable sum of money (Foot 2003, 183–184). Foot argues that in such a case no one would expect a small moral consideration to outweigh a considerable financial consideration and that in such dilemmas "a small moral consideration often slips quietly out of sight" (Foot 2003, 184). In addition to this example, Foot offers two further examples in which the demands of etiquette outweigh the demands of morality. The first example describes how a host would usually continue to serve drinks to a guest who will be driving home even when they have reached the point where their alcohol consumption will impair their ability to drive safely (Foot 2003, 184). The second example, taken from Dostoyevsky's *The Brothers Karamazov*, describes how out of jealousy, Zosima has forced another officer into challenging him to a duel. However, realizing that he has acted disgracefully, Zosima waits for his opponent to fire before tossing away his pistol and apologizing. This apology brings an angry response from his second, as it goes against the dueling code to apologize midduel (Foot 2003, 185). In addition to the examples of conflicts between the demands of etiquette and morality, Foot also describes how, "a man will say that although it is wrong to do a certain thing he 'has to' or 'must' do it in order to stave off disaster to himself, or his family, or his country. And many people are ready to do what they know and admit to be wrong for far less than this, as for instance in spending money on frivolities while other people starve" (Foot 2003, 185).

It is not only that nonmoral considerations often do override moral consideration, even for the person who cares about morality, but that often we are glad that they do. In his analysis of moral luck, Bernard Williams draws upon the example of Gauguin, who abandoned his family to pursue his art. Williams states that "while we are sometimes guided by the notion that it would be the best of worlds in which morality were universally respected and all men were of a disposition to affirm it, we have in fact deep and persistent reasons to be grateful that that is not the world we have" (Williams, Moral Luck 1981, 23). Susan Wolf defends a similar view. She presents an account of the morally perfect person, the moral saint, to demonstrate that a life of moral perfection is not desirable (Wolf 1982). She argues that the moral virtues possessed by the morally perfect person, concentrated in one person and present to an extreme degree, will have the effect of crowding out those nonmoral virtues and interests which we generally believe to be constitutive factors in a well-rounded character or a life worth living. Directly addressing the question of a sense of humor, she argues that the morally perfect person would be devoid of certain types of humor:

> [A] cynical or sarcastic wit, or a sense of humor that appreciates this kind of wit in others, requires that one take an attitude of resignation and pessimism toward the flaws and vices to be found in the world. A moral saint, on the other hand, has reason to take an attitude in opposition to this—he should try to look for the best in people, give them the benefit of the doubt as long as possible, try to improve regrettable situations as long as there is any hope of success. This suggests that, although a moral saint might well enjoy a good episode of *Father Knows Best*, he may not in good conscience be able to laugh at a Marx Brothers movie or enjoy a play by George Bernard Shaw. (Wolf 1982, 422)

Cora Diamond presents a similar view. Diamond expresses concern that if morality is always allowed to take priority in these conflicts between moral considerations and humor, then something of value and importance to our sense of the human good will be lost:

> [H]ow far should the jokey side of us [. . .] be squashed into the space which morality (conceived in this or that particular way) is willing to allow? [. . .] If some answers to such a question are felt to be puritanical or moralistic, that feeling is (I am suggesting) not primarily a response to the content of the answer but rather to how the question itself is conceptualized—to the underlying ideas about human life and human good. Under cover, as it were, of "the authority of Morality," something with its own rights is being denied them: that is the feeling. (Diamond 1997, 215)

Craig Taylor further develops this view in his analysis of moralism. Taylor argues that one form of moralism is the tendency for morality to encroach into areas of our lives where it has no authority. Humor, he argues, is one such area. He states, "we sometimes say of some potentially offensive joke, 'That is not funny,' when it quite patently is funny and we cannot stop ourselves from laughing. The point is that once morality is allowed the kind of adjudicating role [. . .] it may be difficult to really appreciate much that is humanly valuable, including many of the things that are funny" (Taylor 2012, 71–72). In support of his argument that morality should not hold an adjudicating role, Taylor draws upon an argument presented by Bernard Williams. In response to Charles Fried (Fried 1970, 27), who thought it necessary to provide a moral justification for why a person should save the life of their wife over the life of a stranger who is in equal peril, Williams argues, "this construction provides the agent with one thought too many: it might have been hoped by some (for instance, by his wife) that his motivating thought, fully spelled out, would be the thought that it was his wife, not that it was his wife and that in situations of this kind it is permissible to save one's wife" (Williams, Persons, character and morality 1981, 18).

If morality is not to play an adjudicating role, then this raises the question of how we should resolve the conflict between moral considerations and considerations of humor. Taylor argues that it should come down to the relative strength of the competing considerations. He argues, "In some cases a joke will be morally objectionable but very funny and it will be natural to say that morality should give way. In other cases the situation will be the reverse" (Taylor 2012, 73). The conflict will be resolved, Taylor concludes, based upon the "relevant limits of their domains" (Taylor 2012, 73). In the next section, I will explore these limits. I will draw on the broader debate regarding the conflict between moral considerations and nonmoral considerations to argue that although morality does not have an adjudicating role, and as a result we may tell jokes without the thought that the joke is also morally justified, morality does set the boundaries for humor. To develop this position, I will explore the argument for admirable immorality that is presented by Michael Slote (Slote 1983).

II.

If a sense of humor is considered admirable, such as a well-crafted cynical or sarcastic wit, then this gives us a reason for thinking that it should, on occasion, outweigh moral considerations. It may seem counterintuitive to think that something immoral can also be admirable, but Michael Slote counters this intuition by presenting what he calls "admirable immorality," cases of character traits which are admirable and yet intrinsically connected to something immoral. Slote presents a strong, weak, and intermediate version of his admirable immorality thesis. He dismisses the strong version of the thesis as it requires an example of a character trait which is unquestionably immoral but at the same time admirable, such as admiring cruelty or wickedness, a view which Slote argues "cannot plausibly be defended" (Slote 1983, 79). Slote rejects the weak version of the thesis as in these cases we can conceptually separate what we admire from what is immoral and admire it independently of the immorality. Slote presents the example of a robber's daring as a case of the weak version of the thesis, where the daring can be conceptually separated from the immorality of the deed (Slote 1983, 79). The intermediate version of the admirable immorality thesis, the version of the thesis that Slote defends, covers cases where the admirable character trait is not directly immoral but is intrinsically connected to something which is immoral so that the character trait cannot be conceptually prised from the immoral act. Slote presents four examples in which he believes these criteria have been met: The case of admiring Gauguin's passion for his art even though this passion leads him to abandon his family to go to Tahiti to paint[2]; the admiration for a father who, motivated by parental love, deliberately misleads the police about the whereabouts of his son, knowing his son has committed a serious crime; admiration for Churchill's single-minded pursuit of allied victory, even though this single-mindedness led to the firebombing of German cities; and admiration for the strong stomached leader who is willing to set aside his own moral objections to torture in order to obtain information about the whereabouts of bombs in the hope of saving innocent lives[3] (Slote 1983, 79–107).

It could be argued that some of these examples represent conflicts between competing moral considerations rather than conflicts between moral and nonmoral considerations, and so do not represent examples of admirable immorality. For example, we could think that the father has a duty to protect his son; that Churchill had a duty to put allied lives first or that there is a consequentialist moral justification for winning the war that justifies his actions; and that a leader has a moral duty to protect the lives of innocent citizens, or there are consequentialist justifications for him using torture.[4] Owen Flanagan suggests that even the Gauguin example, which is perhaps the most challenging to define in terms of competing moral considerations, could be accommodated within a moral picture that places emphasis on self-realization (Flanagan 1986, 44). However, such an account seems to require a distortion of traditional accounts of morality. Moral systems that place emphasis on self-realization usually locate self-realization within a broader account of a balanced character or a flourishing life, one that is probably not consistent with a broader picture of Gauguin's life; a life plagued by drink, brawling, depression, and the effects of syphilis contracted from a prostitute (Cooper 2020) (Gauguin Gallery 2016). Gauguin's life seems to be one driven by, and perhaps consumed by, passion rather than one consistent with a moral account of self-realization. Describing Gauguin, and even admiring him, as someone committed to his art seems a more accurate description than someone committed to morality. Cases of admirable immorality are also evident in humor. As we have already seen, Wolf describes a cynical or sarcastic sense of humor, which we may admire, running counter to the optimism and search for goodness which is required by morality, citing the examples the Marx Brothers' movies or George Bernard Shaw's plays.

Owen Flanagan objects to Slote's claim that there are admirable traits that are intrinsically connected to immorality on the grounds that even for the cases of the intermediate thesis of admirable immorality the character traits can be admired independently of the immorality (Flanagan 1986). For some cases of humor, we may be able to conceptually praise the admirable aspect of the humor, for example, the wit or insightful comment, from the immorality and admire it independently. As a result, we can keep what we admire without requiring any immorality. However, for the example offered by Wolf of a cynical or sarcastic sense of humor the admirable element cannot be separated from the immorality as the humor in question is dependent upon a negative outlook or a failure to find the best in people. If we move the focus from character traits to types of humor, we can see further examples of aspects of humor we admire even though there is a feature of the humor which runs counter to morality. Practical jokes are an example of this. Practical jokes are by their nature mischievous; the humor is dependent upon causing someone embarrassment or discomfort, actions which we would usually consider to be immoral. If we were to deliberately embarrass someone or make them feel uncomfortable without any humorous outcome, we would consider this to be unacceptable, especially if we derived pleasure from it. However, it is often considered valued if it is a source of humor, and we may admire a well-executed practical joke.

The admiration we feel for certain types of humor is grounds for us being glad that morality does not always override humor. However, morality still acts as a boundary on the scope of the humor, as if the immorality is too severe then the admiration we feel for the humor is lost, even if the joke in question is still funny. As Flanagan points out in response to the cases of admirable immorality presented by Slote, "We admire traits, such as artistic passion, patriotism, and parental devotion on the assumption that they are not excessive, on the assumption that they are moderated by other devotions and sensitivities within the psychological economy of a whole character" (Flanagan 1986, 43). Marcia Baron further demonstrates the limits of our admiration. In response to Slote's Gauguin example, she highlights that we would no longer admire Gauguin's passion for his art if that passion had reached monomaniacal proportions and he was willing to kill for art supplies or have his son killed because he thought capturing the scene of the murder would make for a masterpiece (Baron 1986, 563). An example of a loss of admiration for humor can be seen in the re-evaluation of the jokes made at Monika Lewinsky's expense following her relationship with Bill Clinton. In a 2014 Vanity Fair article Lewinsky wrote, "In 1998 when news of my affair with Bill Clinton broke, I was arguably the most humiliated person in the world" (Lewinsky 2014). David Letterman, who had frequently made jokes at Lewinsky's expense, when interviewing Barbara Walters in 2014, commented "myself and other people with shows like this made relentless jokes about the poor woman. And she was a kid, she was 21, 22 . . . I feel bad about my role in helping push the humiliation to the point of suffocation" (Late Show with David Letterman 2014).

In the examples of admirable immoral humor that I have addressed the degree of the immorality is limited. A cynical or sarcastic sense of humor, or causing people slight embarrassment at being the victims of practical jokes, are not severe violations of morality. However, we should not be tempted into thinking that there is no immorality involved. There are, of course, cases in which people do not mind being the butt of the joke or even find enjoyment in it, but this is not always the case. A defense against this may be to find fault with the person who is embarrassed or annoyed. There may be the suggestion that they should "lighten up" or "learn to take a joke," and although there is undoubtedly merit in not always taking yourself too seriously, sometimes being embarrassed or annoyed is an entirely reasonable response. Yet to refrain from telling jokes for these reasons would end a lot of humor which we consider of value.

Determining where the moral boundaries lie can require a form of practical wisdom. There are going to be clear-cut cases in which we find an immoral joke funny, and yet the immorality means that we do not find the humor admirable, situations where we might say, "I know I shouldn't laugh, but I can't help myself." Such cases can be where the humor tips over from being embarrassing to humiliating, such as the example of the jokes at Monika Lewinsky's expense. However, there are cases where a nuanced judgment is required, and as a result, there will be disagreements about just where the boundary lines should be drawn. There are also cases where a degree of luck is involved, as the joke may be risky and our judgment about whether it has overstepped a moral boundary can depend on how it is received. An example of this sort of risky joke was recalled by the Irish journalist and broadcaster, Brian Keenan, who was held hostage in Beirut for over four years. While being held captive, he was often moved between locations, which involved him being bound in tape and transported in the boot of a car. He recounted how after being released he was traveling in a taxi with fellow former hostage John McCarthy. The taxi driver on recognizing them said over the intercom, "Sorry to interrupt you gentlemen, but I couldn't help asking . . . wouldn't you be more comfortable travelling in the boot?" (Keenan 2009). This was clearly a risky joke, given the potential sensitivity of the subject matter, and had the joke caused distress then an apology would seem appropriate; however, Brian Keenan found it amusing.

For many examples of immoral jokes, the consequences of the joke will determine whether a moral boundary has been crossed. In cases of jokes which draw upon negative stereotypes or humor which makes light of serious situations, it is important to investigate what role such jokes play in reinforcing or promoting prejudices or undermining serious topics. However, we do not need to believe that there will be negative consequences for a joke to be considered beyond the bounds of morality. If a racist joke is told to a group of people who are unlikely to be swayed in their opinions by the racist content of the joke, this does not mean that there is nothing wrong with the telling of the joke. A joke resting upon an ugly stereotype or mocking a serious topic may be sufficient grounds for us to consider the joke to of crossed an important moral boundary even if there are no negative consequences. As Ted Cohen highlights:

> It may be that a mammoth raft of literature, propaganda, fiction, poetry, religious writing and preaching, and casual conversation can produce or sustain a general opinion of things, including an opinion of kinds of people—surely it would be foolish to deny that; but it is farfetched to indict a movie or a novel or a joke on those grounds. And worse: when it turns out that you can find no convincing evidence to support this claim about the effects of such jokes, you seem obliged to give up your moral complaint. And you shouldn't do that. (Cohen 1999, 82)

III.

The previous section explored cases where the admirability of a character trait or action can be grounds for moral considerations to be overridden. However, the example raised by Foot of "spending money on frivolities while other people starve" (Foot 2003, 185) does not meet this description. In such cases, the act, or the associated character traits, is not admirable, and yet it is commonplace for it to override the moral consideration of helping people who are starving. The moral boundary previously described is also not present as the moral cost in such cases is considerable. If in such cases moral considerations can be overridden even when it is not in favor of an admirable act or character trait, then can the same be true for cases of humor? To answer this question, I will refer to the distinction between the two different types of conflict between moral considerations and nonmoral/immoral considerations, the *moral/nonmoral conflict,* and the *moral/immoral conflict.* Cases of immoral humor typically fall into the first category, the *moral/immoral conflict,* where there is a direct conflict between the immorality of the humor and moral considerations. The case of spending money on frivolities instead of helping people who are starving falls into the second category, as the act of spending money on frivolities is not immoral in itself. Still, the resources used on such frivolities could instead go to help those in need. The conflict, therefore, is over the allocation of resources rather than a direct conflict between morality and immorality. Conflicts of this nature raise questions about the limits of our moral duties. In cases of the *moral/immoral conflict,* we have a moral duty not to do things which are immoral in themselves, even if this moral duty can be overridden. However, in cases of the *moral/nonmoral conflict,* it is harder to determine what our moral duties are. There is a distinction to be made between actions which we are morally duty-bound to perform and supererogatory actions. Whether helping those who are starving is a moral duty or an act of charity, and hence supererogatory, is a matter for debate, a debate which is beyond the scope of this chapter, but one conclusion that can be drawn is that for cases of this kind it is not that moral considerations are overridden, and there is not a moral boundary to limit to the scope of the immorality, but rather that the cases instead show the limits of the moral demands upon us. For the cases of immoral humor that are examples of the *moral/immoral conflict,* such a conclusion would not apply, as it is not a matter of how we use our resources but instead a direct conflict between morality and immorality.

So far, I have looked at cases of immoral humor where the primary or sole aim of the humor is to amuse. However, there are also cases in which immoral humor is aimed at causing harm. For example, when reinforcing a negative stereotype, being cruel, or undermining a serious situation is not merely the means to bring about amusement or a consequence of the humor but is a desired end. In many cases, the humor is just used for immoral ends, in which case it would rightly be condemned, but there are cases when the immoral humor is being used to further a moral end. For example, humor which we would usually consider to be cruel, such as jokes that relentlessly mocked someone's appearance, could be morally justified if they were employed to try to undermine the authority of a dictator. In such cases, the usual moral boundaries that apply to immoral humor would not apply, but the justification would not be due to a regard for the value of the humor but due to the broader moral justification. The humor acts as a tool and can be judged in a similar way in which other morally questionable tools can be used when being employed to achieve broader moral aims, such as the use of violence.

CONCLUSION

In this chapter, I have examined the conflict that can exist between morality and humor. I have argued that morality should not play an adjudicating role in determining what jokes should be told, and as such jokes should not need to be morally justified, but that morality does provide the boundary that limits the degree of immorality. Parallels can be drawn with other areas of judgment. For example, we may not think we need to morally justify watching a film that contains violence, but we may think there should be limits placed on the level or the nature of the violence that can be shown in a film. This account of the relationship between morality and humor highlights the important role that humor plays in our lives by acknowledging that it shouldn't always be overridden when it comes into conflict with morality, or need to be justified by moral considerations, but still allows for a moral limit to be in place.

NOTES

1. A notable representation of this debate can be found in Singer 2011.
2. This example was originally presented by Bernard Williams (Williams, Moral Luck 1981).
3. This example was originally presented by Michael Walzer (Walzer 1973).
4. A more detailed discussion about whether these examples can be defined as a conflict between competing moral considerations can be found in Slote 1983, Flanagan 1986, Baron 1986.

REFERENCES

Baron, Marcia. 1986. "On Admirable Immorality." *Ethics, Vol. 96, No. 3 (April)* 557–566.
2018. *BBC*. 23 April. Accessed June 9, 2020. https://www.bbc.co.uk/news/uk-scotland-glasgow-west-43864133.
Cohen, Ted. 1999. *Jokes: Philosophical Thoughts on Joking Matters*. Chicago: University of Chicago Press.
Cooper, Douglas. 2020. *Paul Gauguin*. 3 June. Accessed June 10, 2020. https://www.britannica.com/biography/Paul-Gauguin.
Diamond, Cora. 1997. "Moral Differences and Distances: Some Questions." In *Commonality and Particularity in Ethics*, edited by Lilli Alanen, Sarah Heinamaa and Thomas Wallgren, 197–234. Basingstoke: Macmillan Press.
Flanagan, Owen. 1986. "Admirable Immorality and Admirable Imperfection." *The Journal of Philosophy, Vol. 83, No. 1 (Jan)* 41–60.
Foot, Philippa. 2003. "Are Moral Considerations Overriding?" In *Virtues and Vices and Other Essays in Moral Philosophy*, 181–188. Oxford: Basil Blackwell.
Fried, Charles. 1970. *The Anatomy of Altruism*. Cambridge, Mass: Harvard University Press.
2016. *Gauguin Gallery*. Accessed June 1, 2020. https://www.gauguingallery.com/gauguins-health.aspx.
Keenan, Brian. 2009. Quoted in *"Life is sweet for Brian Keenan" by Joanna Moorhead, The Guardian*. 12 September. Accessed 5 2020, www.theguardian.com/lifeandstyle/2009/sep/12/brian-keenan-dublin-hostage.
2014. *Late Show with David Letterman*. CBS/Worldwide Pants, 13 May.
Lewinsky, Monica. 2014. "Shame and Survival." *Vanity Fair*, June. www.vanityfair.com/style/society/2014/06/monica-lewinsky-humiliation-culture.
Marshall, Alex. 2020. *The New York Times*. 12 June. Accessed June 14, 2020. https://www.nytimes.com/2020/06/12/arts/television/blackface-litte-britain-tv-enfield.html.
Michallon, Clémence. 2019. *The Independent*. 11th January. Accessed June 9, 2020. https://www.independent.co.uk/arts-entertainment/tv/features/friends-netflix-gay-chandler-fat-monica-trans-dad-carol-lesbian-wedding-kiss-homophobic-transphobic-a8695511.html.
Phillips, D.Z. 1977. "In Search of the Moral 'Must': Mrs Foot's Fugitive Thought." *Philosophical Quarterly, vol. 27, no.107, April* 140–157.
Singer, Peter. 2011. "Rich and Poor." In *Practical Ethics, 3rd Edition*. Cambridge: Cambridge University Press.
Slote, Michael. 1983. "Admirable Immorality." In *Goods and Virtues*, 77–107. Oxford: Oxford University Press.
Taylor, Craig. 2012. *Moralism: A Study of Vice*. Durham: Acumen.
2008. *The Guardian*. 27 October. Accessed June 1, 2020. https://www.theguardian.com/media/2008/oct/27/russell-brand-jonathan-ross-andrew-sachs-calls.
Walzer, Michael. 1973. "Political Action: The Problem of Dirty Hands." *Philosophy & Public Affairs, Vol. 2, No. 2 (Winter)* 160–180.

Williams, Bernard. 1981. "Moral Luck." In *Moral Luck: Philosophical Papers 1973–1980*, 20–39. Cambridge: Cambridge University Press.
Williams, Bernard. 1981. "Persons, character and morality." In *Moral Luck: Philosophical Papers 1973–1980*, 1–19. Cambridge: Cambridge University Press.
Wolf, Susan. 1982. "Moral Saints." *The Journal of Philosophy, Vol. 79, No. 8. (August)* 419–439.

Part III

SOCIAL MORAL JUDGMENTS OF AMUSEMENT

Chapter 7

You Shouldn't Have Laughed!
The Ethics of Derogatory Amusement
Andrew Morgan and Ralph DiFranco

1. CONSIDER AN EXAMPLE

Consider an instance of derogatory humor, delivered by comedian Michelle Wolf at the 2018 White House Correspondents' Dinner, aimed at President Donald Trump's Press Secretary, Sarah Huckabee Sanders:

> I actually really like Sarah. I think she's very resourceful. Like she burns facts and then she uses that ash to create a perfect smokey eye. Like maybe she's born with it, maybe it's lies. It's probably lies. (Wolf 2018)[1]

Wolf's joke proved to be controversial. While many of her fellow comedians praised her, Wolf also received criticism. The White House Correspondents' Association issued a public apology for her jokes, claiming that they were not in the spirit of the dinner's mission (@whca, April 29, 2018). Perhaps you found Wolf's joke amusing, perhaps not. If you did, is your amusement morally defective? You may think that such amusement is defective because the joke is derogatory. But what makes humor derogatory, and is all derogatory humor morally objectionable? The aim of this chapter is to provide some answers to these questions.

We begin by roughly characterizing what we take humor to be and the variety of forms it can take. Then, in section 3, we propose a form of derogation—expressive derogation—that is distinct from derogatory effects. When one derogates in the expressive sense, one both makes manifest and endorses a derogatory attitude. Expressive derogation explains what makes humor derogatory across a wide variety of contexts regardless of the particular psychological effects it happens to cause. In section 4, we employ this proposal to identify which instances of humor involve endorsing derogatory attitudes. Sections 5 and 6 build on this theory of endorsement to explain when derogatory humor and amusement, respectively, count as morally objectionable. In section 7, we discuss the problems with Steven Gimbel's harm-based account of the morality of humor and highlight the strengths of our own view.

2. THE VARIETIES OF HUMOR

In this section, we begin by offering a rough starting point for a definition of humor, and by identifying just a few of the different forms that humor can take. First, we think it is important to distinguish humor itself from the characteristic responses to it, such as laughter and feelings of amusement. As we understand it, humor consists of acts or artifacts designed to cause amusement. In comparison, characteristic responses may be elicited by mere amusing occurrences, events that cause amusement in observers but are not designed to produce such effects. For instance, absent-mindedly stepping into a puddle could easily evoke amusement in observers, yet behavior of this sort does not by itself constitute the production of humor. At the same time, an instance of humor may on some occasions fail to evoke any response whatsoever, as when one tells a joke that falls flat.

Some forms of humor are verbal while others are nonverbal. When we engage in verbal humor, we use natural language to convey some propositional content to our audience that is designed to elicit amusement. Nonverbal humor consists in the use of imagery designed to evoke amusement. Here imagery should be understood broadly so as to include content in a variety of different sensory modalities, including, inter alia, visual, and auditory imagery. Some humor is entirely verbal, as in the case of written jokes, and some is entirely nonverbal, as in comical mime acts and sketches featuring characters without dialogue (e.g., Mr. Bean, The Tramp). Of course, many instances of humor feature both verbal and nonverbal elements. A successful stand-up routine often crucially depends on paralinguistic elements such as prosody, facial expressions, and gestures, in addition to the words uttered. While our focus is primarily on verbal humor much of what we say extends to nonverbal humor as well.

Our topic in this chapter is derogatory humor, that is, humor that subordinates a target or ranks a target lower than some (purported) superior along some normative dimension. By "target" we mean to refer to that which is put down, mocked, ridiculed, or satirized, rather than to the intended audience (though in some cases, of course, the two may be identical).[2] The targets of derogatory humor may include individuals (as when someone mocks George's clumsy speech), groups (e.g., ridiculing white people for their alleged inability to withstand spicy food), or institutions (like jokes that comment satirically on the legal system, professional sports, marriage, etc).[3]

This definition of "derogatory humor" follows a tradition that can be traced to Plato, according to which humor crucially involves expressing a sense of superiority (for discussion of so-called superiority theories see Gimbel 2018, 7). However, we are not suggesting that all humor must by definition involve ranking, asserting one's dominance, or anything of the sort. On the contrary, we assume that derogatory humor is a proper subset of the humor category. Like all humor, derogatory humor can be merely verbal, but it often involves nonverbal imagery as well. Disparaging impersonations, pejorative mimicry, and other depictions rely on imagery in a way that mere verbal humor need not. For instance, imagine a speaker who mocks a target by speaking in a shrill tone of voice—purporting to mimic them. This is a way of foisting an auditory image on an audience that they need not generate themselves in order to feel the mocking rhetorical force.

As a kind of expressive act, the primary way that derogatory humor functions to subordinate or rank lower is by being expressive of derogatory attitudes and perspectives.[4] In the next two sections, we argue that explaining derogatory humor's expressive power requires distinguishing two notions of derogation.

3. DIAGNOSING DEROGATION

Though many different phenomena might be described as "derogatory," we will here focus on distinguishing three: having derogatory attitudes, performing derogatory expressive acts, and causing derogatory psychological effects. In the past, literature on derogation has tended to focus on psychological effects such as activating biases, prompting negative evaluations, inciting violence, evoking objectionable imagery, shocking, and offending.[5] In contrast, we use the term "expressive derogation" to refer to the way that speakers can use language to express derogatory attitudes and thereby also signal endorsement of those attitudes. What then makes an attitude derogatory? Derogatory attitudes may take the form of propositional attitudes, affective states, perspectives, emotions, and various noncognitive states. What they all have in common is their inherently comparative stance: a derogatory attitude always ranks a target lower than some purported superior, along some dimension of normative evaluation.[6] Thus, when speakers derogate in the expressive sense, they thereby affirm a commitment to a derogatory comparative stance. As we will see in section 5, there is an important difference between merely communicating *that* one has a derogatory attitude and expressing in this endorsing way.

While derogatory effects often result from expressive derogation, these two forms of derogation can also come apart. For example, imagine a young child hears a racist joke and repeats it to her friends. The child doesn't understand the attitudes embodied in the joke and harbors no derogatory attitudes herself. Therefore, telling the joke involves no derogatory expression on the part of the speaker. But if members of the target group overhear the child tell the joke, they might well understand it and consequently feel hurt and offended. Other members of the child's audience may experience objectionable imagery or the activation of biases, whether or not they fully understand the expressive qualities of the joke. Therefore, derogatory psychological effects can be generated despite the absence of a derogatory expressive act. In describing the moral features of such a situation, we would probably not want to say that the speaker is blameworthy, though we would feel that it is important to correct her.

Importantly, the reason why the child's act does not constitute derogatory expression is not just because she does not possess the attitudes. Rather it is because she is, in an important sense, not a competent speaker. In contrast, if we imagine a competent speaker who tells the same joke in order to fit in with a group of racist friends, this deliberate act can constitute derogatory expression even if the speaker himself doesn't happen to share the derogatory attitudes. We will return to cases like this in the next section.

We can also imagine a thoroughly racist speaker who utters the joke while he is alone—either aloud in private speech or silently in inner speech. This speaker fully understands and endorses the racism in the joke (which is exactly why he enjoys telling it and laughing to himself). In such a case, expressive derogation is present.[7] However, there may be no actual derogatory effects, for there is no audience to hear him. And if the speaker is already as racist as he can be, his private telling of the racist joke will make little difference to his own psychology or resulting behavior. Nevertheless, it seems like something he shouldn't be doing (probably one of many racist things he shouldn't be doing) and for which he is blameworthy.

4. DEROGATORY HUMOR AS EXPRESSIVE ACT

The phrase "derogatory expression" may refer to an act whereby one expresses a derogatory attitude or to the expressive vehicle one uses in acts of derogatory expression.[8] This distinction is analogous to the two uses of the term "slur": when interpreted as a verb "slur" refers to acts whereby one disparages a group, but when interpreted as a noun phrase "slur" (or "slur word") refers to a conventional vehicle designed to disparage a group (Anderson and Lepore 2013, 351). A speaker may utter a neutral label for a group (e.g., "Jew" or "Italian") in a contemptuous or dismissive tone such that they disparage members of the group *qua* group members (Jeshion 2013, 239). In so doing, the speaker could thereby slur the target without uttering a slur word.

Likewise, humorous expression admits of an act/vehicle distinction. "Joke" may refer to a token act—a telling of a joke—or to a type of vehicle used in such acts. For example, stereotypes are conventional depictions of groups that often serve as vehicles for derogatory humor.[9] If someone performs a caricatured depiction of a gay man that features stereotypical speech patterns and gesticulations their act makes use of a conventional derogatory vehicle. Though acts whereby one produces derogatory humor often make use of conventional vehicles, they need not always do so. Wolf's joke from the Correspondent's Dinner served to humorously derogate Sarah Huckabee Sanders without using any preexisting derogatory stereotypes, slur words, or other conventional vehicles for derogation.

Our focus in this chapter is on humorous acts that constitute expressive derogation. In virtue of what does a joke or humorous caricature derogate in the expressive sense? In general, a depiction of a target can be expressive, in part, if it invites a viewer to share a perspective. Such expressive depictions can enable sympathy in a number of different ways. For instance, a painting might be expressive of rage by virtue of depicting a situation which is palpably such that were we in it, we would feel rage (Green 2007, 195). Or consider a photograph of someone that was taken from a low angle in such a way as to make the subject appear large and strong. Such a depiction facilitates admiring the subject, and thus looking at such a photo puts us in a good position to share in that admiration (Green 2007, 210).

Stereotypical depictions of a group are likewise sympathy-enabling. Because intentionally enabling and inviting others to share an attitude is usually a form of endorsement, producing the sympathy-enabling expressive qualities of stereotypical depictions is rarely a neutral, nonderogatory act. For instance, one cannot claim in good faith that an impression that employs a racist stereotype of African Americans is merely a neutral attempt to show how African Americans appear to racists, to elicit laughter, or to express affiliation with the target group. All else being equal, such attempts to deflect criticism will be made in vain. For example, consider the 2019 scandal involving Virginia Governor Ralph Northam. Northam was pressured to resign after a yearbook photo surfaced of someone wearing blackface makeup on his 1984 medical school yearbook page. Though he denied that the photo was of him, Northam admitted that he had darkened his face with shoe polish when dressing up as Michael Jackson the same year for a dance competition, and only later came to appreciate what was objectionable about his costume after a conversation with one of his staff (Hayes 2019).

It would not be an adequate defense for Northam to say he dressed up as Jackson out of admiration or because he enjoyed performing Jackson's signature dance moves. Blackface minstrelsy is a conventional vehicle for expressing a racist ideology, governed by specific norms aimed at producing depictions that invite viewers to share this racist perspective (e.g., exaggerated physical features, speech patterns). Acts by competent agents that make use of this convention express the derogatory attitudes and therefore constitute expressive derogation, regardless of whether or not the performer themselves possesses the relevant attitudes (Lott 1993). If it seems strange at first to attribute derogation to an agent who does not possess derogatory attitudes, consider Kate Manne's distinction between sexism and misogyny as a useful model. Misogynistic acts can function to enforce harmful norms and expectations whether or not the agent themselves possesses sexist attitudes (Manne 2018). More generally, we suggest that derogatory expressive acts (whether misogynistic, racist, ableist, homophobic, sizeist, etc.) can play an oppressive functional role regardless of the speaker's attitudes and intentions.

Whether or not one's behavior reflects how one personally thinks or feels about the target, racist impressions are still sympathy-enabling. They proffer derogatory attitude to the audience, thereby signaling endorsement and inviting sympathetic imitation. Unless a stereotypical impression is done in a sufficiently ironic or satirical context, such that one's intention to satirize, ridicule, or otherwise protest depictions of this sort is thereby also made manifest, one's impression will constitute expressive derogation. In general, humor expressively derogates whenever it enables sympathy with a derogatory attitude by inviting the audience to share that attitude through the use of expressive behavior (e.g., caricatures, imitative performances, slurring utterances and gestures, symbolic acts, and other behavior that presupposes a derogatory ideology).

How is it possible for humor featuring pejorative depictions of a group (stereotypes, offensive caricatures, slurs, etc.) to ever avoid constituting expressive derogation? In nonderogatory pejorative depictions, the context must make abundantly clear that the agent producing the depiction disavows the particular attitudes expressed in the depiction. In such cases, it is firmly in common ground that the audience is to neither empathize nor sympathize with those who view the target as depicted. Out-group members who employ stereotypes in humor can sometimes avoid expressive derogation in contexts where it is clear that they have a subversive aim, but often the presumption of such an aim will not be present. In the latter case, their humor will expressively derogate. When contexts change, even the same comedian telling similar jokes can start to generate derogatory expression where there was none before. Consider the example of Louis CK, a comedian whom audiences used to trust as an ally of oppressed groups. After he admitted in 2017 to sexually harassing women, reactions to Louis CK's humor started to shift. As Pakistani-Australian comedian Sami Shah explains:

> We used to hail [CK] as brilliant for his ability to go to dark places, to say things that are hilariously absurd and grotesque . . . we used to trust him as an individual and go, "His heart's in the right place . . . and therefore, when he says these things we know it's not coming from a place of malice, we know it's coming from a place of comedy"—and that's where the context lay. Now, we don't consider Louis CK to be as empathetic, trustworthy or considerate a person, and therefore when he goes back to the same places, he doesn't have the credibility to go there anymore. (Shah quoted in Hegarty 2019)

Nonderogatory uses of stereotypes and other pejorative depictions have a clear subversive aim; one is attempting to undermine the stereotype, to show that it is a vicious fiction (Anderson 2015). This is why marginalized people often have a subversive aim when they utilize stereotypes of their own group. The presumption that self-deprecating humor featuring stereotypes has a subversive aim explains why we are inclined to regard such humor as morally unobjectionable, perhaps even morally valuable. For example, a comedian who is a member of a marginalized group may adopt stereotyped speech patterns and mannerisms commonly associated with their own group in the context of a stand-up routine that challenges bigoted perceptions of the group in question. Along these lines, Chun (2004) argues that a caricatured English dialect, *Mock Asian*, which embodies stereotypical features of non-native English speakers from East-Asian countries, can be used to critique racist perceptions of East-Asian people. This dialect includes phonological features such as /r/-deletion ("number" is pronounced "numba") and coda simplification ("it's" is pronounced as "is"), as well as syntactic features, for example, the absence of the copula ("you too tall") and the absence of articles ("I want eggroll") (Chun 2004, 272). In a stand-up bit, Korean-American comedian Margaret Cho describes a situation in which a magazine published an article about her diet without consulting her. Cho creates a fictional version of herself and tells the story of her upbringing using Mock Asian (reported in Chun 2004):

> When I was a little girl? And I grow up on the rice paddy? . . . We are so hungry all the time. And we have no money and I want to go to the market to buy a chicken head, but I have no money eh—so I have to sell my finger. . . . but I still have tendency to put on weight. Which is why I really hope I catch malaria. (282)

Rather than promoting a racist stereotype, Cho's bit "critiques stereotypes of Asian women as idealizations of passive, petite, and self-sacrificing femininity," and comments on mainstream ideological links between Asia and poverty perpetuated by the U.S. media (Chun 2004, 283).

In other cases, the goal of using a stereotype might be to foster solidarity by invoking shared experiences. However, humor involving the use of stereotypes by members of the stereotyped group is not always innocuous. We can imagine a member of a marginalized group performing a stereotypical impression of their own group in a comedy routine in an attempt to pander to a racist audience. In this case, the speaker's derogatory impression lacks a subversive aim. Thus, their depiction of their own group constitutes expressive derogation. Moreover, as Anderson (2015) observes, even in cases where the performer has a subversive aim, it may not be easily discernible. L'Official (2017) describes a somewhat complicated case: Ben Vereen's homage to the Black vaudevillian performer, Bert Williams, during Ronald Reagan's Inaugural Gala in 1981. After singing one of Williams' popular songs while wearing blackface (as Williams himself often did), Vereen performed a skit in which he offers to buy the crowd a drink, but is denied service by the bartender due to his race. Next, Vereen sang a much more somber song while wiping the paint from his face in an attempt to shed light on the pain caused by blackface minstrelsy (L'Official 2017). Only the first part of Vereen's performance was televised, and as a result, Vereen was criticized for pandering to a mostly white conservative audience. L'Official suggests that even in light of Vereen's subversive agenda, his full performance still would have been highly controversial, since it is unclear whether the audience would have understood his subversive intent in the second half. In the absence of a coordinated effort by members of the target community to appropriate conventional derogatory vehicles, it can be extremely difficult to make use of them in nonderogatory ways.

Having a subversive aim when reproducing an objectionable stereotype in the context of a joke, or when performing a pejorative impression intended to be humorous, is a necessary, but not sufficient condition for making such depictions nonderogatory. Well-meaning allies may perform a stereotypical impression in the context of a good faith attempt to undermine bigotry, yet fail. Consider an incident in 2014 that occurred after Dan Snyder, owner of the Washington NFL team, then known as the 'Redskins', announced that he would create a charitable foundation for Indigenous communities. Synder's announcement came at a time when the team had been publicly criticized for using a slur against Indigenous people as their team name. In reference to Snyder's announcement, the twitter account for *The Colbert Report* tweeted, "I am willing to show #Asian communities I care by introducing the Ching-Chong-Ding-Dong Foundation for Sensitivity to Orientals or whatever" (Barrineau 2014). Despite the fact that this tweet was seemingly intended as satire, the show's host, Stephen Colbert, was criticized for the use of slurs for East-Asian people and the incident led to "#CancelColbert" trending on twitter (Barrineau 2014).[10] Such incidents suggest that when using slurs and other racist language for the purpose of creating humor, speakers run the risk of derogatory expression even when their satirical aim is clear.

5. EXPLAINING THE MORAL DEFECTIVENESS OF DEROGATORY HUMOR

If one holds that the wrongness of humor is exhausted by harmful consequences, then it might seem that its explanation poses no special ethical problem. After all, a joke that is perfectly innocuous in most contexts may inflict a great deal of harm when told at the wrong moment, for example, right before a lifesaving surgery. Making humorous commentary while attending a ceremony, such as a wedding or funeral, often involves centering oneself in such a way as to interfere with the event's purpose (Gimbel 2018, 141–2). Moreover, whether a joke causes derogatory effects depends largely on features of the audience. A "perfectly harmless" joke may cause shock or offense in an audience that is overly sensitive, or who has particular negative associations with the topic material. The most "offensive" joke may have little to no effect on an audience that is desensitized, or who is already as bigoted as they can be.

If a joke causes predictable derogatory effects that are harmful, then that is certainly part of the explanation for why telling it may be morally wrong (just as causing harmful effects constitutes at least part of the explanation for why any act may be wrong).[11] The substantive philosophical question at issue here is whether derogatory humor can also be wrong just by virtue of what it expresses, and if so, what could serve to make it wrong in this effect-independent way. As the example from the previous section of the speaker who tells racist jokes in private illustrates, harmful effects cannot be the whole story.

We suggest the following principle:

Inheritance: whenever harboring a derogatory attitude φ would make an agent morally defective then, ceteris paribus, it is wrong to express φ.

According to this principle, whenever telling a joke involves expressing a derogatory attitude that is itself morally objectionable, the act of telling the joke inherits that wrongness.[12] This is true even if telling the joke does not happen to generate derogatory effects on a particular occasion. Importantly however, *Inheritance* does not itself assume that all derogatory attitudes are intrinsically bad. Some may be morally neutral (such as harboring a derogatory attitude toward broccoli), while others may be morally admirable (such as harboring a derogatory attitude toward a specific dominant group that is actively supporting systems of oppression).

A derogatory attitude is morally objectionable to the extent that it involves a normative comparison that is substantively unjust or undeserved. Paradigm examples of morally objectionable derogatory attitudes involve lowering a target group in virtue of its morally irrelevant features (race, gender, sexual orientation, age, ability, religious affiliation, etc.). Whenever telling a joke involves expressing attitudes that unjustly ascribe a lower moral status to a target group or individual, *Inheritance* evaluates the action of telling that joke as wrong.

This does not mean that it is always wrong to *communicate that* one has a morally objectionable derogatory attitude. An important step toward changing one's derogatory attitudes is often admitting that one has them. It is the additional *endorsement of* those attitudes present in derogatory communicative acts that causes them to rise to the level of expression and, as captured by *Inheritance*, can make such acts morally objectionable. In general, humor that mocks or ridicules usually, if not always, constitutes an evaluation. It is hard to see how one could produce derogatory humor and not thereby take an evaluative stance, at least implicitly. Any modern attempt to reproduce a nineteenth-century era blackface minstrel performance, for instance, will have moral implications. The performer is either showing an audience a form of humorous racial caricature in order to mock or criticize it (as Vereen tried to do in his 1981 performance, and as Spike Lee does in his 2000 film *Bamboozled*) or one is disparaging Black people. Because of the way that it invites audiences to share a perspective by enabling sympathetic responses, the production of humor almost always involves communicating endorsement.

To sum up: *Inheritance* evaluates as morally objectionable the expressive act an agent performs when producing derogatory humor, whenever the attitudes thereby expressed are themselves morally objectionable. The agent's expressive act will inherit the moral qualities of the attitudes it expresses whether performed in public or in private. Thus, *Inheritance* explains what is objectionable about derogatory jokes whether they are uttered aloud in public, aloud in private, or silently by means of inner speech. Such acts can be morally defective even if the agent does not actually possess the attitudes in question, and regardless of whether the act leads to any actual harmful effects. While *Inheritance* is a principle about the expression of intrinsically wrong attitudes, we suspect that a mirrored version of the principle could serve to motivate the expression of morally praiseworthy derogatory attitudes (we return to this issue in section 8).

6. EXPLAINING THE MORAL DEFECTIVENESS OF DEROGATORY AMUSEMENT

While it is fairly easy to see how a competent speaker's *telling* a derogatory joke could involve derogatory expression, what are we to say about the amusement of the audience? The first step is to distinguish *feelings* of amusement from *expressions* of amusement. Amusement *felt* in response to a derogatory joke could stem from different sources. Often the reason for the felt amusement response is that the hearer shares the derogatory attitudes expressed by the joke (at least to some extent). If those derogatory attitudes are morally objectionable, the feelings of amusement that they generate in turn contribute to the moral defectiveness of the hearer. However, if feelings of amusement are to be understood broadly enough, they can also stem from sources like surprise, psychological discomfort, a sense of the absurd, or even a desire to have a pleasant social interaction (Keltner 1996, 394; Gervais and Wilson 2005, 399). Insofar as a feeling of amusement arises from some source *other than* the possession of a morally objectionable derogatory attitude, it seems plausible to say that the hearer is not to be morally criticized for it.[13]

In addition to the feeling of amusement, we can also consider expressions of amusement—its physical manifestations—the most paradigmatic of these being laughter. Just as a speaker's telling of a derogatory joke involves derogatory expression, so also does it seem right to say that a hearer's laughter in response to a derogatory joke can involve derogatory expression (De Sousa 1987, 290).[14] However, not all laughter is created equal. In particular it is useful to contrast so-called Duchenne laughter from non-Duchenne laughter. Duchenne laughter involves the contraction of a nonvoluntary muscle (the *orbicularis oculi*) and therefore its production is not entirely under our control (Hurley et al. 2011, 19–23). This lack of control is why a hearer may experience a laughter response even if she does not share the derogatory attitudes expressed by the joke. Just as feelings of amusement in response to derogatory jokes can stem from sources other than a shared derogatory attitude, so also can the physical manifestations of amusement. Insofar as a laughter response is involuntary, it needn't be blameworthy (Gimbel 2018, 137).

However, even Duchenne laughter can be voluntarily *suppressed* (De Sousa 1987). If a hearer indulges his Duchenne laughter in response to a derogatory joke, allowing it to continue without attempting to suppress it or otherwise distance himself from it, this expression of amusement can come to constitute an endorsement of the derogatory attitudes expressed by the joke. In such a situation, the amused audience member can count as *endorsing* the derogatory attitudes expressed by the joker, even if the amused audience member doesn't *possess* those attitudes himself. Insofar as the derogatory attitudes in question are morally objectionable, *Inheritance* will count the hearer's voluntarily unsuppressed Duchenne laughter as morally objectionable as well. Similarly, merely reporting the slurring utterance of another speaker can constitute positive evidence of endorsement, if the reporter does not take care to sufficiently distance themselves from the slurring speaker's perspective (Camp 2018, 52).

On the other hand, non-Duchenne laughter is both voluntarily producible and voluntarily suppressible. Thus, it is a more straightforward example of an endorsing expression of amusement. Insofar as a joke expresses morally objectionable derogatory attitudes, a hearer's non-Duchenne laughter response will constitute a morally objectionable expression of endorsement (even if they do not actually possess the attitudes). Imagine a nonsexist hearer who intentionally laughs at a misogynistic joke in an effort to fit in with his sexist friends. This laughter is an expression of endorsement that is morally objectionable insofar as the attitudes expressed by the original joke were themselves morally defective, regardless of the fact that the laugher himself does not possess the attitudes.[15]

Laughter is not the only form that our expressions of amusement can take. Amusement can cause us to smile, shift our gaze, tilt our heads, touch our faces, among others.[16] The discussion of Duchenne and non-Duchenne laughter above suggests a more general account:

(1) If a physical manifestation of amusement is voluntarily produced, then it constitutes an endorsement.[17]
(2) If a physical manifestation of amusement is produced involuntarily, then it does not constitute an endorsement.[18]
(3) If a physical manifestation of amusement is voluntarily suppressible, then the failure to suppress it constitutes an endorsement.
(4) If a physical manifestation is not voluntarily suppressible, then the failure to suppress it does not constitute an endorsement.

Notice that amusement can be derogatory not only when it is felt or expressed in response to humor but also when it is a response to mere "amusing" occurrences. Imagine a bigot who laughs whenever he observes members of the group he despises suffer some misfortune. His feelings of amusement, and his expressions of amusement, are due at least in part to the derogatory attitudes he harbors and therefore constitute endorsement of them. According to *Inheritance*, expressing endorsement of an attitude is wrong insofar as the attitude endorsed is wrong. Thus, we can define wrongful manifestations of amusement as follows:

(5) Physical manifestations of amusement in response to wrongful derogatory jokes or mere amusing occurrences are wrong iff
   (i) The original joke expressed a morally objectionable derogatory attitude OR the derogatory attitude causing the amusement is morally defective AND
   (ii) The physical manifestation of amusement is produced voluntarily OR the physical manifestation of amusement is voluntarily unsuppressed

Even in cases where an audience member's feelings of amusement are not caused by the possession of a wrongful derogatory attitude, they may still have a moral reason to stifle their laughter in some public contexts. Consider a case in which amusement—and its public manifestation—in response to a joke is caused by something other than the joke's derogatory content (e.g., the joke is well-structured and clever despite being expressive of a derogatory attitude). Here a laughter response does not itself encode information about what it is a response to. In the event that one laughs at a derogatory joke about trans people, for instance, to reply that one was laughing only because the joke was well-structured is not an adequate defense. In such cases laughter signals one's privileged status and perhaps serves to distance oneself from trans people. Thus, in public contexts, there is a moral reason to suppress, stifle, and apologize for laughter responses to jokes that expressively derogate vulnerable groups.[19]

7. UNOBJECTIONABLE DEROGATORY HUMOR: ADVANTAGES OVER GIMBEL'S ACCOUNT

We have argued that humor and amusement are morally objectionable to the extent that they involve the expression of morally defective derogatory attitudes. At the same time, we have already seen that some humor about marginalized groups can be nonderogatory. But one might still wonder whether all *derogatory* humor is morally objectionable. In his attempt to answer this question, Gimbel (2018) distinguishes pure humor from impure humor. An instance of humor is "pure" when it consists of clever playfulness designed only to amuse an audience (Gimble 2018, 65). In contrast, "impure" humor is designed to accomplish goals beyond generating amusement, such as promoting an ideology (Gimbel 2018, 65).

Gimbel uses the term "rough humor" to refer to humor that ridicules its target. He claims that rough humor is unobjectionable to the extent that it is pure. Rough humor becomes morally objectionable only when its "play frame" is ruptured, and as a result, its "roughness penetrates into the real world in a way that causes a certain sort of harm" (150).[20] A joke's play frame consists of "a special aesthetic stage removed from normal life . . . on which to perform the gag" (Gimbel 2018, 39). As long as jokes are performed on this special stage Gimbel claims they are *always* playful, cannot harm, and are therefore never objectionable (such jokes are "pure"). However, attempts at pure humor that *do* rupture their play frames are morally objectionable because they cause harm (thereby becoming "impure"). For example, if a rape joke serves no greater moral purpose, and a reasonable person could predict that telling such a joke would be likely to inflict harm by alienating and creating a hostile environment for victims, then telling such a joke would be morally wrong (Gimbel 2018, 163). As long as no such harmful effects are likely to occur, the joke can remain within its play frame and therefore constitute an instance of morally permissible, pure humor (Gimbel 2018, 153).

The first problem with Gimbel's harm-based account is that it seems far too permissive (Hick 2018). For instance, if Gimbel is correct, blackface minstrel theater should be acceptable as long as the performance is clever and playful, and no one in the audience is actually harmed. Recall the case of Ralph Northam, who admitted that in 1984, he wore blackface when dressing up as Michael Jackson for a talent show. On a charitable interpretation of his behavior, Northam's only goal was to create a playful depiction of Jackson. Moreover, it is not clear that his actions caused any significant harm, and his performance seemed to be well received at the time (Northam claims to have won the competition). Thus, Gimbel's account predicts that Northam's behavior was unobjectionable. Yet Northam was widely criticized. Thus, Gimbel's account does not comport with widely shared negative reactions to racial caricatures.

Additionally, rough humor has no audience when produced in private or inner speech. A speaker may have many reasons for telling jokes in such solitary contexts. They may want to practice a performance, or they may simply be silently uttering a joke for their own amusement. If the speaker is already as prejudiced as he can be, his jokes cannot *increase* his potential to cause harmful effects. On our view, jokes in such contexts may still be objectionable, since causing harm is not a necessary condition on a joke's being morally wrong. In contrast, Gimbel's account mistakenly predicts that in all such cases the production of humor that derogates a marginalized group is morally permissible. The fact that racist jokes are objectionable in private and inner speech contexts is due to the speaker's expression of a morally objectionable attitude. Such expression may occur regardless of whether one's joke is "pure" or "impure."[21] We take the ability to explain the wrongness of racist jokes in private and inner speech contexts to be an advantage that our view has over Gimbel's.

We agree with Gimbel that humor featuring marginalized groups is often morally permissible, and sometimes even morally valuable. Gimbel (2018) suggests (we think rightly) that ethnic humor may foster intimacy in relationships and we should not "condemn this surely ethically good act" (129). Gimbel cites Berger (1995) who holds that members of a group may tell ethnic jokes about themselves as a way of integrating themselves into the group and establishing group solidarity (95). This usage synergizes well with our account of nonderogatory humor in section 4 above. However, the second problem with Gimbel's account is that it places the burden of proof on the targets of ethnic humor (to prove they have been harmed) and allows speakers to defend themselves merely by citing their good intentions. In contrast, we believe that an adequate account of the ethics of derogatory humor will follow in the footsteps of Kate Manne's call to "make misogyny [and racism, and homophobia, and ableism, etc.] more epistemologically tractable" (Manne 2018, 60). Instead of needing to determine an agent's feelings or intentions in order to determine whether their behavior is misogynistic or racist, all one needs to know is whether a member of the target group might reasonably interpret the behavior as hostile.

Given Gimbel's harm-based account of what's wrong with ethnic humor, determining whether an instance of humor constitutes unobjectionable, good-natured ribbing requires first making a judgment about the speaker's intentions: did they intend to merely display cleverness or do they have some ulterior motive? Then we have to determine whether there are autobiographical facts about the audience that would have thinned the play frame, and whether any audience members were therefore harmed by the joke. According to Gimbel, as long as the speaker has no ill intent and the joke inflicts no harm (or only causes harms that are outweighed by some moral good), then the joke is permissible.[22] We suggest that a better way to determine whether jokes about a marginalized group are morally permissible is to simply defer to the members of the target group themselves. If a target decides that the joke is unacceptable, then caution is warranted—members of dominant groups ought to refrain from telling it. However, if the target group decides that the play frame is thick enough, then the joke is permissible. Call this the *Deference Account* (DA).

What does deference entail? First, deferring requires assigning more moral significance to marginalized peoples' preferences regarding how they are to be depicted and less to the comparative aesthetic value of the humor. Deferring also requires making a good faith attempt to be empathetic toward marginalized people, especially with respect to their attitudes toward jokes aimed at their group. Of course, attempts to defer may generate an epistemological problem: we may not always know whether we have a group's approval. Further, marginalized groups are not monoliths—some group members may regard a joke as acceptable while others do not. Therefore, DA does require aspiring derogatory comedians to pursue a comprehensive understanding of the target group's preferences, to the best of their ability, as complicated as those preferences may be.

At the same time, we deny that deferring means simply polling members of a group and acquiescing to the majority. Thus, DA should not be taken to suggest that as long as more than half the members of a group G approve of a joke about Gs, then telling the joke is permissible, or that as long as more than half disapprove, the joke is impermissible. One reason to avoid the simplistic polling view is that an internal minority within the group may be disenfranchised. Often, the most vocal members of a group have the most power within the group. Thus, DA requires being sensitive to the reality of intersectionality: a marginalized group may contain a proper subset of members who are themselves marginalized within the group (in addition to being oppressed *qua* member of their group with respect to the broader society). We should make a good faith effort to become aware of their preferences as well. If, for instance, the majority of African American hearers judge that a joke about African Americans is permissible, while many African American women object, we ought to take into account the latter's preference. In light of such cases, when a joke is contentious or we cannot be certain how group members feel about it, caution is warranted—we ought to refrain from telling it.

Because Gimbel's account explains wrongness solely in terms of harm, proving that an action is wrong requires proving that harm occurred. However, since the sort of harm Gimbel is interested in usually consists of a subjective experience (e.g., offense, demoralization, activating traumatic memories), an account like his simultaneously makes it difficult for marginalized people to provide evidence that they have experienced harm. While sometimes made manifest in an individual's behavior (e.g., facial expressions, tone of voice, or bodily posture), a harmful experience need not be publicly accessible. Moreover, targets of derogatory humor may have an incentive to not show any evidence of distress or embarrassment in situations where the joker occupies a position of authority and power. A student from an underrepresented group may feel pressure not to speak out when a professor makes an offensive joke because of the asymmetrical relationship between them, or she may want to avoid being labelled a "buzzkill." The *Deference Account* does not burden marginalized people in the way harm-based accounts do, since according to DA actual harm is not necessary for a joke to be impermissible. Proving that harm has been suffered should not be necessary for proving that a joke is objectionable.[23]

Another benefit of DA is that ascertaining the permissibility of a joke does not require discerning the speaker's intentions. Oppressed groups should have dominion over both pure and impure jokes. Thus, determining whether a speaker's intent was benign or malicious, whether they intended only to produce mirth or advance a proposition or ideology, is not necessary for determining whether the joke is morally defective. Instead, DA would invoke a "reasonable target" standard, in the spirit of Kate Manne's analysis of misogyny. We can ask whether a member of a marginalized group might reasonably interpret the joke or expressions of amusement as hostile. "This is as opposed to doing psychology to glean an agent's intentions, or having to take their word for it" (Manne 2018, 60).

Finally, while Gimbel is right to suggest that humor can be a powerful tool for use in illuminating social problems marginalized groups face, the extent to which dominant groups should assist in alleviating those problems and the type of help they ought to provide should be determined exclusively by the marginalized groups in question. Assuming that humor can have a liberating effect, it should be up to marginalized people to choose whether and to what extent they want this type of help from dominant groups. We suggest that it is better to let marginalized people unilaterally decide which jokes are appropriate tools for promoting their own liberation.

8. CONCLUDING REMARKS

Some may object that the cost of a morally perfect society, according to DA, is the loss of the aesthetic value and amusement impermissible jokes would have generated. We believe that this loss is more than outweighed by the duty to respect marginalized groups' authority to determine how they are represented. It would not be a great tragedy if most cis-het speakers went the rest of their lives without telling jokes about LGBTQ+ people, if most white speakers did not tell jokes about racial minorities, or if most men did not tell jokes about women. Deferring to marginalized groups may mean not telling jokes about them, but it does not follow that no such jokes can ever be told. Putting the DA into practice means, inter alia, hiring more writers, directors, actors, and comedians who are members of marginalized groups. A morally perfect society is not one with fewer jokes, it is one with more diverse jokers.

The *Inheritance* principle also explains how derogatory group-based humor may be morally valuable. If the attitudes one expresses by means of a joke are themselves morally praiseworthy, that enables their expression to be morally praiseworthy as well. To return to the example with which we began this chapter, consider once again Michelle Wolf's joke about Sarah Huckabee Sanders. If we stipulate that derogatory attitudes, like contempt, directed at Sanders in virtue of the lies she told while serving as the White House press secretary are fitting and morally apt, and Wolf's derogatory joke about Sanders is expressive of such attitudes, then we should regard Wolf's joke as morally praiseworthy.

NOTES

1. Hick (2018) also discusses this example.
2. We take self-deprecating humor—humor that takes the speaker themselves, or a group or institution of which they are a member, as its target—to be a proper subset of the class of derogatory humor.
3. Our focus in this chapter is on derogatory humor that subordinates *human* targets. However, nonhuman organisms, objects, geographical regions, among others, could certainly be the targets of derogatory humor as well.
4. Our expansion of the discussion of derogatory humor beyond racist and sexist humor is inspired by Anderson (2015).
5. For examples of studies specifically measuring the effects of derogatory humor, see Ford et al. (2014) and Woodzicka et al. (2015).
6. One way of derogating that we will not discuss at length in this chapter involves ranking a target lower in importance or significance than is warranted. For more on the moral implications of "unseriousness," see Brian Mondy's chapter 5 in this volume.
7. For a discussion of how speaker meaning and expression are possible in inner speech and private speech, see Morgan (2019).
8. Bar-On (2015) distinguishes acts of expression from vehicles that agents use to express psychological states.
9. Here we have in mind the notion of a "social stereotype" developed by Fricker (2007), for whom such stereotypes consist of an "*image* which expresses an association between a social group and one or more attributes, and which thereby embodies one or more generalizations about that social group" (37).
10. For a closer look at the political function and moral implications of satirical humor, see Larsen and Sackris's chapter 9 in this volume.
11. For an ethical analysis of the harms of humor, see Tristan Nash's chapter 7 in this volume.
12. This principle covers a much broader range of expressive acts, not just humorous ones. We think it also provides a plausible explanation for the wrongness of many instances of slurring and other pejorative utterances.
13. For instance, Smuts (2010) argues that one may laugh at a well-structured joke without thereby approving of the attitudes the joke conveys.
14. It is useful to keep in mind the distinction between behavior that is expressive and that which constitutes self-expression (see Green 2007). Laughter is expressive of amusement, given that it was designed to signal amusement. However, laughter that is faked does not constitute self-expression, that is, it does not both signal and show one's own amusement.
15. For more on the related phenomenon of "forced" laughter, see Dan Shargel's chapter 1 in this volume.
16. See, for example, Keltner (1995) for just one study of the physical manifestations of amusement and how they differ from the expressions of embarrassment.
17. By "voluntarily produced" we mean to include *both* behaviors that can be produced at will and those that can be suppressed at their onset by willing.

18. By "produced involuntarily" we mean to include behaviors that are not produced at will *and* cannot be suppressed at their onset by willing.

19. Here we disagree with Smuts (2010) and Gimbel (2018) who hold that laughter is always innocuous when caused by a derogatory joke's structure or cleverness, and not a derogatory attitude.

20. Gimbel mentions a harm-based account by John Morreall, according to which the wrongness of humor featuring stereotypes "is . . . proportional to the harm those stereotypes are likely to cause" (2009, 108).

21. We are suspicious of Gimbel's pure/impure distinction. Gimbel holds that pure ethnic jokes employ an "icon," that is, a flattened, dehumanized caricature that does not purport to depict any actual group (Gimbel 2018, 111). Gimbel contrasts ethnic jokes featuring icons with jokes about real people (Gimbel 2018, 143). However, it is not clear how any ethnic joke, understood in this way, could be about an actual group (Hick 2018). But ethnic jokes are about *actual* groups, not merely possible or imaginary groups. Moreover, even if one does not take icons and stereotypes to represent an actual group, listeners may take them to be representative of an actual group. The fact that stereotypical depictions have this sympathy-enabling quality is one reason to not reproduce them at all.

22. Gimbel (2018, 153) includes a flow chart that summarizes the procedure for determining the moral permissibility of telling a joke just described.

23. This is not to suggest that harm is irrelevant to the question of whether derogatory humor, and more generally derogatory expression, should be legally prohibited (as opposed to just socially prohibited). Theorists writing about whether derogatory expression (e.g., hate speech) should be legally prohibited tend to restrict their discussion to public speech that causes harm (see Waldron 2012). We take no position here on the question of whether the law should sanction or prohibit any type of humor.

REFERENCES

Wolf, Michelle (2018). "Michelle Wolf performs stand-up routine at White House Correspondent's dinner," *ABC News*, YouTube. Filmed April 28, 2018. Posted April 28, 2018. URL=<https://www.youtube.com/watch?v=L8IYPnnsYJw≥

Anderson, Luvell (2015). "Racist Humor." *Philosophy Compass* Vol. 10, 501–509.

Anderson, Luvell and Lepore, Ernie (2013). "What Did you Call Me? Slurs as Prohibited Words." *Analytic Philosophy* Vol. 54, 350–363.

Bar-On, Dorit (2015). "Expression: Acts, Products, and Meaning." In *Meaning Without Representation: Expression, Truth, Normativity, and Naturalism*, edited by S. Gross, N. Tebben, & M. Williams. Oxford: Oxford University Press, 180–209.

Barrineau, Trey (2014). "'Colbert Report' tweet stirs up anger." *USA Today*. March 27, 2014. https://www.usatoday.com/story/life/tv/2014/03/27/stephen-colbert-tweet-angers-asians/6991725/

Berger, Arthur Asa (1995). *An Anatomy of Humor*. New Brunswick, NJ: Transaction.

Camp, Elisabeth (2018). "A Dual Act Analysis of Slurs." In *Bad Words: Philosophical Perspectives on Slurs*, edited by D. Sosa. Oxford: Oxford University Press, 29–59.

Chun, Elaine W. (2004). "Ideologies of Legitimate Mockery: Margaret Cho's Revoicings of Mock Asian." *Pragmatics: Quarterly Publication for the International Pragmatics Association* Vol. 14, 263–289.

De Sousa, Ronald (1987). *The Rationality of Emotion*. Cambridge, MA: MIT Press.

Ford, Thomas E., 1 Woodzicka, Julie A., Triplett, Shane R., Kochersberger, Annie O., and Holden, Christopher J. (2014). "Not all groups are equal: Differential vulnerability of social groups to the prejudice-releasing effects of disparagement humor." *Group Processes & Intergroup Relations* Vol. 17, 178–199.

Fricker, Miranda (2007). *Epistemic Injustice: Power and the Ethics of Knowing*. Oxford: Oxford University Press.

Gervais, Matthew and Wilson, David S. (2005). "The Evolution and Functions of Laughter and Humor: A Synthetic Approach." *The Quarterly Review of Biology* Vol. 80, 395–430.

Gimbel, Steven. (2018). *Isn't That Clever: A Philosophical Account of Humor and Comedy*. New York: Routledge.

Green, Mitchell S. (2007). *Self-Expression*. Oxford: Oxford University Press.

Hayes, Christal (2019). "'You cannot get shoe polish off': Virginia governor darkened his face in Michael Jackson costume." *USA Today*. February 2, 2019. URL=<https://www.usatoday.com/story/news/politics/2019/02/02/ralph-northam-virginia-governor-blackface-michael-jackson/2756133002/≥>

Hegarty, Siobhan (2019). "When the lines between offensive comedy and off-limits jokes are blurred." *ABC Life*, May 2019. URL= <https://www.abc.net.au/life/knowing-when-comedy-crosses-a-line/11090890>

Hick, Darren Hudson (2018). "Review of Isn't That Clever: A Philosophical Account of Humor and Comedy." *Notre Dame Philosophical Reviews*, May 17, 2018. URL=<https://ndpr.nd.edu/news/isnt-that-clever-a-philosophical-account-of-humor-and-comedy/>

Hurley, Matthew M., Dennett, Daniel C., and Adams, Reginald B., Jr. (2011). *Inside Jokes: Using Humor to Reverse-Engineer the Mind*. Cambridge, MA: The MIT Press.

Jeshion, Robin (2013). "Expressivism and the Offensiveness of Slurs." *Philosophical Perspectives* Vol. 27, 231–259.

Keltner, Dacher (1995). "Signs of Appeasement: Evidence for the Distinct Displays of Embarrassment, Amusement, and Shame." *Journal of Personality and Social Psychology* Vol. 68, 441–454.

Keltner, Dacher (1996). "Facial Expressions of Emotion and Personality." In *Handbook of Emotion, Adult Development, and Aging*, edited by C. Magai and S. H. McFadden. New York: Academic Press, 385–401.

L'Official, Pete (2017). "When Ben Vereen Wore Blackface to Reagan's Inaugural Gala." *The New Yorker*, January 6, 2017. URL= <https://www.newyorker.com/culture/culture-desk/revisiting-ben-vereens-misunderstood-blackface-inaugural-performance>

Lott, Eric (1993). *Love and Theft*. Oxford: Oxford University Press.

Manne, Kate (2018). *Down Girl: The Logic of Misogyny*. Oxford: Oxford University Press.

Morgan, Andrew (2019). 'Plato's Revenge: Moral Deliberation as Dialogical Activity.' *Pacific Philosophical Quarterly* Vol. 100, Issue 1, pp. 69–89.

Morreall, John. (2009). *Comic Relief: A Comprehensive Philosophy of Humor*. Malden, MA: Wiley-Blackwell.

Smuts, Aaron (2010). "Do Moral Flaws Enhance Amusement?" *American Philosophical Quarterly* Vol. 46, 151–162.

Waldron, Jeremy (2012). *The Harm in Hate Speech*. Cambridge, MA: Harvard University Press.

White House Correspondence Association (@whca), "#WHCA Statement to Members on Annual Dinner," Twitter post, April 29, 2018. https://twitter.com/whca/status/990773612226412545?lang=en.

Woodzicka, Julie A., Mallett, Robyn K., Hendricks, Shelbi, and Pruitt, Astrid V. (2015). "It's Just a (sexist) Joke: Comparing Reactions to Sexist Versus Racist Communications." *Humor: International Journal of Humor Research* Vol. 28, 289–309.

Chapter 8

Amused by the Outrageous
The Morally Tempering Effect of News Satire
Rasmus Rosenberg Larsen and David Sackris

> "Every week the nominees in this category do the impossible: They make the news funny!"
>
> —Joint statement by Eric Bana and Connie Britton introducing the 70th Emmy Award for Outstanding Variety Talk Series.[1]

Political satire has been a frequent element in Western culture dating back to ancient Greece. While its aim, impact, and form has varied greatly—from Aristophanes' play *Lysistrata* exposing the farcical elements of patriarchic norms, to La Fontaine's *Fables* ridiculing superstition and religion—in the past three to four decades, a novel form of political satire has won unprecedented popularity in the United States, the so-called *news satire*. News satire is set as a televised faux newscast, and it portrays real political issues in a satirical fashion. Though the first occurrence of televised news satire in the United States can be traced to *Weekend Update* in 1975, the more popular instances of the past decades are *The Daily Show, The Colbert Report, Last Week Tonight, Real Time, Full Frontal, Late Night,* and *The Opposition*.

Although news satire has been around for some time, the genre is probably best represented by *The Daily Show* (TDS) and *The Colbert Report* (TCR).[2] In fact, the unprecedented popularity of said shows led to a surge of research in media studies with the primary aim of addressing two questions: (1) Is news satire, as put forth by *TDS* and *TCR*, different in kind from other political satire? (2) If it is different in kind, to what extent (if any) does this difference manifest itself in viewers? For example, does it uniquely motivate or demotivate viewers to participate in the political process? (e.g., Baumgartner and Lockerbie 2018; Kim and Vishak 2008; Young 2008).

A survey of this growing literature yields decidedly ambiguous conclusions: In terms of the first question, there is some reason to think *TDS* and *TCR* differ from classic political satire, such as that presented in *The Tonight Show* and *The Late Show*, in that *TDS* and *TCR* are more informative and fundamentally political in a way that the latter two shows are not (e.g., Baumgartner and Lockerbie 2018; Hoffman and Young 2011; Kim and Vishak 2008; Xenos and Becker 2009). However, the literature has reached no clear conclusions with regards to the second, more important question, namely, as to whether news satires such as *TDS* and *TCR* create a highly motivated voter base, or if said shows merely pander to, or even propagate, political slackers looking for a cheap laugh.[3]

While news satire may be informative and provocative, one of its main goals is to make the morally outrageous amusing. For instance, when Donald Trump ran for office in the 2016 presidential election on the Republican ticket, news satire shows would shape the majority of their content around the steady stream of moral outrage caused by said candidate. While the examples of such satirical bits are many, the following is well representative of the content at the time: on October 7, 2016, the *Washington Post* published a video recorded in 2005, which had Mr. Trump bragging about sexist behavior around women, professing that "When you're a star, they let you do it . . . Grab them by the pussy. You can do anything." Trevor Noah, the current host of *TDS*, thus commented on this episode with a smirk: "What kind of person grabs the pussy? That doesn't sound pleasurable for either party involved."[4]

Admittedly, this is funny. But more interestingly, Trevor Noah and his *TDS* colleagues managed to do what seems almost impossible, turning something that their viewers (presumably) see as a sexist, morally base behavior into something worthy of amusement.

However, the question that has been vexing media researchers still stands: What effects, if any, do jokes like these have on viewers in terms of their political efficacy and participation?[5] Not only do scholars disagree on this issue, they also seem to lack common, reliable theories and methods for answering such a question. Plausibly, the key measure for political participation in a constitutional democracy is voting. However, when participants in news satire studies are asked whether they, for instance, plan on actually voting, their answers are highly unreliable. For example, Baumgartner and Morris (2011) found that young voters generally overestimate their likelihood of voting, whereas 91 percent reported that they *would* vote, the *actual* voter participation (in the 2008 general election) among eighteen to twenty-four-year olds was 49 percent (74).

As a result of this unreliability, researchers have to use (actuarial) proxies for voting when trying to gauge the effect of news satire. They typically ask questions such as How likely are you to participate in a political rally? How likely are you to volunteer for a political organization? How likely are you to discuss the upcoming election with a friend? How likely are you to sign a petition? (e.g., Chen and Sun 2017).

As most scholars recognize, these questions are unlikely to adequately measure the impact of *news satire* on political *participation*: Just as peoples' intention to vote are radically different from their actual voting, there is likely a similar difference between intending to sign a petition and actually coming across a relevant one and signing it.

In this contribution, we suggest a different approach to measuring and assessing the impact of news satire on the political process. Instead of asking the broad question of "What effect does news satire have on participatory democracy?," we shall form a (testable) theory that seeks to qualify and guide an initial answer to the question: "What effect *should we expect* news satire to have on participatory democracy?" Perhaps by first developing a theory that lends itself to prediction, can we then develop better test/research paradigms. At the very least, perhaps such a theory can serve to explain why research into this area has yielded such mixed results.

In what follows, we argue that we should expect news satire to have an *attenuating effect* on one's political position, viewpoints, beliefs, motivation, among others. That is, we theorize that a systemic consumption of news satire should lead to tempered states toward and about the political and moral issues one normally would be outraged about. Put in more formal terms, we shall outline a theory that predicts that if *person x* is exposed to a *news story y* that would typically invoke moral outrage, *person x* will be less outraged by *y* when the content of *y* is conveyed in a news satire format (i.e., we theorize that amusement *causes* attenuation of outrage). For example, if a person was initially morally outraged by Mr. Trump's sexist behavior (e.g., by reading the *Washington Post* story), our theory predicts that such a person as becoming *less* morally outraged if that same information is later presented in a humorous light as part of a news satire segment.

In formalizing our theory, we draw on Jesse Prinz's *sentimentalist* moral psychology, which posits that moral judgments are necessarily and sufficiently constructed out of a variety of emotions. When we are negatively aroused by a specific behavior, we are morally appalled; when positively aroused, we are morally approving. We argue that it follows from Prinz's theory that people are incrementally less outraged if moral issues are treated in a humorous fashion: such treatments result in mixed emotions, which result in a tempering effect on the viewer. We qualify our theoretical explanation with existing empirical work on satire, as well as research in moral psychology. We tentatively conclude that it may not be unproblematic to turn serious moral and political issues into laughing matters.

1. THE UNDERLYING SENTIMENTALIST ASSUMPTION IN MEDIA STUDIES RESEARCH

Most researchers into the effects of news satire share a basic assumption: if news satire plays a motivational or demotivational role in relation to the political process, it will be through the *triggering of emotions* in its viewership.

For example, Hart and Hartelius (2007) fear that if news satire (e.g., *TDS* and *TCR*) generates emotions of cynicism, it will depress political participation among viewers. Baumgartner and Morris (2006) argue that negative emotions toward political candidates generated by news satire lowers political efficacy, that is, it reduces peoples' trust in the political process. Further, Lee and Kwak (2014) argue that if news satire has a motivating effect, it would also be through the generation of negative emotions. In support of their hypothesis that arousing negative emotions, in particular the emotion of anger, will be correlated with political activity, they state: "Indeed, emotions can supply energy with which to undertake actions, and empirical evidence predominantly supports the role of emotions in motivating political behaviour" (Lee and Kwak 2014, 312).

Other researchers make a similar assumption: Chen and Sun (2017) propose that if political humor does motivate action, it will be through the generation of anger. They state, "we specifically examine a negative emotion (i.e., anger) not only because political satire is likely to induce anger but also because it has been widely studied in public opinion and found to have a strong association with participatory behaviours" (3014).

It appears, then, that these media studies researchers share the assumption that *negative emotions* are the primary driver of political participation. This suggests that they believe that emotions play a primary role in judgment formation: individuals determine that they ought to participate (or not) in the political process as a result of certain (strongly or weakly) felt emotional states. We believe this assumption is telling in regards to the moral psychological (value) theory media studies researchers *implicitly* endorse. To us it appears as if they place fundamental importance on emotion as having a constituting role in moral judgment, orientation, and motivation. Such an approach is typically referred to by philosophers and psychologists as a *sentimentalist* approach to moral theory.

2. PRINZ AND THE SENTIMENTALIST OOZE OF MORALITY

Building on these observations, we suspect that researchers generally operate with an implicit commitment to a *sentimentalist* value theory. In this section, we substantiate such a theoretical framework with the aim of generating more precise research hypotheses, as well as more qualified interpretative claims about current research on news satire.

Throughout the history of Western philosophy and psychology, the human capacity to make moral judgments has predominately been described as a rational disposition (e.g., Kavathatzopoulos 1991). In the past two decades, however, behavioral and cognitive scientists have found empirical evidence that appears to demonstrate that affect, emotion, and feeling play a coextensive and formative role in moral judgments; findings that have proven difficult to square with the dominant *reason-based* theories of morality (e.g., Greene, Sommerville, Nystrom, Darley, and Cohen 2001; Haidt, Koller, and Dias 1993; Pascual, Rodrigues, and Gallardo-Pujol 2013; Strohminger 2014). Following these findings, an increasing number of moral philosophers and psychologists have argued that the long-neglected *sentimentalist* theories of morality must now be reconsidered (e.g., Blackburn 1998; Greene 2013; Haidt 2012; Prinz 2007; Slote 2010).

Sentimentalist theories of morality, or *moral sentimentalism*, typically refers to a cohort of ethical and meta-ethical theories historically rooted in seventeenth and eighteenth-century British Empiricists such as Earl of Shaftesbury, Francis Hutcheson, Thomas Reid, Adam Smith, David Hume (Driver 2013). What sentimentalist moral theories of this kind convey is that emotion, feeling, mood, sentiment, and/or affect, in one way or the other, are pivotal in moral judgment, belief, and behavior. In this way, moral sentimentalism contrasts with moral rationalism in that the latter entirely bypasses the constitutive role of emotion; at most, moral rationalists will make room for emotion as an *outcome* of moral reasoning, but reject the possibility of a formative impact on morality as a whole. For example, you may feel anger when you read about political corruption in the newspaper, but according to rationalists this is only because you *reasoned* that corruption was wrong. Opposed to such a view, moral sentimentalism (broadly construed) argues that it is because you are affectively appalled by political corruption that you therefore judge it to be immoral. In the former case, reason plays a *prehoc* role, and in the latter case, reason plays a *posthoc* role.

Most versions of moral sentimentalism share the view that emotions can be a sufficient condition for moral judgments. What they disagree on is the degree to which emotions are necessary for morality, and whether they accept the strongest version of moral sentimentalism, namely, that emotions are both necessary and sufficient for morality, that is, the theory that a moral judgment or belief is nothing more than realizing the disposition to react emotionally to specific social situations.[6]

One of the most cited of the contemporary sentimentalist theories is Jesse Prinz's *sentimentalist constructivist* account (e.g., Prinz 2006; 2006; 2015;

2016), which posits that moral judgments and beliefs are wholly—that is, necessarily and sufficiently—constituted by emotional dispositions and processes. When we judge something to be morally right or wrong, Prinz argues, what is driving this viewpoint is never our rational analysis of the situation, but rather a felt experience of either positive or negative valence.

Prinz goes a long way to demonstrate that there is significant empirical evidence in support for his constructivist account. While we might agree—from mere introspection—that our moral judgments are always associated with emotions (e.g., you *feel* that murder is wrong), Prinz instead points to the science. Indeed, the vast majority of empirical research in moral psychology seems to support the view that moral judgments always coincide with emotion processes. That is, when we make moral judgments, it is always the case that some emotions are processing (for a recent review, see Prinz 2015).

Prinz acknowledges that this body of evidence is only suggestive insofar that it can also serve to support the *rationalist* hypothesis that emotions are necessary outcomes of moral judgments: when we have reasoned that something is wrong/right, it will always be the case that we will have a corresponding emotional reaction. Thus, in some sense, the data readily supports both rationalist and sentimentalist accounts, and Prinz foresees that perhaps the data will always be enmeshed in ambiguity insofar as we cannot have a moral judgment without also being (cognitively) *aware* of it, and as soon as we are subjectively *thinking* about morality, the relevant data (brain scans) will always show this cognitive aspect alongside the emotion processes (e.g., Prinz 2015).

Because of these ambiguities, Prinz also considers another strand of evidence taken from studies of moral testimony. In their hallmark studies of verbal moral justifications, Haidt and colleagues (1993; 2000; 2001) found that when people make moral judgments, they are often incapable of rationally justifying their moral position, but will, on the other hand, reliably emphasize their emotional states toward the issue. And even when test subjects both realize and recognize their incapability of rationally justifying their moral beliefs, they rarely choose to revoke or revise their position. For example, when asked about the morality of hypothetical scenarios concerning cannibalism, patriotism, incest, among others (e.g., Is it morally acceptable for two siblings to have consensual, protected sexual intercourse?), most individuals were capable of giving an immediate moral judgment, though the majority were incapable of justifying their viewpoint when asked to explain, for example, what exactly makes consensual, protected incest wrong. When pressured, people often responded with sentences such as "I know it's wrong, but I just can't tell you why." Haidt and colleagues referred to this as *moral dumbfounding*: when one makes a moral judgment driven by emotion, while being lucidly aware of having no good reasons for their viewpoint (for replications, see Hindriks 2015; Uhlmann and Zhu 2014).

Taken together, Prinz argues that this body of evidence—that is, that (1) emotions always coincide with moral judgments, and (2) individuals tend to be satisfied with their initial, immediate feeling about a moral issue—supports his constructivist version of sentimentalism: that emotions are necessary and sufficient for moral judgment and beliefs.

But what are the actual psychological mechanics of a moral judgment? Is it just arbitrary which emotions serve to deem one issue immoral and another moral? Prinz argues that while the actual occurrent emotion is what makes us immediately perceive a given situation as a moral one, the mechanics are strictly rule based:

First, the moral judgment of a situation is controlled by the valence of the occurring emotion. Similar to most canonical theories in affective science, Prinz posits that all emotions are inherently valenced, that is, emotions are always perceived with a binary value: either they are negative or positive. For instance, disgust is always perceived as negative, and joy is always perceived as positive. What determines the final judgment of a moral issue, then, is to what extent it is associated with emotions of positive or negative valence. We may be disgusted by hearing about a genocide in the evening news or feel sincere joy when our daughter gets engaged. In the former case, we have formed a judgment of moral *disapprobation*, and in the latter case a judgment of moral *approbation*.

Second, since emotions are realizations of dispositions (i.e., we have the disposition to feel anger, and when we do feel anger, that disposition is realized), Prinz argues that moral judgments are similarly realizations of dispositions to undergo specific feelings in particular situations. In other words, Prinz believes that moral beliefs are essentially emotional dispositions (what he calls *sentiments*) that can be triggered by specific perceptual content. Thus, when we truthfully believe that murder is wrong, what we are really conveying is that we have a disposition to emote negatively when we perceive a murder. Analogously, when we truthfully say that we morally approve of giving to charity, what we are really saying is that we will emote positively when we see such an act of kindness.

Prinz thus argues that moral judgments take the following dispositional structure: "To believe that something is morally wrong (right) is to have a sentiment of disapprobation (approbation) towards it" (Prinz 2006, 33).

This position warrants some further critical considerations. For example, if emotions are *sufficient* for moral judgment, it then seems to follow that *all* emotional processes implicitly convey moral judgments. But this is clearly counterintuitive. When feeling tremendous joy and pleasure eating a delicious cheesecake, it would seem wrong to say that we thereby also feel moral approbation toward the cheesecake. Prinz thinks cases like these demonstrate a fact about the moral realm, namely, that moral judgments are about human behaviors:

> A moral sentiment is a disposition that causes us to feel emotions of other-blame (i.e., anger or disgust) when another person performs an action of a certain type (or has a certain trait, etc.), and emotions of self-blame (i.e., guilt or shame) when we ourselves perform that action. A moral judgment is an emotional state that issues from such a bidirectional disposition. Thus, to tell whether a state of disgust is a moral judgment we must know whether it comes from a moral sentiment. That, in turn, depends on whether the object of our disgust would have caused shame if we ourselves have been responsible for it. (Prinz 2016, 64)

Yes, we can feel joy when eating a particularly delicious cheesecake, but in such a case, we are not making a moral judgment. For our purpose here, it seems fairly uncontroversial to claim that news satire typically targets human behavior (i.e., given its political content). So, when we are angered by the behaviors of a political candidate, on Prinz's theory this anger is a moral judgment. We now turn to analyzing the (social) role of news satire through the lenses of Prinz's sentimentalist theory.

3. NEWS SATIRE, MEDIA STUDIES RESEARCH, AND OUR COMPLICATED EMOTIONAL LIVES

To round up what has been said so far: In section 1, we concluded that media studies researchers appear to assume that emotions motivate political behavior, for instance, citizens participate in politics in part because of negative emotions such as anger, disgust, among others. Furthermore, as we just argued in section 2, such emotions may constitute a moral judgment (on a sentimentalist theory). Our working premise for analyzing the effects of news satire, then, is to look at the formation of moral judgments in relation to political participation and efficacy.

With this framework in mind, we return to one of the core questions being asked by media studies researchers: does news satire motivate or demotivate viewers to participate in the political process? Our analysis of the literature tells us there are currently *three related*, yet different questions being investigated:

> *Question A*: Are viewers of news satire *more likely* to participate in the political process, and if so, is this because viewers of news satire *feel a high level of political efficacy* as a result of watching, and being informed by news satire? (e.g., Chen and Sun 2017; Hoffman and Young 2011; McBeth and Clemons 2011).

Question B: Are viewers of news satire *more likely* to participate in the political process, and if so, is this because viewers of news satire feel negative emotions (e.g., moral outrage) as a result of watching, and being informed by news satire? (e.g., Chen and Sun 2017; Lee and Kwak 2014).

Question C: Are viewers of news satire *less likely* to participate in the political process, and if so, is this because viewers of news satire *feel cynicism about the political process and their efficacy* as a result of watching, and being informed by news satire? (e.g., Baumgartner and Morris 2006; Hart and Hartelius 2007).

While these research questions all build on intuitive predictions (e.g., increased participation due to moral outrage), testing or answering these questions, however, is not at all straightforward. Significant difficulties arise on a number of parameters, where one obvious limitation is that there are numerous factors in play when determining whether someone will, and why they did, participate or have trust in the political process.

Take, for example, *political efficacy*. Feelings of political efficacy are highly correlated with core personal aspects such as level of education, creed, culture, gender, and mundane factors such as how regularly one follows the news. Some researchers therefore conclude that all of these factors somewhat disarm the purpose of looking at news satire in isolation, since, as Young and Esralew (2011) argue, such viewership cannot be separated from other political efficacy factors:

> Our data suggest that *The Daily Show* and late-night comedy in general are part of a diet of healthy political characteristics and behaviors, all of which correlate positively with political participation, discussion, and debate viewing. Among the other, even stronger characteristics of participatory and politically talkative citizens are following politics, education, strong party identification, and exposure to various traditional forms of political media, including National Public Radio, political talk radio, cable news, and newspapers. (2011, 113)

We might even say that the three different research questions are caught in a "chicken and egg" problem: are individuals more likely to watch shows like *TDS* and *TCR* because they are more interested in politics to begin with, or do individuals become more interested in politics because they watch *TDS* and *TCR*?

Finding an unambiguous answer to this question is enmeshed in a number of staunch practical hurdles. For example, it is exceedingly difficult to design a study that can actually measure what these researchers are looking for (i.e., the *unique* impact of news satire). Indeed, the average viewer of *TDS* and *TCR* is, in fact, already more educated and more closely follows politics than the average nonviewer, making it difficult to find a proper sample group for reliable testing (e.g., Compton 2011). In addition, it is not clear what it means to be a regular viewer or consumer of news satire, and the majority of Americans get their political information from a variety of news sources, making it problematic to assess the impact of news satire alongside other information streams (Baumgartner and Morris 2011, 69). As a result, designing a study that tests for the unique effects of watching news satire on political behaviors like voting, participating in rallies, or one's likelihood to discuss politics, becomes next to a practical impossibility.

Furthering the problems with pursuing this research is that there appear to be discrepancies in the way research questions are formed. For example, the cause-effect relationship predicted by researchers of *Question A* and *Question B* may be inseparable in the sense that feelings of political efficacy and moral outrage may both promote political participation. On a different note, but still problematic, is that the cause-effect relationship in *Question B* and *Question C* differ in terms of the emotion and the behavior it leads to: research on *Question B* seems to purport that news satire is motivating due to emotional outrage, while research on *Question C* predicts demotivation due to emotional cynicism.

We believe these incongruences between the leading research questions (and their implied predictions) should get us thinking about alternative questions. Judging their current approach, it seems that media researchers haven't seriously considered the following possibility: that watching news satire invokes a number of competing emotions, and that those emotions have differing valences, some positive and some negative. As a result, viewing satire is likely to manifest in *mixed emotions*: moments of anger, moments of comic joy, moments of cynicism, among others. If the primary goal of news satire is to make people laugh, that is, to have every segment build around comical punchlines, then we should expect any anger generated by the content portion of the segment to be diluted by that final humorous punchlines.[7] Similarly, we should expect any cynicism generated to similarly be diluted by that final punchline. *Question B* and *Question C* both identify emotions that theorists expect to govern behavior. But what if both emotions (i.e., anger and cynicism) are consistently generated as mere instances among a mix of other emotions? In such a case, what might we expect to be the conclusive outcome of news satire on political participation?

It appears to us that researchers have yet to consider two important observations regarding human dispositions and the goal of news satire: First, human beings are complex emotional creatures, and as a result have diverging, complex emotional reactions to the same events. And second, the goal of satire is to make people laugh, whatever else it may end up doing. If we take Prinz's moral sentimentalism seriously—together with these two observations—a central question then seems be what can be predicted about the *emotional* effects of news satire in regards to political efficacy and motivation?

4. MORAL SENTIMENTALISM AND NEWS SATIRE

In this section, we seek to answer the question concerning the potential impact of news satire on political efficacy and motivation. Before we initiate this discussion, we must first highlight the two hypotheses around which we frame the following conversation about the effects of news satire:

Null-Hypothesis: The view that news satire has *no* unique and/or extraordinary effect on basic political efficacy and motivation compared to traditional forms of news.

Alternative Hypothesis: If the null-hypothesis can be ruled out, that, in fact, news satire does seem to have an effect on underlying political efficacy and motivation, we expect this effect to be one of emotional *attenuation* and behavioral *de-motivation*.

In general, it is a very real possibility that news satire does *not* have a measurably unique impact on its viewers compared to the many other existing information streams (i.e., the *Null-Hypothesis*). However, if we can rule out the *Null-Hypothesis*, then we must have an explanation that can account for any such measurable differences. Such explanation is what informs the *Alternative Hypothesis*, the details of which we outline in this section:

If we assume that moral judgments simply are the result of emotional states (i.e., sentimentalism), it then follows that both positive and negative emotional states play a role in shaping the final moral judgment. For example, when judging a morally relevant situation, say, a homeless boy stealing candy from the local grocery, there will presumably be a number of positive and negative emotions that all weigh into one's final judgment. Maybe one is sympathizing with the dire situation of the boy. Perhaps one is at the same time appalled by the audacity of the boy to steal. Overall, according to Prinz's theory, whichever of the positive and negative emotions dominates the perception (so to speak) will determine the nature of the final moral judgment. So in case one is feeling *more* negatively than positively about the boy stealing candy, the judgment will then be one of moral disapprobation. However, and importantly, it would be wrong to characterize this judgment as unambiguously negative, since, after all, one was also feeling some sympathy for the boy's situation. Moreover, the difference between negative and positive valence is indicative of the *degree* to which one judges the situation to be right/wrong.

Analogously, if a news satire segment about a certain issue generates mixed emotions—for example, maybe it makes you appalled *and* amused—then the final judgment is likewise made up of both positively and negatively valenced emotions. So whatever the final judgment is, it is likely to be one of inherent ambivalence, similar to judging the poor boy stealing candy. That is, even if negative emotions dominate one's final judgment, it is unlikely to be unambiguous because it is coextensive with and tempered by other positive emotions (i.e., amusement) associated with the segment.

Consider again the story from *Washington Post* that reported Mr. Trump bragging about sexually assaulting women. If we hypothesize that *person x* was exposed to this story in *time 1*, we might expect this person's judgment to be one of disapprobation (i.e., negative emotion). Now, consider what happens when person *x* is then exposed to the story again during a news satire segment (e.g., as presented by Trevor Noah and *TDS*). In this case, we would predict that *person x* transitions from having a purely negative judgment in *time 1*, to having a mixed judgment in *time 2*, namely, one of both being appalled by Mr. Trump's actions (i.e., negative emotion), and at the same time associating it with something humorous (i.e., positive emotion). It might be that person x is still judging the situation negatively overall, though we claim that the judgment has transitioned from one of unambiguity to one of ambiguity (see figure 8.1).

Further, we might even have good reason to expect that in some cases the final judgment that results from watching a news satire segment results in a surplus of positive emotion due to the goal of news satire: to make people laugh. Consider then that many media studies researchers (as discussed above) assume that it is primarily the negative judgments that motivates

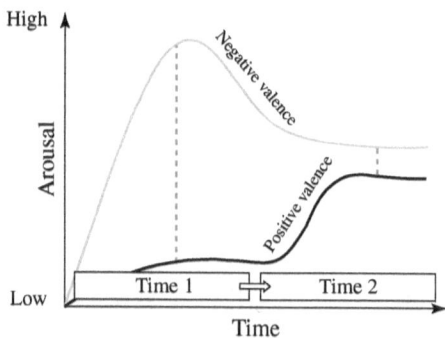

Figure 8.1. How a Moral-Emotional Judgment Might Change Over Time Due to Various Modes of Exposure.

people politically. According to this assumption, then, if the final judgment resulting from news satire is instead *positive* (as opposed to negative), we might thus expect news satire to be politically non- or demotivating.

What many media researchers have focused on in their inquiry into the effect of news satire is the quality of news-related *content*, and not necessarily the effects of a *satirical format*. It is the content that many researchers take to set these shows apart from mere late night stand-up comedians riffing on politics. For example, Hoffman and Young (2011, 164) maintain that the content of news satire is almost as substantial as the content of traditional news, and so for that reason expect the political efficacy generated by watching news satire to be on par with that of watching traditional news programs. Moreover, they reason that since both shows are *informative*, and since the process of being informed is a key part of feeling politically efficacious, news satire must generate predictable rates of political efficacy on par with regular news (for a similar view, see Kim & Vishak, 2008).

From a sentimentalist theoretical point of view, however, we believe this line of reasoning is fundamentally problematic due to significant differences between traditional news and news satire, namely, the latter ends with a humorous punchline, whereas the former does not. Indeed, if the final punchline generates a net positive emotion, or cancels out the negative emotions generated by the content (figure 8.1), we should not expect that content to have much of a motivating effect on viewers, that is, if the working assumption is that anger and outrage really are motivating, humor might *disarm* such emotionally driven processes. In a very real sense, the same content (as presented by both news and news satire segments) might be perceived differently due to its format.

There is empirical evidence suggesting that differences in content perception can be controlled by manipulating the format. In a study of traditional news format, Zillmann and colleagues (1994) found evidence that ending a news segment with a humorous anecdote attenuated the negative feelings generated by a previous *hard news* segment. In their study, participants were shown a news clip that contained emotionally disturbing information (e.g., a story about the rise of highway violence). Some participants were then immediately exposed to a humorous or lighthearted news story. The participants who were exposed to the final humorous story reported feeling less worried about the events described in the hard news portion. As Zillmann and colleagues reports: "Exposure to an amusing closing story fostered diminished accounts of the severity of international conflict and domestic crime . . . The light-hearted frame of mind created by humor appears again to effect a belittlement of threatening issues" (1994, 75).

In addition, work in so-called *positive psychology* has consistently recognized the role that humor may play in blocking or overriding negative emotions. In a survey study, Peterson and Seligman (2004) found that humor played a significant role as a *coping mechanism* for dealing with negative, stressful situations. The authors state that "humor as a psychological strength is particularly visible when an individual or group is facing adversity, inasmuch as it helps to mitigate, suppress, interrupt, or even permanently replace negative impact" (2004, 595). If humor has such disarming effects, it likely plays the same role for viewers of news satire: as long as the negative or outrageous content is punctuated with a joke, we should expect any negative emotions generated by the content to be diminished compared to how the viewer perceived that same content prior to experiencing it in a humorous format.

Conventional wisdom also supports these findings: we often use humor to diffuse a stressful situation or to break the ice in socially uncomfortable situations (e.g., Norrick and Spitz 2008). We expect the humorous feelings to, in some sense, override or cancel out the negative ones and result in a generally more positive atmosphere. In our view, there is little reason to think ending a traditional newscast with a humorous or lighthearted story is fundamentally different from satirizing a serious news story. If we end on a bit of humor, we are more likely to have a positively valenced judgment of the situation.

Now, if we assume—as media studies researchers do—that that negative emotions are likely to motivate political participation, then given the role of humor in news satire, we should *not* expect news satire to be politically motivating. If humor mitigates a perceived threat or typically overrides negative emotions, then we should also expect any feelings of anger generated by that perceived threat to be mitigated as well.

With these observations in hand, however, it is telling to read that most media studies researchers appear to conclude that the *Null-Hypothesis* cannot be ruled out. Indeed, several studies propose that the effects of viewing news satire are fundamentally mixed, and thus, that there is no clear evidence of unique and extraordinary effects compared to other forms of information streams (e.g., Young and Esralew 2011, 100–101). But perhaps the *effect* of news satire that we are searching for is not one of concrete behavior (e.g., motivation), but one of political inertia, attenuation, diffusion, among others. Since news satire has the effect of evoking mixed emotions in the viewer, for example, anger at the corruption in the government as well as amusement at the ineptness of politicians, the final judgment is likely to be emotionally mixed and comparatively weak. If viewers are both laughing and cringing, it is hard to see how we can just single out the cringing emotion and predict its effect on political participation given that it may well be overridden by the laughter.

Thus, when researchers, due to mixed results, seem to be hesitant about ruling out the *Null-Hypothesis*, it might be exactly such mixed results that *should* lead to a ruling out of the *Null-Hypothesis*. Certainly, the attenuating effect of humor could have a significant impact on political participation given the contention that humor essentially cancels out negative emotions. If humor effectively cancels out negative emotions, then political satire may well be less motivating when compared to traditional news sources. If this argument is sound, and we have shown that the *Null-Hypothesis* might be ruled out, this leads us to consider our *Alternative Hypothesis*: that news satire has a *de-motivating* effect on political participation

Some research into news satire indicates that if one agrees with the basic message of the satire (e.g., the person dislikes the ridiculed political party/policy/politician), that person is likely to find the satire *more amusing* than the person who disagrees with the basic message of the satire (e.g., Chen and Sun 2017). Further, there is evidence that for the person who disagrees with the satire, they are more likely to be *angered* by the content (e.g., Chen and Sun 2017; Flanagan 2017). Thus, if shows such as *TDS* and *TCR* are essentially "preaching to the choir," that is, lampooning persons and events that their viewers think are proper targets of ridicule, those viewers are more likely to find the content humorous, and as a result, are less likely to form a motivational negative judgment about the content. Thus, for viewers who agree with the message of the satire, the overall effect might be one of de-motivation insofar as their adverse political perspectives are attenuated.

This leads to speculation about what happens if a person *does not* agree with the content of the segment. For instance, if a person is watching his/her political favorite being ridiculed in a news satire segment, should we expect such a person to feel less positive about the candidate or more negatively about his/her candidate's opponents? Perhaps it passes as a sound prediction that those who disagrees with the satire are likely to feel more negatively about their opponents. If so, news satire appears to operate as a double-edged sword, whereas some viewers are attenuated in their political views, and other viewers are strengthened in their adverse beliefs concerning their political opponents.

Finally, and this is even more speculative, our *Alternative Hypothesis* seems to imply that news satire may be bad or counterproductive for the politics such segments appear to promote or support. With this in mind, consider then that most of today's news satire segments cater to a liberal-leaning viewership. Does this mean that liberal voters who consume news satire are less likely to perceive issues and events that should be bad-for-liberals as thoroughly negative? We think this might be the case. When liberal viewers consume news satire, they may indeed perceive these bad events with a comparatively more positive feeling, and therefore become less worried about it. And when people are less worried, they may be less politically motivated; that is, less likely to participate politically (e.g., by voting, organizing).

5. CONCLUSION

In this chapter, we demonstrated that by pairing news satire with perspectives from sentimentalist moral theory, we were able to form novel predictions about the effects of news satire on its viewer base. Such predictions, we hope, might translate into likewise novel research hypotheses and designs for future experimentation. But what might constitute such a better experimental design?

We believe the approach taken by Zillman and colleagues (1994) almost twenty-five years ago is on the right track. Their approach was simple: some viewers were shown news programs about a negative issue that was dovetailed with a humorous news story, and other viewers were shown the same news program with the final, humorous segment cut out. They were then asked to indicate how severe they viewed the problem addressed in the news report, how concerned they were about negative future developments concerning that issue, and how concerned they were that the issue would affect them negatively.

An analogous experiment could be performed with news satire: viewers could be shown a negative story as covered by the conventional televised news and as covered by, for instance, *TDS*. They could then be asked the very same type of questions as in Zillman and colleagues (1994). If viewers are less worried about the issue as presented by *TDS*, then we find some useful answers. Perhaps *TDS* is less likely to motivate, as a result of disarming the outrageous with shrewd amusement. Notice that such a procedure completely cuts out the problem of doubtful self-reports, which the majority of research on this topic relies on, since respondents do not need to rate their likelihood of participating in as of yet unplanned protests, their likelihood of writing to their (possibly unknown to them) congressperson, or even their likelihood of discussing the issue on social media. Perhaps all we really need to know is how the viewer *feels* at the end of the segment, whether they really were amused by the morally outrageous.

NOTES

1. *Television Academy*, November 1, 2019, https://www.youtube.com/watch?v=qVZtQO4Sypc

2. TDS aired for the first time in 1996 and is still running. TCR ran from 2005 to 2014.

3. For the proarguments, see Chen, Gan, and Sun (2017), Kim and Vishak (2008), Baumgartner and Lockerbie (2018), Hoffman and Young (2011). For the conarguments, see Holbert, Lambe, Dudo and Carlton (2007), Morris and Baumgartner (2008). One caveat is that the methods used to investigate this question are limited and incongruent. This will be discussed.

4. Sadaf Ahsan "'It's not the locker room, it's you, motherf—er': Trevor Noah says Trump's comments 'glorify' rape," *The National Post*, October 11, 2016.

5. Political efficacy denotes the degree to which individuals see themselves as a competent knower of/about political issues and that their participation in the political process matters. For an explanation of political efficacy, see Holbert, Lambe, Dudo, and Carlton (2007).

6. For a philosophical overview of the various philosophical positions in sentimentalism, see: Prinz 2007, 13–21.

7. John Stewart consistently maintained that the primary goal of *TDS* (under his tenure) was to make people laugh, not inform them. See, for example, his widely watched appearance on the CNN show "Crossfire": Retrieved from *YouTube*, November 8, 2019: https://www.youtube.com/watch?v=aFQFB5YpDZE

REFERENCES

Baumgartner, J. C. and J. S. Morris. 2011. "Stoned Slackers or Super-Citizens? The *Daily Show* Viewing and Political Engagement of Young Adults." In *The Stewart/Colbert Effect: Essays on the Real Impact of Fake News*, edited by Amarnath Amarasingam, 63–78. Jefferson, NC: MacFarland and Company.

Baumgartner, J. C., and Brad Lockerbie. 2018. "Maybe it is More Than a Joke: Satire, Mobilization and Political Participation." *Social Science Quarterly* 99 (3): 1060–1074.

Baumgartner, J. C., and J. S. Morris. 2006. "*The Daily Show* Effect: Candidacy Evaluation, Efficacy, and American Youth." *American Politics Research* 34 (3): 341–367.

Blackburn, Simon. 1998. *Ruling Passions: A Theory of Practical Reasoning*. New York: Clarendon Press.

Chen, Hsuan-Ting and Ping Sun. 2017. "How Does Political Satire Influence Political Participation? Examining the Role of Counter- and Proattitudinal Exposure, Anger, and Personal Issue Importance." *International Journal of Communication* 11: 3011–3029.

Compton, Josh. 2011. "Surveying the Scholarship on *The Daily Show* and *The Colbert Report*. In *The Stewart/Colbert Effect: Essays on the Real Impact of Fake News*, edited by Amarnath Amarasingam, 9–23. Jefferson, NC: MacFarland and Company.

Driver, Julia. 2013. "Moral Sense and Sentimentalism." In *The Oxford Handbook of the History of Ethics*, edited by Roger Crisp, 358–376. New York: Oxford University Press.

Flanagan, Caitlin. 2017. "How Late Night Comedy Fueled the Rise of Trump." *The Atlantic*, May 2017 Issue. https://www.theatlantic.com/magazine/archive/2017/05/how-late-night-comedy-alienated-conservatives-made-liberals-smug-and-fueled-the-rise-of-trump/521472/

Greene, Joshua D., R. Brian Sommerville, Leigh E. Nystrom, John M. Darley, and Jonathan D. Cohen. 2001. "An fMRI Investigation of Emotional Engagement in Moral Judgment." *Science* 293 (5537): 2105–2108.

Greene, Joshua. 2013. *Moral Tribes: Emotion, Reason, and the Gap Between Us and Them*. London: Penguin Press.

Haidt, Jonathan, Fredrik Björklund, and Scott Murphy. 2000. "Moral Dumbfounding: When Intuition Finds No Reason." *Lund Psychological Reports* 1 (2), Department of Psychology, Lund University.

Haidt, Jonathan, S. H. Koller, and M. G. Dias. 1993. "Affect, Culture, and Morality, or is it Wrong to Eat Your Dog?" *Journal of Personality and Social Psychology* 65 (4): 613–628.

Haidt, Jonathan. 2001. "The Emotional Dog and its Rational Tail: A Social Intuitionist Approach to Moral Judgment." *Psychological Review* 108 (4): 814–834.

Haidt, Jonathan. 2012. *The Righteous Mind: Why Good People are Divided by Politics and Religion*. New York: Pantheon Books.

Hart, R. P., and E. J. Hartelius. 2007. "The Political Sins of John Stewart." *Critical Studies in Media Communication* 24 (3): 263–272.

Hindriks, Frank. 2015. "How Does Reasoning (Fail to) Contribute to Moral Judgment? Dumbfounding and Disengagement." *Ethical Theory and Moral Practice* 18 (2): 237–250.

Hoffman, L. H. and D. G. Young. 2011. "Satire, Punchlines, and the Nightly News: Untangling Media Effects on Political Participation." *Communication Research Reports* 28 (2): 159–168.

Holbert, R. L., J. L. Lambe, A. D. Dudo, and K. A. Carlton. 2007. "Primacy Effects of *The Daily Show* and National TV News Viewing: Young Viewers, Political Gratifications, and Internal Political Self-Efficacy." *Journal of Broadcasting & Electronic Media* 51 (1): 20–38.

Kavathatzopoulos, Iordanis. 1991. "Kohlberg and Piaget: Differences and Similarities." *Journal of Moral Education* 20 (1): 47–54.

Kim, Young M., and John Vishak. 2008. "Just Laugh! You Don't Need to Remember: The Effects of Entertainment Media on Political Information Acquisition and Information Processing in Political Judgment." *Journal of Communication* 58 (2): 338–360.

Lee, Hoon, and Nojin Kwak. 2014. "The Affect of Political Satire: Sarcastic Humor, Negative Emptions, and Political Participation." *Mass Communication and Society* 17: 307–328.

McBeth, M. K., and R. S. Clemons. 2011. "Is Fake News the Real News? The Significance of Stewart and Colbert for Democratic Discourse, Politics, and Policy." In *The Stewart/Colbert Effect: Essays on the Real Impact of Fake News*, edited by Amarnath Amarasingam, 79–98. Jefferson, NC: MacFarland and Company.

Norrick, N. R., and Alice Spitz. "Humour as a Resource for Mitigating Conflict in Interaction." *Journal of Pragmatics* 40 (10): 1661–1686.

Pascual, Leo, Paulo Rodrigues, and David Gallardo-Pujol. 2013. "How Does Morality Work in the Brain? A Functional and Structural Perspective of Moral Behavior." *Frontiers in Integrative Neuroscience* 7: 65.

Peterson, Christopher, and Martin Seligman. 2004. *Character Strengths and Virtues: A Handbook and Classification*. Washington, DC: American Psychological Association.

Prinz, Jesse J. 2006. "The Emotional Basis of Moral Judgments." *Philosophical Explorations* 9 (1): 29–43.
Prinz, Jesse J. 2007. *The Emotional Construction of Morals*. New York: Oxford University Press.
Prinz, Jesse J. 2015. "Is the Moral Brain Ever Dispassionate?" In *The Moral Brain: A Multidisciplinary Perspective*, edited by J. Decety and T. Wheatley, 51–67. Cambridge, MA: MIT Press.
Prinz, Jesse J. 2016. "Sentimentalism and the Moral Brain." In *Moral Brains: the Neuroscience of Morality*, edited by Matthew Liao, 45–73. New York: Oxford University Press.
Slote, Michael A. 2010. *Moral Sentimentalism*. New York: Oxford University Press.
Strohminger, Nina. 2014. "Disgust Talked About." *Philosophy Compass* 9 (7), 478–493.
Uhlmann, Eric L., and Luke Zhu. 2014. "Acts, Persons, and Intuitions: Person-Centered Cues and Gut Reactions to Harmless Transgressions." *Social Psychological and Personality Science* 5 (3): 279–285.
Xenos, M. A., and A. G. Becker. 2009. "Moments of Zen: Effects of *The Daily Show* on Information Seeking and Political Learning." *Political Communication* 26 (3): 317–332.
Young, Dannagal G. 2008. "The Privileged Role of the Late-Night Joke: Exploring Humor's Role in Disrupting Argument Scrutiny." *Media Psychology* 11 (1): 119–142.
Young, Dannagal G., and Sarah E. Esralew. 2011. "Jon Stewart a Heretic? Surely You Jest. Political Participation and Discussion Among Viewers of Late-Night Comedy Programming." In *The Stewart/Colbert Effect: Essays on the Real Impact of Fake News*, edited by Amarnath Amarasingam, 99–115. Jefferson, NC: MacFarland and Company.
Zillman, Dolf, Rhonda Gibson, Virginia L. Ordman, and Charles F. Aust. 1994. "Effects of Upbeat Stories in Broadcast News." *Journal of Broadcasting and Electronic Media* 38 (1): 65–79.

Chapter 9

Eutrapelia and the Normativity of Social Humor

Andrew Jordan and Stephanie Patridge

In this essay, we explore Aristotle's social virtue of *eutrapelia* (εὐτραπελία), which is sometimes translated as ready-wit or wittiness. We think that it can help explain some features of our judgments about humor that might otherwise be mysterious or puzzling, and bridge some normative gaps in our preferred account of humor, a fitting-attitude account. To help motivate the puzzle that our discussion of *eutrapelia* aims to help solve, let's start with an apparent tension in our responses to humor. On the one hand, some of our humor responses suggest that we think that humor is an objective phenomenon. For example, we say things like "that was hilarious!" or "that was *really* not funny!" Further, we tend to engage in genuine disagreements about humor. Upon hearing a friend's uproarious laughter at a joke, we might find ourselves chastising him "come on, it isn't *that* funny," or even "you shouldn't laugh at that sort of thing." Finally, we have a fairly well-established practice of professional comedic criticism. You can read professional assessments of stand-up comedy routines, comedic films, and literary works, and in many cases, even get a numeric rating of the work's funniness. As a result, we might be drawn toward a theory that conceives of funniness and its related properties as properties of comedic objects.[1] On this sort of view, when we say "that's funny" we are making an assessment of the comedic object and what aesthetic properties is has.

On the other hand, some of our responses to humor suggest that we think that humor judgments don't aim to get an object right. For example, there is a great deal of variety in how humans respond to humor. Some find slapstick films funny; others do not. Some are amused by puns; others not so much. And we tend to be fairly comfortable with this sort of variation. If you invited a friend to improv comedy show, who replied that they just don't like silly humor, you may find your friend's response disappointing. After all, we want our friends to share our sense of humor, and we want to share activities we find amusing with others (Cohen 1999, 32). Were you to convince your friend to give it a try anyway, after which they responded "I told you, I don't like improv" it would be quite odd for you to seriously impugn your friend's sense of humor solely on this score. As a result of this second set of observations, we might be drawn toward a theory that conceives of humor as being in the eye of the beholder, and so to not see funniness as a property of objects. On this sort of view, when we say "that's funny" we are actually saying something about ourselves, namely that *we* find it funny.

We think that there is something right about both sets of observations. And we have elsewhere argued that the most attractive way to account for the first set of observations—our tendency to behave in ways that suggest the funny is a real property of objects of humor—is by adopting a fitting-attitude theory of amusement (Jordan and Patridge 2012). On our view, the funny is a response-dependent property, and something is funny to the extent that it provides a reason of the right kind for a related sentiment, what we might call comic amusement.[2] It is in this sense that a sentiment must fit its object: the object must provide a reason for the sentiment.

But we still have some reservations about whether a fitting-attitude theory can fully capture the relevant phenomenon. Elsewhere we have argued that a specific fitting-attitude view can accommodate the second set of observations, namely the wide latitude we afford to humor judgments. Specifically, we have argued that we should see the reasons for amusement as ones that are noncompelling (Jordan and Patridge 2018). On this way of seeing humor-relevant reasons, they make our humor responses intelligible or reasonable (they ground or justify them) but they do not rationally require individuals to be amused by genuinely funny things (they are noncompelling reasons). That is, even if there is an object-directed reason to be amused, one would not be open to rational criticism simply because they fail to be amused. That is, one need not upon pain of irrationality or of unreasonableness find improv comedy funny, even if it is. It's up to you. Still, on our view not all instances of comic amusement would be reasonable. Some things are not funny, that is, they do not provide a reason of the right kind to be amused, and so it can be legitimately said "hey, that's not funny." Other things will be less funny than we find them and so it can be legitimately said "it's not *that* funny!" In this way, our view can support both the thought that humor is not anything goes, while still allowing for quite a bit of latitude in our responses to humor.

But even that modified fitting-attitude view seems ill-equipped to capture another commonplace thought—that a general insensitivity to humor, for example, being humorless, is a failing and that there are grounds for criticizing such an individual. If humor-relevant reasons are noncompelling, and the humorless person just is the person who generally is not amused, then it might seem that there is nothing much to say here. It's up to him: He's getting things right enough. This is the first significant normative gap that we hope to fill here.

In addition, while we think that a fitting-attitude theory of the funny can do a fairly good job of making sense of what we call artistic humor, it seems less well suited to help us understand the phenomenon of what we call social humor. While we do not want to make too much of this distinction, for our purposes it is suitable to conceive of artistic humor as the sort of thing that we tend find in art objects, for example, literature, film, plays, and stand-up comedy routines. By "social humor" we mean humor as it manifests itself in the course of our ordinary social activities, say when we are hanging out with friends or colleagues. As we explain, we think that social humor does not seem open to the same sort of object-directed analysis that artistic humor is, and so seems less suited to our FA analysis. For this reason, we think that making sense of the normativity of social humor requires treating it as a relatively distinctive aesthetic-social phenomena. This is the second of two significant normative gaps that we hope to fill in here.

In this essay, we aim to make some progress in filling the aforementioned normative gaps—explaining judgments about the humorless person and capturing certain features of social humor—by borrowing from Aristotle's writing on a social virtue of *eutrapelia* (εὐτραπελία). We think that Aristotle's discussion of *eutrapelia* is instructive for thinking about the normative contours of social humor and that it provides useful normative resources to criticize those who are generally insensitive to artistic humor, the humorless person. As a result, we think that it can fill the two normative gaps left in our fitting-attitude theory of humor. We will begin this task by offering a rough account of virtue theory and the role that *eutrapelia* plays in such a theory. Though we caution, when focusing specifically on Aristotle's views, we do not intend here to break any new interpretive ground. Our interest here is in the aforementioned normative upshots of adding a neo-Aristotlian conception of *eutrapelia* to our FA theory; again, that it can make sense of distinct features of social humor and our tendency to find fault with those who are generally insensitive to humor, including art humor.

I. *EUTRAPELIA* AS A SOCIAL VIRTUE

> Those who carry humor to excess are thought to be vulgar buffoons striving after humor at all costs and aiming rather at raising a laugh than in saying what is becoming ... while those who can neither make a joke themselves nor put up with those who do are thought to be boorish and unpolished. Those who joke in a tasteful way are ready-witted [*eutrapelia*]. (Aristotle, 1941, *NE* 1128a5-10)

In *Nichomachen Ethics* 4.8 [1127b33-1128b9], Aristotle identifies *eutrapelia*, (εὐτραπελία) as a key practical virtue.[3] *Eutrapelia* tends to be translated into English as "ready-wit," "wittiness," or "good humor," but we think that each of these English translations at best misses the point of *eutrapelia*, and at worst engenders misconceptions. So we'll use *eutrapelia* to refer to the virtue, though we sometimes use "wittiness" when talking about people. For example, in his book *Greek Laughter: A Study of Cultural Psychology from Homer to Early Christianity*, Stephen Halliwell writes that *eutrapelia*

> means literally "ease at turning." It is a word which in the classical period has a broader sense of "flexibility," adaptability, easy-going character, etc., and a narrower sense of "wit(tiness)." The connection between the two is presumably that "wit" could readily be associated with facility for repartee, and ability to adapt one's humour quickly to the shifting requirements of banter. (Halliwell 2008, 312)

Key to understanding *eutrapelia* is the fact that Aristotle includes it as one of three social virtues. It involves being able to laugh,[4] to be amused, and joke around appropriately in social contexts, where those contexts may be subtly changing minute by minute in part because of the sort of humor that is injected into them. That Aristotle identifies *eutrapelia* as a social virtue, shows that he thinks that one's ability to engage appropriately in social humor is normatively important. Indeed, for Aristotle, and other virtue theorists, the virtues have pride of place in an account of an ethical life.

Virtue theorists also tend to emphasize the highly context-dependent nature of right action, and so resist the articulation of abstract action-guiding moral principles. Instead, they tend to focus on questions like "what kind of person should one be?" or "what kind of life should one aim to live?"[5] These sorts of questions are answered primarily by thinking about the human good in terms of virtuous (or perhaps excellent) character traits. Though virtue theorists think that determining how to act in a given situation is normatively important, they tend to agree that right action is best understood in terms of what it means to be a good human. As a result, virtue theorists focus their normative thinking on questions about good human character traits. If one is living the best human life, if one is virtuous, then one will, as a matter of course, tend to act well. So that Aristotle identifies *eutrapelia* as a practical virtue—one of only a few that he identifies in the *Nichomachen Ethics*—shows its centrality to his task of figuring out how to be a good human. Though we don't agree with everything that Aristotle says about the virtues in general or *eutrapelia* in particular, we think that he is on the right track in identifying *eutrapelia* as a social virtue that has a central role to play in normative theories of humor.

So what are the virtues? On a broadly Aristotelian reading, the virtues are admirable states of character the exercise of which is taken to be a central component in the best way of living a human life, sometimes referred to as *eudaimonia,* or flourishing. The virtues are relatively stable, cross-situational dispositions to engage in the right kinds of activities, for the right sorts of reasons, while having the appropriate affective attitudes. Consider, for example, the virtue of generosity.[6] In a particular case, generosity may require that one give a person money in part because the person is in need in some particular way. And the exercise of this virtue requires not just action of a certain sort but also implicates the reasons for which a person acts and how they feel in so-acting, and the specific way that they act. Hoarding one's money, giving it away because so doing will increase one's social capital, feeling aggrieved at giving, or being overly demonstrative about giving would all be signs that one is not generous. We say "signs" here because Aristotle clearly thinks that some deviation from the requirements of full virtue is to be expected. Though a certain level of cross-situational consistency is required for one to be generous, even the generous person may miss the mark sometimes. As a result, Aristotle thinks that it is hard to determine exactly when such failures warrant assertions of vice [1109b19-23]. Adding to this challenge is the fact that what virtue requires of us is highly context-dependent. As a result, one cannot know in the abstract exactly how, say, a generous person would act in a given situation. Consider, for example, the complexity involved in thinking about just the bare action component in the case at hand: What should one give? Money? Food? Time? Attention? Something else altogether? Or is tough love what is required in this case? If one should give something, how much should they give in this case? How should they give it? In person? Anonymously? If one should give something in person, how should they do so? How should they speak to the person in need? What sorts of physical gestures should they make? How should they feel about the interaction? Should they be happy to give? Sad at the person's plight? Such questions cannot be answered in the abstract, and instead require attending to the details of the case at hand. Hence, the generous person is guided by their trained practical sensitivities. Such sensitivities are developed by a lifetime of experience and education, attuned by habituation and practice. In the normal course of proper practical development, the virtues becomes a sort of second nature; the generous person sees well enough what is called for in a particular situation and acts, thinks, and feels thusly. We generally agree with Aristotle on these points.

Despite the fact that what a given virtue requires of us is highly context-dependent, Aristotle tells us something fairly concrete about each virtue. The virtues are situated between particular associated vices of excess and deficiency that represent substantive ways of going wrong. Consider, for example, the stingy person. The stingy person tends to not give at all or not give enough when it is called for. And when she does manage to give, she likely begrudges doing so. Stinginess is a vice of deficiency associated with generosity, and hence represents a particular way of going wrong. The other way to go wrong is to exhibit the vice of wastefulness. That vice shows itself in giving more than is called for in a given situation, or in ways that are unhelpful to the case at hand. It is a vice of excess. Wastefulness can also show up when a person gets it wrong with regard to when something is important, and hence, a proper occasion for giving, and when a matter is trivial, and hence, not. So, as a practical matter, we are guided not only by the virtues but also by the vices.

Many will likely find no quarrel with the thought that generosity, or friendliness, or even-temper are worthy character traits that make one's life better, even if we disagree about their exact contours. Less convincing, however, are the virtues of Aristotelian pride, which is associated with the proper receipt of great honors [NE, 1123a35-1125a35], and Aristotelian magnificence [NE 1122a25-1123a30], which is associated with the proper giving of large sums of money. Such virtues are more alien to contemporary readers: it's hard to see how living a life which does not allow one to exercise these putative virtues would be lacking in any substantive way. As a result, many of Aristotle's virtues and vices seem to be more a product of his time, place, ethnicity, gender, and class, than they are an account of what makes a human life worthwhile.[7] For this reason, neo-Aristotelian virtue theorists like ourselves tend to depart from Aristotle in various ways, particularly so when it comes to what character traits are thought to be key for flourishing, and how to make sense of the contours of such traits. Still, virtue theorists adopt the larger evaluative task of making virtue central to one's take on understanding normativity. While one might be tempted to see *eutrapelia* as similarly a product of Aristotle's distinct social position, we think that there is a lot to like about Aristotle's treatment of *eutrapelia*. In the next section, we will sketch a conception of *eutrapelia* that is roughly consonant with Aristotle's and that we think is roughly consonant with common social practices.

II. *EUTRAPELIA* AND SOCIAL HUMOR

For Aristotle, *eutrapelia* is concerned with a kind of humorous social play, what we are calling social humor. *Eutrapelia* is the ability to engage in context-appropriate, mutually pleasurable, humorous exchanges. This is a learned social skill that is highly sensitive to social context. If Aristotle is right to claim *eutrapelia* as a practical virtue, then being good humored or having a ready-wit contributes to a *eudaimonistic* or flourishing life. The ready-witted person will live a more admirable or worthwhile life than those who are not ready-witted. How plausible is this claim? In *Nichomachean Ethics* IV.8, Aristotle claims that "[s]ince relaxation is a part of life which includes passing the time in amusement, there too seems to be an appropriate style of personal relations to do with the content and manner of speaking and listening—what one should and as one should" [2006, 1127b34-1128a2]. And in *Politics* VIII.3, he claims that "Amusement is for the sake of relaxation, and relaxation is of necessity sweet, for it is the remedy of pain caused by toil: and intellectual enjoyment is universally acknowledged to contain an element not only of the noble but of the pleasant for happiness is made up of both" [1941, 1339b15-20]. So it seems that for Aristotle the pleasures associated with leisure and play (which includes social humor) are part of a flourishing life in part because their pleasures are good—as he says, flourishing is both noble and pleasurable. And they act as a kind of medicine that serves to make the toil of life more tolerable: All work and no play makes life dull, dreary, and full of drudgery. Still, Aristotle cautions, leisure and play activities, while worthwhile, are not as good as other more serious pursuits. We are easily misled into seeking these sorts of pleasures as if they themselves were the proper end of life [1139b15-35]. They are not; though they are part of it, they are not the most important part. Aristotle is no hedonist. Further, on Aristotle's view what is worthwhile here is not the mere pleasure of social humor, but the pleasure associated with virtuous exchanges of social humor. That is, not any social pleasure is valuable, it must be proper pleasure. We can get social humor wrong.

Still, why think that we can get social humor wrong? For Aristotle, the answer may partly lie in his conception of humor. For example, in *NE* 4.8 Aristotle characterizes the sort of joking that he has in mind in this section as "a sort of abuse" [2006, 1128a33], the proper object of which is moral and social failings (Curran 2016, 54) that are not truly vicious (Curran 2016, 252).[8] Further, in *Poetics* IV.5 Aristotle distinguishes tragedy from comedy by claiming that comedy "is an imitation of men worse than average" with respect to the ridiculous "which is a mistake or a deformity not productive of pain or harm to others" that causes laughter [1941, 1149a31-37]. And while discussing friendship in *Rhetoric* II.4 Aristotle claims that worthwhile friends can both take and make a joke, where jokes are primarily understood as a sort of making fun of each other [1381a34-37]. So it seems that Aristotle conceives of humor as involving something that looks like a good-natured making fun that does not harm its object. Though we do not think that all social humor is mocking in this way, no doubt a lot of it is. For this reason, it is very easy for us to slip from enjoyable exchange to assault and offense, which makes social humor challenging and shows in part why we need training and virtue to do it well. As Mary Beard points out, just learning to laugh at and be amused by the proper objects is a significant social achievement.

Anyone who has ever brought up young children will remember the time and effort it takes to teach them the standard rules of laughter: in simplest terms what to laugh at and what not to laugh at (clowns, yes; people using wheelchairs, no; *The Simpsons*, yes; the fat lady on the bus, no). (Beard 2014, 44)

Moreover, context matters a great deal when it comes to social humor. It matters, for example, with whom we are joking [1128a2-3]. Is it a friend or a work colleague? Are they particularly sensitive about a certain topic? If so, to make light of them in this regard might verge on cruelty. Are we at a funeral or at the bar? Would telling a joke at this time in this context to these people inappropriately distract attention to ourselves? Would it lighten the mood? Jokes that would be base, puerile, or morally indecent in one context might be just the thing in another context. Those who are poorly trained will laugh and joke at all the wrong things, at the wrong time, and in the wrong way. Reading the nuance of a particular social context so as to see what humor behaviors and responses are appropriate is a learned social skill that is difficult to master.[9]

The witty person takes opportunities for amusing and being amused by others, with a degree of tact and creative ingenuity, and does so with an eye toward the proper maintenance of the social activity. Like the other virtues, Aristotle thinks that we can gain some insight into *eutrapelia* by thinking about its associated vices of excess and deficiency, buffoonery and boorishness. These vices no doubt will be readily recognizable to contemporary readers as genuine vices that show themselves in certain contexts, which we think serves to make *eutrapelia* a fairly convincing social virtue. Consider buffoons. Buffoons are "always on the look-out for what is funny and trying to raise a laugh [in herself as well as others] rather than to speak decorously and avoid offending the person who is being made fun of" [2006, 1128a4-7]. They crack the wrong jokes aimed at the wrong subjects. They joke around too often. They joke around in inappropriate circumstances. They do so in the wrong way, say while laughing too heartily. As Aristotle puts the point, the buffoon is a "slave to what is funny, sparing neither [themselves] nor anyone else if [they] can raise a laugh" [2006, 1128a35-2218b1]. The buffoon is generally insensitive to the harm that laughing at others can cause, which means their joking will often tend toward cruelty. And though Aristotle does not say so, we think that the buffoon tends toward selfishness—they are constantly distracting us from the social activity that we are engaged in and drawing the social attention back to themselves. The buffoon is often socially exhausting. Though, as Aristotle points out, many of us really enjoy a laugh, and so we tend to enjoy the buffoon more than we should, and many of us even have a tendency to wrongly associate buffoonery with *eutrapelia* [1128a10-20].

At the other end of the spectrum is the boor. At the extreme, boors are those who "never make a joke themselves and disapprove of those who do" [2006, 1128a8-9]. Boors resist social opportunities to laugh or be amused and to get others to do so; they are stiffs. The boor, as Aristotle puts the point, "is useless" and "contributes nothing" to these enjoyable social activities [2006, 1128b2-3]. We think that describing the boor as useless is particularly insightful. The boor does not join in the fun. As a result, not only does the boor miss appropriate opportunities to have enjoyable social activities, but they also fail to do the social work necessary to affirm and support such activities for others. To be successful, social humor requires not only participants who are willing to joke around, but it also requires those who are willing to laugh and to be amused. In laughing and being amused, participants affirm the participants and the activity, which gives it the social momentum to be carried on if the participants so wish. If no one laughs, however, the joking around tends to be done. The boor is not amused, and so does not contribute to the activity. Even worse, the boor's refusal to be amused runs the risk of short-circuiting the humorous activity altogether. Like buffoons, boors tend to draw attention away from the enjoyable social activity and to themselves—Why aren't they laughing? This effect will be heightened in cases where the number of participants is small, in cases where the boor wears a disapproving facial expression like a frown, and in cases where the boor (wrongly) interjects "that's not funny." For these reasons, we think that the boor can be worse than useless. Adding to this, in a particularly astute observation Aristotle notes that individuals will very often "listen to" jokes that they would not themselves tell because they are improper in the context [2006, 1128a34-b1]. When it comes to laughing and being amused, people tend to steer quite clear of boorishness. A person of good humor will want the fun to continue, so long as the context supports its continuance. As a result, they will tend to support jokes that are somewhat inappropriate by laughing and being amused and tend to avoid socially calling out the activity or the joker if propriety allows it. Still, Aristotle notes that there are *some* jokes that the good-humored person "would not even listen to," and hence some social activities that they will act to thwart [2006, 1128a34-1128b1]. We think that jokes that appear to wound a participant, or that are particularly venal, say racist jokes, are likely to be among the jokes that one should not tolerate.

So though one might have been initially inclined to think that there are very few normative considerations at play when it comes to social humor, Aristotle's treatment of the practical virtue of *eutrapelia* and its associated vices of buffoonery and boorishness suggests otherwise. Further, we think that his discussion of *eutrapelia* is roughly consonant with our own social practices. Those who joke too little or too much, or at the wrong objects, or in the wrong way do tend to be subjected to normative criticisms, criticisms that are characterological in nature and need not reference moral considerations narrowly conceived. Further, many of these normative criticisms seem roughly to map onto Aristotle's vices of boorishness and buffoonery fairly easily. It is clear that humans care about how good individuals are at navigating social contexts with humor, and there is a robust socially normative conceptual scheme to support such caring. For this reason, we think that there are legitimate virtue theoretic normative standards at play in social humor.

Further, we think that we can learn a bit about how to get social humor right by thinking about ways that it can go wrong, particularly in terms of the vices of buffoonery and boorishness. Again, *eutrapelia* involves a social skill of being able to help create, and to sustain, mutually pleasing, playful social interactions. Both the buffoon and the boor, in their own distinctive ways, either do not participate in the maintenance of, distract from, or even actively undermine social humor.

We think that bringing the social virtues and vices to the center of a normative account of social humor has the additional benefit of helping us to see the phenomenon of social humor more clearly. One key reason that social humor is valuable is that it offers us the opportunity to engage in a shared, enjoyable, playful social activity. Our discussion of the vices of boorishness and buffoonery have shown that it is important that participants engage social humor not only by joking around themselves (which not everyone will do) but also by giving space for others to joke around, and by being amused by those who joke (which is essential for social humor to be enjoyable and sustained over time). As a result, in engaging in social humor participants create, however, temporary and fleeting, a social bond for which they share the responsibility. In telling and receiving jokes with laughter participants both affirm their status as members of a common group and build a common bond. The person joking, in assuming the recipients will get the joke on offer and be amused, signals that the recipient is one of them; the recipients, in laughing and being amused, affirm the person who is joking, and the social humor at play. So in a very real sense the practice of joking around, when successful, operates to affirm the participants as members of a shared community.[10] This is one of the key reasons that we value social humor, praise those who are good at it, and criticize those who are not. While individuals tend to value social humor because engaging in it is pleasurable (even only as a supporter), at least part of that pleasure is a response to its importance in forging social bonds.

III. *EUTRAPELIA* AND THE FUNNY

Thus far our examination of *eutrapelia* has focused mainly on the responses to social humor, for example, laughter and amusement. And one might expect an essay on the normativity of social *humor* to focus at least somewhat on answering questions of the form "but are the jokes funny?" Though we agree that particular instances of social humor can be concerned with the funny, we think that determinations of the funny are very often beside the point of social humor. This, no doubt, will seem jarring to at least some readers. To help illustrate what we mean by this, we focus on a commonplace phenomenon, our tendency to enjoy sharing bad jokes with each other.

Individuals often find themselves in social contexts where they enjoy and are amused by telling each other what they acknowledge to be quite bad jokes. For example, in the bar after the day's conference presentations one might find oneself with a group of academics telling elephant jokes. Here are some examples.

Q: What was the elephant doing on the freeway?
A: About 5 mph.

Q: How do you stop an elephant from charging?
A: Take away his credit card.

Q: Why couldn't the elephants go swimming together?
A: Because they only had one set of trunks.

Q: What did Tarzan say when he saw a herd of elephants?
A: "Look, a herd of elephants!"

Q: What did Tarzan say when he saw a herd of elephants in sunglasses?
A: Nothing, he didn't recognize them.

Q: What did Tarzan say when he saw a herd of giraffes?
A: "You fooled me once, elephants! Not again!"

Clearly, elephant jokes are real groaners. They often juxtapose our knowledge of elephants with a bad pun of some sort. Sometimes they are just nonsense. They are so bad that they in some ways violate the norms of joke telling—for example, the presumption that joke tellers aim to tell funny jokes. So they often look more like anti-jokes or nonsense jokes. Still, despite the fact that elephant jokes are bad jokes, telling them in social groups can be very amusing indeed. And it can be amusing even as participants recognize that the jokes are cringe-worthy. In such contexts, we think that what is amusing is the social activity of which the jokes are a part, and not the jokes themselves. (Readers who happen to like elephant jokes can substitute their own bad joke type here to help see the point, e.g., dad jokes, puns, dead baby jokes, or knock-knock jokes.) This provides at least some reason to think that what we are after in these instances of social humor is not contact with "the funny," but enjoyable social experiences. And it may provide some grounds for rethinking the object-directed way of understanding the normative features of humor-related judgments.

To help further the above point, imagine that a colleague were to walk up to the elephant-joking group and proceed to tell a long series of their own elephant jokes, leaving no room for anyone else to contribute a joke to the activity. While some might be at least a little amused at such a colleague, their amusement will likely not be a response to the jokes' funniness, but instead to the ridiculousness of their behavior. *This* is not how one should behave in these sorts of social spaces. And it seems that annoyance is an equally legitimate response to the floor-hogging colleague; they behave like a buffoon. They selfishly claim the social space for themselves, in order to try to get us to be amused *by them*. But we are engaged in social humor, and this colleague seems to think that it is appropriate to turn our social activity into their own personal stand-up routine. For this reason, the buffoon's elephant jokes will likely fall flat. In fact, we suspect that elephant jokes tend to be more amusing when told as part of a shared social activity, one where several members of the group are riffing on the theme of elephant jokes, than as part of a solo joke-telling activity. This outcome is what we'd expect if social humor were concerned more with being able to successfully and properly navigate a social space in a way that causes amusement than with the saying of funny things.

To help make this point a different way, consider a case where among the ranks of the elephant-jokers is someone we might refer to as a comic snob. The comic snob takes themselves to have a refined sense of humor. They therefore refuse to laugh or be amused by any activity for which they lack an object-directed reason to experience amusement. That is, they will only laugh if they think something is genuinely funny. Were the comic snob to admonish the group "you guys do know that elephant jokes are not funny, right?" the group members would likely be at least a little confused by this gesture. While the snob's admonishment might derail the social humor, the snob certainly would not have identified for the group a sufficient reason to not be amused. The elephant-jokers know that the jokes are not funny. This is precisely the activity they are engaged in—amusing each other by telling bad jokes. In this context, the comic snob is a boor, and the group would rightly admonish the snob to "lighten up." Assuming that the comic snob has a refined sense of comedic judgment, and that they are a keen judge of the funniness of jokes, it nevertheless seems that they do something inappropriate in bringing their fancy humor judgment to the socially low comedic task at hand, the sharing of elephant jokes.

When everyone is laughing, everyone is bonding, and everyone is enjoying themselves, the further question "But is this *funny*?" even if cogent, is often beside the point. Sometimes our amusement is a recognition that a joke is funny. Sometimes it is a recognition that we are involved in an enjoyable social activity, and sometimes it is both. To claim otherwise is to simply disregard too much of our humor practices. Further, given that social humor aims at mutually pleasant interchanges that cause amusement and laughter, a relentless pursuit of the funny is very often beside the point of what is going on. An obsession with the funny in such contexts can very easily become an expression of boorishness or buffoonery as illustrated in the cases of the comic snob and the floor hog.

Still, one might worry that in the elephant joke case, it is not the joke itself that is the object of amusement, but the telling, and while the joke itself might be bad, the telling may not be. In that way one might preserve the idea that the object of social amusement is the funny. We agree that tellings can be funny, even in cases where the jokes themselves are not. For example, the late comedian Jim Bowen is famous for a stand-up routine in which he reads jokes from an ancient collection of jokes, *Philogelos* or "laughter lover," which is "written in unstylish Greek," and dated to the late Roman Empire around the fourth or fifth century CE (Beard 2014, 185). Most of the jokes in *Philogelos* are lost on Bowen's audience, they were written for those with different world views, experiences, and sensitivities. Still Bowen's telling of these mostly mysterious jokes is at least somewhat funny and audiences laughed (though their laughter was often mixed with groans). As in the case of Bowen's stand-up, the elephant jokes might be a case of a funny telling of an unfunny joke. How plausible is such an explanation in our elephant examples? Though we readily admit that this may be what is going on in some cases of social humor, we think that it is unlikely that in the main members of such groups are responding to the funniness of the joke tellings. To help see why, consider what features of tellings tend to be the proper sorts of considerations to support the thought that a telling is funny. Some candidate features will refer to the joke, for example, its representational content, and relevant incongruity. Some will refer narrowly to the telling, for example, the joker's timing, cadence, tone, facial expression, and body language. And some will bring them both into focus, for example, a tension between the joke's representational content and the teller's voice modulation. But if the funniness of the respective tellings are essentially what group members respond to when it comes to social humor, then we would expect them to be very amused by some contributions, the funny tellings, and very unamused by others, the unfunny ones. That is, we'd expect amusement to at least roughly track the funniness of the respective tellings. But we do not think that fits the phenomena of social humor very well. Individuals engaged in social humor tend to laugh, joke, and be amused at least somewhat by the activity in a way that is independent of whether the jokes are funny. And at the very least, social amusement will not tend to track the funniness of tellings very well (the floor hog might in fact be very funny). And we think this illustrates a conceptual point about the relationship between the funny and the success conditions for social amusement. Success in social amusement is not just a matter of getting at the funny, though funniness can contribute to successful social amusement. Though one might try to rescue the thought that it is the tellings that are the aesthetic object by claiming that participants who are amused by bad tellings are responding incorrectly, or that they are not experiencing genuine amusement and instead feigning amusement for aesthetic-moral support, or that funniness-relevant reasons operate quite differently in social humor, each of these moves would require substantive argumentation to get off the ground. Absent such arguments, we think that the most reasonable way to understand the phenomena we have considered here, that is, the floor-hogging buffoon, the boorish comic snob, and our tendency to be similarly amused by everyone who contributes properly to the social humor activity at hand, is that they are responding to individuals' support of or failure to support the relevant, enjoyable social activity. That is, when everyone is laughing, everyone is bonding, and everyone is enjoying themselves, the further question "But is this *funny*?" even if cogent, might sometimes be beside the point of what's going on. Sometimes our amusement is a recognition that a joke is funny. Sometimes that we are involved in an enjoyable social activity, and sometimes it is both. To claim otherwise is to simply disregard too much of our humor practice.

IV. *EUTRAPELIA* AND FITTING-ATTITUDE THEORY

At the opening of this chapter, we suggested that a neo-Aristotelian approach to the social virtue *eutrapelia* might help to resolve two normative gaps in our preferred theory of the funny, a fitting-attitude theory. One issue was the worry that many of our responses to social humor seem less object-directed than art humor, and so it seems less well suited to an FA theory. As we have characterized it, social humor is a shared activity that aims to create opportunities for pleasing interchanges that cause participants to be properly amused. Hence, we should expect that an adequate account of the funny will have less to say about the normativity involved in social humor. The sort of normativity at stake in social humor is often better explained not by determining if what is said in such exchanges is in fact funny, but by determining if the participant has successfully navigated a social context in a way that caused people to laugh and be amused and/or helped support and sustain other's attempts at such navigation by, say, allowing them space to joke around, laugh, and be amused within proper limits. *Eutrapelia* is a virtue that relates to this kind of social feat, which can be performed well or badly; funniness will sometimes bear on one's success here and sometimes not. The good-humored person is highly skilled in this regard. They take opportunities for amusing and being amused by others, and do so with a degree of tact and creative ingenuity, but what those opportunities are and what form they will take will be contingent on features of the context including the particular interests, needs and maybe even sense of humor of the other participants. Adding a virtue theoretic account that includes the virtue of *eutrapelia* to our normative conception of humor can thereby help resolve one significant gap in our fitting-attitude theory of the funny.

The other normative gap that we identified in our fitting-attitude theory concerns the humorless person. At the opening of this essay, we noted that individuals can diverge significantly in their sense of humor, and that people tend to be fairly comfortable with this fact. Again, we might be disappointed were a friend to refuse our invitation to go to an improv show on the grounds that they just do not like silly humor. But most would not think that their friend is being irrational or unreasonable, even if they sincerely believe that improv comedy is the best kind of comedy. Some people just do not like improv, and we get that. In an attempt to take this aspect of our humor practices seriously, we have argued that reasons for amusement are noncompelling. That is, that improv comedy is funny does provide your friend a reason to accept your invitation. And, on our view, were the show funny, it would be because it provides an objected-directed reason for being amused. But these sorts of reasons, we have argued, are noncompelling. They make amusement apt, or fitting, or reasonable, but they do not rationally require that one be amused. Hence, there is room for personal taste in humor (and we think in aesthetic properties more generally). However, that seems to leave us in an unhappy position, as it is unclear how we could capture the idea that someone who finds very little, or almost nothing funny is the proper subject of criticism. While we think that an account of humor should make room for the thought that different people have different senses of humor, we also think that a general insensitivity to humor would be a normative failing. We think that by borrowing some of the normative resources that are made available on the sort of neo-Aristotlean virtue theoretic account that we have developed here in connection to social humor, we can resolve this tension. While the person who has a general insensitivity to humor is not subject to rational criticism for failing to be amused by any particular instance of the funny—such reasons are noncompelling—one who has a general insensitivity to humor, be it social humor or art humor, is boorish. That is, they are still the proper subject of characterological criticism.

NOTES

1. We use the term "funny" throughout to stand in for a host of putative humor-related, aesthetic properties, for example, hilarious, humorous, witty, and amusing.

2. The qualification that the reason must be of the right kind is meant to capture the intuitive sense that not all reasons for amusement are properly tied to the comedic aspects of the object. To rework an example from an earlier paper, if Sarah Silverman were to sincerely hold a gun to Maria Bamford's head and demand "be amused, damn it!" that act may give Bamford a reason to be amused. But the reason is directed at the potential harm that might befall Bamford and not at the comedic features of the object.

3. We would like to thank Stephen Hanson for his helpful comments on Aristotle.

4. By "laughter" we mean "laughter that signals amusement." There are two kinds of laugher: Duchenne and non-Duchenne laughter.

"The Duchenne display involves symmetrical, synchronous, and smooth contractions of both the zygomatic major and the orbicularis oculi muscles of the face. The zygomatic major is the muscle in the cheeks that pulls the lip corners upwards and backwards, while the orbicularis oculi is the muscle that surrounds each eye socket and causes wrinkling of the skin at the outer sides of the eyes ('crow's feet') . . . [O]nly genuine enjoyment smiles also involve the orbicularis oculi, which is less subject to voluntary control. Smiles that involve other facial muscles besides these two generally indicate the presence of other (often negative) emotions besides pure enjoyment" (Brown and Schwartz 1980).

Apparently, humans are fairly good at detecting the difference between the two in social exchanges.

5. For a more nuanced examination of the relationship between virtue ethics and right action, see Hursthouse (1999), esp. Ch 1.

6. For ease of explication, we here give this virtue a wider gloss than Aristotle's virtue of liberality, whose scope seems limited to small sums of money [NE, 1120a23-1121a10].

7. This may be no surprise, as the task in the *Nichomachean Ethics* is more to make sense of the common wisdom of his day so that one can become good, than to understand what the good is as an intellectual matter.

8. We here avoid taking a theory of humor from Aristotle's scattered and undeveloped comments on what we might call the ridiculous, or the laughable, or the funny. Aristotle does not say enough about social humor and comedy for us to have confidence that he has a developed theory of humor. His task in NE 4.8 seems to be in thinking through pleasing, joking intercourse with one another. It is clear that he thinks that a main way we do this is by making fun of ourselves and others.

9. Interestingly, Aristotle expresses some confusion about what sets social humor's normative standard, and asks if we should tell jokes that will amuse and not offend the listeners—putting the normative standard to the actual hearers—or should we tell jokes that a witty would find amusing—putting the normative standard on

virtuous hearer? While he ends up siding with the latter position, he doesn't defend or advocate it in a way that suggests that he holds it strongly [1128a26-3].

10. Still, we agree with Peter Kivy's (2003) claim that it simultaneously expresses others' status as outsiders, those who are not part of the joking group but also those who are but are not amused either because they don't get them or for some other reason.

REFERENCES

Aristotle. 1941. *The Basic Works of Aristotle*. Translated by Richard McKeon. New York: Random House.

Aristotle. 2006. *Aristotle: Nichomachean Ethics, Books II-IV*. Translated by C. C. W. Taylor. New York: Oxford University Press.

Beard, Mary. 2014. *Laughter in Ancient Rome: On Joking, Tickling, and Cracking Up*. Oakland: University of California Press.

Brown, S. L. and Schwartz, G. E. 1980. "Relationships Between Facial Electromyography and Subjective Experiences During Affective Imagery." *Biological Psychology*, 11, 49–62.

Cohen, Ted. 1999. *Jokes: Philosophical Thoughts on Joking Matters*. Chicago: The University of Chicago Press.

Curran, Angela. 2016. *Routledge Philosophy Guidebook to Aristotle and the Poetics*. New York: Routledge.

Halliwell, Stephen. 2008. *Greek Laughter: A Study of Cultural Psychology from Homer to Early Christianity*. New York: Cambridge University Press.

Hursthouse, Rosalind. 1999. *On Virtue Ethics*. New York: Oxford University Press.

Jordan, Andrew, and Patridge, Stephanie. 2012. "Against the Moralistic Fallacy: A Modest Proposal for a Modest Sentimentalism about Humor." *Ethical Theory and Moral Practice*, 15, no. 1, 83–94.

Jordan, Andrew and Patridge, Stephanie. 2018. "Fitting Attitude Theory and the Normativity of Jokes." *Erkenntnis*, 83, no. 6, 1303–1320.

Kivy, Peter. 2003. "Jokes are a Laughing Matter." *The Journal of Aesthetics and Art Criticism*, 61, 5–15.

Part IV

ANCIENT PERSPECTIVES ON THE MORAL JUDGMENTS OF AMUSEMENT

Chapter 10

Amusement, Happiness, and the Good Life in Plato's Dialogues

Oksana Maksymchuk

In the *Nicomachean Ethics* and *Politics*, Aristotle explicitly treats the subject of amusement.[1] He defines amusement as a form of relaxation, akin to sleeping and drinking, explaining that it provides a welcome respite from past exertions. While we pursue such a relaxation as if it were valuable for its own sake, Aristotle observes, it is only valuable for the sake of serious activity. In contrast to Aristotle, Plato does not explicitly offer a pithy definition of amusement, nor does he concisely explain its value. While he regularly treats the subject of amusement, its problematic nature, and its place in a human life, a thorough analysis of all aspects of his treatment would present a daunting interpretative and reconstructive task. This chapter takes a more modest approach to Plato's treatment of amusement by focusing on a particular type of activity conventionally considered a mere amusement, which Plato attempts to elevate to the status of serious activity. This activity, central to Plato's dialogues, is the characteristic activity of a philosopher. The term *philosophizing*, which I use throughout, helps underscore popular culture's ambivalent attitude to this type of activity and those who engage in it.

Limiting the scope of my analysis to Plato's conception of philosophy as an activity deserving of exclusive commitment and lifelong pursuit allows the study to get a clearer view of what Plato thought was problematic about amusement and those who dedicate their lives to it. First, on Plato's account, due to the triviality of its objects and objectives, amusement cannot constitute a human being's proper occupation and thus does not merit exclusive commitment. Second, even if one pursues amusement nonexclusively, such a pursuit involves opportunity costs in the form of attention, time, and resources, thus indirectly undermining one's ability to reach mastery in one's proper occupation. A further surprising feature of Plato's view that my analysis brings out is that the proper basis for drawing the distinction between amusement and serious activity is not practical utility, nor the agent's own view of what she is doing based on factors such as her perceived enjoyment, nor the fact that one is relaxing and restorative and the other strenuous and depleting. Rather, the distinction lies in the value of the activity and its contribution to a good human life, determined in part by the objects and objectives of the activity, and in part by one's orientation to these objects and objectives. On this account, persons can be genuinely mistaken about whether they engage in amusement or in a serious activity and it takes an expert with an insight into what is good to diagnose and correct them.

The chapter begins by setting up the contrast between amusement and serious activity in the context of one of the main questions raised by Plato's dialogues: what does it mean to do philosophy and what is the relationship between philosophy and a good human life? It continues with an examination of Callicles' account in the *Gorgias* of philosophizing as a childish amusement unworthy of exclusive commitment. It then turns to the *Republic*, showing that Plato takes on board some key structural features of Callicles' analysis of amusement, even as he disagrees about philosophy's own status and explains why most people (including Callicles) are so bad at distinguishing between amusement and serious activity. I conclude the chapter by addressing a potential problem for my reading, presented by Socrates' portrait of a laughing philosopher in the *Theaetetus*, which suggests that the philosopher does occasionally engage in philosophy as a form of amusement. I show that even in this case, the amusement of the philosopher is an experience he would rather be without as it is occasioned by the suboptimal epistemic and ethical condition of their interlocutor, as well as by the philosopher's recognition of his own human limitations.

1. AMUSEMENT, SERIOUS ACTIVITY, AND THE POINT OF PHILOSOPHIZING

One central aspect of Plato's thought is his systematic defense of the activity his dialogues describe and model for the readers—the activity of philosophizing. Most of the time, it is Plato's Socrates who explicitly considers the possibility that what he and his interlocutors are doing is a mere amusement, and not a serious activity.[2] His concern often assumes a form of the question: are we merely joking around and playing like children, or are we doing something serious, he asks?[3] Occasionally, he raises this question to bring out the implications of an interlocutor's theory—for example, if Theaetetus (or Protagoras) is right, and all perceptions are true for any perceiver, making each an infallible measure of all things, then philosophizing conceived as Socratic midwifery would be a silly game, a mere amusement.[4] Most often, however, his question plays a rhetorical role, urging the interlocutors to change direction, cut to the chase or abandon a nonstarter argument by reminding them that they are not merely horsing around, but engaging in something serious.

Instead of mere play, Socrates prefers to think of his activity as a search or a hunt.[5] The event of an aristocratic hunt, often depicted in the classical Greek myths and poetry, is not a solitary activity, but one in which one engages alongside others for the sake of capturing a trophy animal. The hunt may often involve amusement, the playful taunting and testing of one's fellow hunters' skills and showing off of one's own. Indeed, Socrates' trademark style in the early dialogues is "irony," which is very amusing unless one happens to be the butt of his jokes.[6] But ultimately, the point of the activity is to grasp what is being sought, or at any rate, to get closer to it.[7] If amusement were philosophizing's only point, then it would make sense to abandon any particular dialogue if it stops being amusing. Herein lies the force of Socrates' exhortations: things have just gotten hard, we have reached a frustrating impasse, and it is tempting to give up. If this were a mere amusement, we would be right to quit now, as children quit a game that has ceased to be fun. Whether we quit or press on reveals what we think we are after when we engage in philosophy. So do we stop, or do we keep going?

Famously, most early dialogues end in an impasse, also known as *aporia*, all explicit attempts at grasping what is being sought revealed as falling short. Socrates usually bears the responsibility for the aporetic outcome, as it seems to be a direct consequence of his questioning.[8] Nevertheless, it is often the interlocutor who is responsible for ending the conversation. While Socrates expresses his interest in continuing the difficult search, his interlocutors decline his request.[9] Many beginner students, when encountering Plato's early aporetic dialogues for the first time, form an impression that Socrates' questioning amounts to little more than stalking and harassing his interlocutors, ultimately showing the pointlessness of the so-called *Socratic method*. "There he goes again," they sigh "wasting his time and ours as well. The interlocutors are right to refuse to take part in his game. Why are we reading this, again?"

Plato's concern about philosophy's bad reputation as a pointless amusement is far from outdated. The recent crisis in the humanities reflects just one dimension of a wider negative attitude to the type of activity that we may broadly term "philosophizing"—the activity that resists easy monetization and does not, directly and all by itself, generate any readily discernible profit or utility. In ordinary contemporary English language usage, the term *philosophizing* expresses censure, dismissal, or mockery. Philosophers are readily contrasted with the so-called *practical men*, those who have the will and the power to change the world in accordance with their desires and plans.[10]

Similarly, in Plato's Athens philosophizing was regularly dismissed as one of the many idle amusements pursued by the wealthy aristocratic youths, and inappropriate for serious full-grown citizens who have important matters of politics and business to deal with. When Socrates in the *Apology* admitted to having had dedicated his life to philosophical activity, as evidenced by his neglect of his financial interests and familial obligations,[11] his single-minded commitment must have struck his fellow Athenians as inappropriate if not outright ridiculous. Whereas Aristophanes' *Clouds* depicts Socrates' philosophizing as the stuff of comedy during his lifetime, Plato recasts him as a figure of a new type of tragedy in such dialogues as the *Apology* and the *Phaedo*, in which Socrates is prepared to execute his own death sentence rather than give up his philosophical activity.[12]

While the portrayal of a philosopher as a wooly eyed misfit does not originate with Aristophanes, the comic playwright had made it a popular trope.[13] On this view, still alive today, the philosophers pursue their activities with laughter-inducing aplomb and seriousness, as if those activities were worth dedicating one's life to. But whereas the Athenian rich could get away with wasting their lives on idle amusement without suffering any unenviable consequences for their choices, for an average person growing up in the capitalist market economy, the consequences of such near-sighted commitment are more tangible. In contemporary comic strips, philosophy PhDs perpetually flip burgers, exemplifying the low-value society places on the type of expertise they had spent most of their early adulthood cultivating.[14] The very fact that people find such comics amusing suggests that there is a satisfaction involved in seeing the philosopher punished for their indulgent lack of foresight, in the manner of Aesop's fable about an ant and a grasshopper.

The image of a person who transitions from amusing themselves with philosophizing to working a minimum-wage job brings us to the next point of contrast between amusement and other types of human activities, for not every type of unamusing activity is thereby fulfilling and serious. Some activities are considered necessary drudgery rather than anything worthwhile for a human being to engage in. These are the activities that had been traditionally outsourced to animals and human slaves, and in the sci-fi utopias of the "future" would be outsourced to robots. On Plato's view, any labor that one performs for the sake of material livelihood or earning a wage is not only innocuously unworthy of a human being, but detrimental to the cultivation of virtue, and to human happiness.[15] Because most people do not have the luxury to opt out of this type of work, Plato's warning about its dangers only extends to his audience of the wealthy gentlemen who might think that labor offers fulfillment, seeking employment in the fields or in a factory in the manner of Leo Tolstoy and Ludwig Wittgenstein.

Yet far fewer aristocrats in Plato's time had been seduced by a life of menial labor and wage-earning than by a life of amusement. The Greek poets depicted the mythical Golden Age as a labor-free paradise.[16] Unlike some authors in the Judeo-Christian tradition, they made no promises that the original lost unity with the divine could ever be recovered through work and suffering, and thus, offered no ideological backing for the unconditional value of labor beyond providing for one's basic needs. By contrast, a life of amusement seems appealing independently of any ideology because of the pleasure such a life usually involves. Those who pursue amusement seem to do so willingly, choosing it over other activities available to them. Providing people with an income sufficient for survival, so goes the popular conservative refrain, would destroy their motivation to work. By contrast, almost no change in material circumstances would affect a healthy person's motivation to seek out amusement in one form or another.[17] Yet on Plato's view, amusement cannot make one any happier than menial drudgery can—it is merely a more pleasant way to waste one's life.

So if not idle amusement, nor wage-earning, what is the activity that could make one happy? Plato argues that it is doing what is one's own, an activity that fits one's natural type, and doing it as well as one's nature allows.[18] Any activity that appropriately fits one's capacities as a human being is worth dedicating one's life to and a candidate for serious activity. A worthwhile activity becomes a serious activity when one engages in it in an appropriate way, with a proper orientation to the values and goals that make the activity what it is. A person who merely dabbles in worthwhile activities or pursues a single potentially worthwhile activity merely for the sake of amusing herself, fails at achieving happiness similarly to a person who seriously and studiously engages in unimportant trivial activities.

Dedicating oneself to serious activity directly and noninstrumentally contributes to the well-being of the person engaged in it. When asking the question: "Why is P a happy person?" the answer would be "Because she does X," where X is the serious activity P has dedicated her life to. The danger of amusement, as we shall see from examining Callicles' account partially endorsed by Plato, is that the people who dedicate their lives to the pursuit of amusements do so at the expense of cultivating the skills and dispositions necessary for serious activity. Yet they seem to engage in their suboptimal amusing pursuits willingly. Free to live good fulfilling lives, they nevertheless lead lives that do them no good and are not worthy of them. Unlike the menial laborers and wage-earners with limited leisure who waste their lives as a matter of necessity, the amusement-seekers blow their chance at achieving happiness despite the privileges and resources they enjoy. They do this because they misunderstand what constitutes a good human life and what would make them happy. Correcting their evaluative error would turn them away from a life of amusement and to the life of serious activity in which amusement would no longer play a central role.

2. THE DANGERS OF A LIFE OF AMUSEMENT IN THE *GORGIAS*

In the *Gorgias*, Callicles predicts Socrates' eventual demise due to his childish pursuit of philosophy (*Gorg.* 486b2). Criticizing Socrates for wasting his time and talents on "refuting trivia," he urges him to apply himself to serious matters, as befits an adult. On Callicles' account, there are two things of value in a human life—money and power. The serious activities are those that contribute to the acquisition of these goods. By implication, all other activities are either mere amusements, or else necessary but unavoidable drudgery. Philosophy, on his account, is one such amusement, not merely tangential to living a good human life, but detrimental to such a life if pursued without due measure. Callicles' criticism of Socrates exposes the view that Plato found worth explaining, even as he rejected it: that philosophy as a way of life is a waste of one's time and effort, and that the activity that the philosopher indulges in is a rarified and costly form of amusement.[19]

The analysis Callicles offers in order to persuade Socrates to abandon philosophy attempts to change Socrates' mind about what constitutes a good human life and, consequently, what activities and pursuits are involved in living well. He makes his evaluative framework clear when he proposes that the only goods that matter are material resources and power, and that a better and a more capable man is justly entitled to a greater share of these goods than an inferior man. On his account, it is the active political life that enables the naturally better man to secure for himself what he deserves.[20] By contrast, a philosophical life neutralizes a capable man by distracting him from developing the skills relevant for practical success:

> This is the truth of the matter, as you will acknowledge if you abandon philosophy and move on to more important things. Philosophy is no doubt a delightful thing (*charien*), Socrates, as long as one is exposed to it in moderation (*metriōs*) at the appropriate time of life (*hēlikia*). But if one spends more time with it than he should, it's a man's undoing. For even if one is naturally well favored but engages in philosophy far beyond that appropriate time of life, he can't help but turn out to be inexperienced in everything a man who's to be admirable and good and well thought of is supposed to be experienced in. Such people turn out to be inexperienced in the laws of their city or in the kind of speech one must use to deal with people on matters of

business, whether in public or private, inexperienced also in human pleasures and appetites and, in short, inexperienced in the ways of human beings altogether. [. . .] My own reaction to men who philosophize is very much like that to men who speak haltingly and play like children. [. . .] Listen to me, my good man, and stop this refuting. "Practice the sweet music of an active life and do it where you'll get a reputation for being intelligent. Leave these subtleties to others"—whether we should call them just silly or outright nonsense—"which will cause you to live in empty houses," and envy not those men who refute such trivia, but those who have life and renown, and many other good things as well. (*Gorg.* 484c5–486d1)

At the start of the passage, Callicles acknowledges that philosophical activity is *charien*, graceful, and elegant, under two conditions: the practitioner engages in it moderation, and at an appropriate time of life. Callicles grants that if pursued in a measured disciplined way, "it's not shameful to practice philosophy while you're a boy," the right season for play and games (*Gorg.* 485a4). By contrast, for grownups, there is no proper way to pursue philosophy at all: "when you still do it after you've grown older and become a man, the thing gets to be ridiculous" (*Gorg.* 485a6) and deserving of a flogging (*Gorg.* 485c3).

Callicles implies that it is especially shameful for a philosopher to live as he does because his condition is self-imposed due to his mistaken view of what is enviable (*Gorg.* 486d1). A poster child for missed opportunities and wasted potential, he "lives the rest of his life in hiding, whispering in a corner with three or four boys, never uttering anything well-bred, important, or apt" (*Gorg.* 485e2). The full-grown philosopher is similar to a child (*Gorg.* 485b2, 485d8) and "unmanly" (*Gorg.* 485c2), "neglecting the things [he] should devote himself to" (*Gorg.* 485e4) and missing his share of the goods he deserves. His "inexperience in ways of human beings" (*Gorg.* 484d5) renders him useless and unfit for life.

While Plato disagrees with Callicles' substantive views about value, a good human life, and the role that philosophy can play in envisioning and securing it, he agrees with Callicles about the danger of spending one's life on something that is, objectively speaking, merely an amusement. Like Callicles, Plato thinks that untimely and excessive pursuit of amusement prevents its practitioner from living the life worthy of him. But Plato disagrees with Callicles about philosophy belonging to the category of amusements. On his view, the philosopher's characteristic activity, when correctly understood and pursued, would be revealed as most serious and important even by Callicles' lights insofar as it renders the philosophical life best and most successful.

3. EDUCATION, PROPER WORK, AND THE POSSIBILITY OF ERROR

In the previous section, I examined Callicles' reasons for thinking that philosophy is a mere amusement, the pursuit of which should be restricted to children. This section uses the insights gleaned from Callicles to flesh out Plato's view of the danger faced by someone who commits himself to the pursuit of amusement beyond the appropriate age and without due measure. Drawing on the *Republic*, I show that Plato's main reason for suspicion is that amusement, if improperly regulated, would interfere with one's proper work, thus undermining one's ability to do well as a human being. The strictly regulated educational curriculum of the *Republic* is in part motivated by the problem posed by Callicles about the importance of distinguishing between activities that constitute doing well and those that are at best tangential to it. Because private individuals are not in the position to make the correct distinctions on their own, the philosophical rulers must make determinations for the citizens' work and leisure with a view to the overall good of the *polis* and of the citizens themselves.[21]

Plato infamously insists that in a well-run city, each person must only do his or her proper work. The "one person, one job" principle is best known for generating the prohibition against meddling in the work that is not one's own, which becomes a central feature of the definition of justice in that dialogue (cf. *Rep.* 433d1). However, Socrates also gives it a positive formulation when he explains that each of the city's professionals must "work all his life at a single trade for which he has a natural aptitude and keep away from all the others, so as not to miss the right moment to practice his own work well" (*Rep.* 374b5). He observes that "no one can become so much as a good player of checkers or dice if he considers it only as a sideline and doesn't practice it from childhood" (*Rep.* 374c4). In a later passage, Socrates says that the citizens who qualify for the best type of work as philosopher kings and queens will dedicate themselves to every stage of their education "continuously, strenuously, and exclusively" (*Rep.* 539).[22] If strenuousness and perhaps even continuity admit of degree, exclusivity does not. Just how seriously Socrates takes the exclusivity requirement in the case of the best citizens can be gleaned from his insistence that the guardian women must not only be relieved of the traditional household duties but also of most duties associated with childcare (*Rep.* 460b3-d4). Their "mothering" must be kept to the absolute biologically necessary minimum.

So what is the problem that Plato's seemingly authoritarian prescription of "proper work" and his recommended regimentation of work and leisure presents a solution to? On a more general level, it is a problem of misused potential and misdirected talents that cost both the city and the citizens the well-being they are capable of achieving. But specifically in the case of Socrates' usual audience of wealthy youths, who enjoy considerable freedom and may think that the state has no business telling them how to live and what to do, it is the problem of the unreliability of one's judgment in determining what is one's own.

Humans have no natural infallible sense of "one's own"—of what in fact will promote their flourishing and make them happy. They must use other senses to guide them—such as the sense of pleasure, comfort, or absorption. Yet these senses, although helpful indicators of one's proclivities and talents to an expert, may confuse and mislead a nonexpert. For example, the sense of discomfort that a person experiences when engaging for the first time in a challenging activity may seem to her an indicator that the activity is not "her own," while the sense of ease, pleasure, and fun associated with an amusing activity may be taken by her to mean that she has found her calling. She may resist the former and dedicate herself to the latter. But this could well be a mistake. As her competencies and talents are activated and shaped by her engagement in the challenging activity, she may find it pleasant, absorbing, and fulfilling down the road, finally recognizing it as "her own." If she cannot inhabit that distant temporal perspective yet, that may be because she is not, in the present moment, the self she will become through her practiced craftsmanship.

The unreliability of personal evaluative assessment of what is one's own underlies Plato's insistence on the need for specialized expertise in assigning citizens their proper work.[23] Plato's educational experts identify worthwhile activities and provide guidance, training, and support to those whom they identify as worthy matches for those activities.[24] While on Plato's view, one cannot simply make a willful decision to treat one's prescribed work as an amusement regardless of what the work consists in, a citizen who had been expertly matched with her own proper activity and groomed for it from early childhood will enjoy her work as an adult and find it meaningful and fulfilling. Indeed, in the *Republic*, Plato insists that the best type of life is not only one that is objectively most worthwhile and dedicated to the best things that it is possible for a human to be involved with,[25] but also the most pleasant (*Rep.* 587b5–588b3), thus sharing many phenomenological features that make amusements appear choice-worthy.

Plato's insistence that nonexperts cannot reliably distinguish between amusement and serious activity brings us back to Callicles' charge in the *Gorgias* that philosophy is a mere amusement that deals in trivialities, and not something that should be seriously pursued by a capable person. Callicles' indictment of philosophy rests on a misconception of what is good, and thus, what it takes for a human being to flourish. But Callicles is not wrong to insist that philosophy could be pursued in the wrong way and at the wrong time;

nor is he wrong to suggest that dedicating one's like to mere amusement and neglecting the types of activities that constitute doing well is shameful and blameworthy.[26] Plato takes up these features of Callicles' account when he insists that successful initiation into any activity must happen at an appropriate time in one's life, and that the process must fit the pupil's natural talents and unfold in relation to their emergent abilities. In pursuing an activity at the wrong time and in the wrong way, one may mistakenly pursue a potentially serious activity as if it were a mere amusement, and a mere amusement as if it were a serious activity. This sort of mistake would compromise one's wellbeing and make one's life not worth living.

Philosophizing, on Plato's account, is an objectively worthwhile activity that could, if properly pursued, be the source of greatest pleasure for the right kind of person, and to this person, it would also appear more interesting and absorbing than any amusement. In the *Republic*, Socrates explicitly argues that those who are selected for philosophical training should be "orderly and steady by nature" (*Rep.* 539d2), and begin their training at the age of thirty, after having gone through laborious learning, training, and having passed multiple character tests. He explains his reasoning as follows:

> [. . .] When young people get their first taste of arguments, they misuse it by treating it as a kind of game of contradiction. They imitate those who've refuted them by refuting others themselves, and, like puppies, they enjoy dragging and tearing those around them with their arguments. [. . .] Then, when they've refuted many and been refuted by them in turn, they forcefully and quickly fall into disbelieving what they believed before. And, as a result, they themselves and the whole of philosophy are discredited in the eyes of others. [. . .] But an older person won't want to take part in such madness. He'll imitate someone who is willing to engage in discussion in order to look for the truth, rather than someone who plays at contradiction for sport. He'll be more sensible himself and will bring honor rather than discredit to the philosophical way of life. (*Rep.* 539)

In the passage, Socrates distinguishes between two types of philosophizers, those whose pursuit is something fine, and those whose activity is akin to madness. He draws the distinction on similar grounds as Callicles did in the *Gorgias*: the activity could be fine if done appropriately, at the right age, in due measure, but if it is pursued at an inappropriate age, in the wrong way, for the wrong reason, and beyond due measure, the activity and its practitioners deserve censure and correction. Plato is keenly aware that even serious earnest philosophizing may resemble dreamy speculations (*Rep.* 369c5, 592a6; *Laws* 739c1-e5); or a combative sport (*Prot.* 339e3). Indeed, from the perspective of a nonexpert, there may be nothing more to the activity.[27] But this is not all that the activity consists in. While phenomenologically speaking, natural born correctly nurtured philosophers would enjoy their activity even more than ordinary people enjoy ordinary amusements, what motivates them would not be their love of enjoyment, but rather their love of truth.

Plato agrees with Callicles that most people who happen to philosophize in nonideal cities would be well-advised to quit. In Plato's ideal city, the *Kallipolis*, access to philosophical education is tightly regulated, and only a small subset of the guardians are deemed worthy of receiving it. The young who pursue philosophy as if it were a mere amusement pose a special threat to themselves and to others. In the *Apology*, Socrates describes those who take up philosophizing in the wrong way and for the wrong reasons: "the young men who follow me around of their own free will, those who have most leisure, the sons of the very rich, take pleasure in hearing people questioned; they themselves often imitate me and try to question others" (*Apol.* 23c). Despite their attempts to mimic Socrates, their activity is ultimately very different from Socrates'. They do it for fun, because they enjoy hearing the local authority figures embarrass themselves. By contrast, Socrates questions his fellow Athenians for serious reasons, such as turning the Athenians from their present obsession with money and power and compelling them to care about virtue (*Apol.* 31b5, 38a3, 41e2); getting the so-called *experts* to realize their ignorance and continue their inquiry into matters of value (*Apol.* 38a1-5); and reminding humanity of its inherent limitations (*Apol.* 23b1-5). What appears a mere amusement to most people, including his imitators, is so important to Socrates that he says he would rather be put to death than give it up (*Apol.* 28d2-29a2, 29d2-5, 38a2-7).

It may be thought that insofar as the activity is objectively worthwhile, it does not matter whether a practitioner engages in it as if it were an amusement. After all, isn't that the point of the advice to approach one's work as if it were play? Socrates-imitators provide an illustration of why this life-hack does not work. In bringing inappropriate goals, standards, and purposes to their so-called *philosophizing*, they miss the point of the activity and thus fail to engage in it. Similarly, in the *Republic*, the democratic type of man "sometimes occupies himself with what he takes to be philosophy" (*Rep.* 561d1). Because he treats his pursuit as just one activity among others, failing to see its distinctive value, his philosophizing does him no good. His inability to discriminate between his activities lowers all of them to the status of mere amusements, making them a waste of time.

In the dialogues, Plato's characters present two conceptual possibilities for understanding the characteristic activity of a philosopher: some see it as an amusement, pointing out that it threatens to render its practitioner practically useless; others pursue it as a serious activity that merits nearly exclusive commitment over the course of one's entire life. To the first group, Plato concedes that when philosophy is pursued by the wrong people, at the wrong age, for the wrong reasons, and in the wrong way, it may turn out a worthless pursuit, a mere amusement at best and a potentially harmful one at worst. However, when pursued properly by a suitable person for the right reasons and in a well-ordered way, it is a serious activity, and one that would constitute a person's proper work even within a city-state as imperfect as Socrates' own Athens.

4. PLATO'S LAUGHING PHILOSOPHER

If philosophy is important and worthy of being taken seriously, shouldn't philosophers also be serious? And alternatively, if a philosopher appears a figure who laughs, plays, and jokes around, does this undermine philosophy's claim to seriousness, revealing it as a mere amusement after all? These questions are raised by Socrates' portrait of a laughing philosopher in *Theaet* (174c6–175d7). The image seems to pose a problem for my argument that Plato responds to Callicles by elevating philosophy from a mere amusement to an activity that could constitute one's own proper work in a *polis*.

One way of dissolving the problem of the laughing philosopher is to distinguish between the philosopher's motivation and what makes him a successful practitioner of his craft.[28] On this reading, a philosopher may be in it for the amusement that the activity offers, but what makes him good at philosophizing is that he successfully goes after the truth, grasps what is good, makes the relevant divisions in accordance with the structure of reality, and so on. This solution, albeit tempting, does not fit Plato's argument that what motivates a philosopher is reason's fundamental desire for truth. A mature philosopher who is in it for the sake of amusement is getting philosophizing wrong and thus cannot engage in it successfully. So if philosophizing for the sake of an amusing experience is incoherent on Plato's view, what else could explain a philosopher's laughter?

The *Theaetetus* is unique in that instead of modeling the philosopher's behavior by representing Socrates, it also has Socrates describe "the philosopher." In a long passage known as the Digression, Socrates mentions different social situations in which the philosopher laughs: at *Theaet*. 174d2, he cracks up at parties and gatherings at the ridiculousness of what occupies most people, the so-called *social currency* of gossip, flattery, and obsession with money and status; and at *Theaet* (175c1-d5), the philosopher also laughs when he engages in a distinctively philosophical activity of questioning an interlocutor. In the latter case, the butt of the philosopher's joke is a politically savvy man with "a small, sharp, legal mind," confused by philosopher's questioning into speechlessness. It is this condition, Socrates says, that causes the philosopher's laughter (*gelōs*).[29]

The situation described in the *Theaetetus* is anticipated by Callicles, who observes that just as a philosopher appears a laughingstock in the courthouse and the assembly due to his lack of relevant experience, so a savvy political man presents himself as a laughingstock in the kinds of conversations philosophers are practiced in (*Gorg.* 484e1-3). Sure, he admits, the philosopher is better than a seasoned politician at "refuting trivia"—but his advantage is itself a trivial one. The philosopher's laughter, on Callicles' view, is not only an outward sign of his ignorance about what matters but also of a failure of self-knowledge. Comically, he thinks he is not only better than others but also better off than them.

While laughing takes many forms and could mean many things, the laughter of the philosopher in the *Theaetetus* has a specific structure of "laughing at." The one who "laughs at" assumes a position of superiority or high ground over a person or phenomenon that provokes laughter. In the *Theaetetus*, Plato flips the tables on Callicles and others who praise the politically savvy man and take the philosopher for a naïve fool. Plato presents the political man's worldly success as a small thing undeserving of the pride he takes in it and the envy that the many experience at it, a laughing matter from the perspective only a philosopher is capable of taking up. By contrast, the philosopher's concerns emerge as wider in scope than any human being's, and the philosopher as the only one, besides God, fit to pass judgment on what is worth valuing. Unlike the political man, who takes himself and his concerns very seriously, the philosopher takes neither his own human self, nor the human aspects of his existence too seriously. The philosopher can laugh at himself and his human concerns, his sense of superiority arising out of his self-knowledge.[30]

The philosopher's laughter, far from revealing philosophizing as an amusement, reveals everything else as an amusement in comparison to the serious matter of philosophizing. One who pursues philosophy honors the most divine aspect of his being, namely, his reason, thus assimilating himself to what is immortal and best.[31] By contrast, the politically savvy man not only pursues laughable sorts of things, such as money and power, as if they had some inherent value—he also does the opposite of what he intends. His aim is to do well, but the more capable and successful he becomes at satisfying his worldly desires through accumulating wealth and power, the more he sabotages his own goal of well-being.[32]

This leaves us with the question of why the philosopher makes his laughter conspicuous instead of cracking up at the ignorance of the ignorant in private. The irreverent mockery with which the Socrates of the *Apology* addresses his opponents suggests that a philosopher's laughter in the face of the vicious has a truth-revealing, other-directed, and protreptic function.

Since the people the philosopher laughs at are usually those we would consider conventionally successful, his laughter is a form of "speaking truth to power." While it poses an enormous risk to the philosopher insofar as it activates the interlocutor's anger at being publicly shamed, it also opens the possibility of a cure in the form of self-doubt. Furthermore, the philosopher's laughter helps the audience see the interlocutor as a mock-worthy figure, potentially inoculating them against the temptation to imitate such an apparent role model.

5. CONCLUSION

In the chapter, I have argued that Plato considers amusement as a potential danger to a good life insofar as it may prevent a person from doing their own proper work in a *polis*. This does not make amusement impermissible, on Plato's account—indeed, there may be room for some kinds of amusement in a complete life of virtue. But such amusing activities are to be carefully curated and orchestrated by experts to ensure that they are appropriate to the age, talents, and natural proclivities of the citizens. They may never take center stage in the life of virtue.

Drawing on Plato's attempt to redefine philosophy as the best candidate for a proper activity for a human being instead of a mere amusement as it was often perceived by his contemporaries, I also show that Plato is concerned about the possibility of confusion about whether what one is doing is a mere amusement or a worthwhile serious activity. This confusion could lead one to waste one's life. On Plato's view, distinguishing between amusements and serious activities is a task that requires knowledge of what is good and what it means to be a human being, among other things. The philosopher emerges not only as a person doing the most serious work of all, becoming as good and godlike as possible herself. She is also the only one who can tell whether a person is amusing herself and wasting her life on trivialities, or whether what she does is genuinely worthwhile. This helps explain why a philosopher sometimes laughs at the recalcitrant interlocutors. Her laughter is truth-revealing, exposing not only their ignorance about what matters but also their failure of self-knowledge.

NOTES

1. See esp. *Nic. Ethics* IV.8, VI.7, and X.6 and *Pol.* VIII.3, 5, 7.

2. Plato never figures as a character in his own dialogues, and thus he never speaks in them in propria persona. In this chapter, I follow one widely accepted (but

contestable) scholarly convention of taking the character Socrates to express many of the views that Plato held himself.

3. See *Crat.* 406b5-c2; *Rep.* 349a4; *Theaet.* 167e1-6, 168d2-5, 177d4-7; *Soph.* 234e3-235a3, 237c1; *Euthyd.* 277d6-278e2; *Laws* 688b5. In the *Phaedrus*, Socrates draws a further distinction between vulgar and noble amusements, placing philosophical writing into the latter category due to its limitations as a truth-revealing device (see esp. *Phaed.* 277–78). By contrast, "live" dialectical philosophizing retains its status as a serious activity.

4. Cf. *Theaet.* 161e2-162a2.

5. For the comparison between philosophical inquiry and hunting, see *Crat.* 420b; *Stat.* 264a, 285d, and 297d; *Phileb.* 20d; *Lach.* 194b; *Lysis* 218c; *Laws* 654e, and esp. *Rep.* 432.

6. For a classic discussion of Socratic irony and the role it plays in the moral education in the dialogues, see Vlastos 1991, Lane 2006 and 2011.

7. As Socrates' response to Meno's paradox of inquiry suggests, one must often proceed by accepting hypotheses about what is being sought, without yet knowing what it is. The hunt so conceived is of a very particular kind, in that one does not know in advance what entity is being hunted.

8. For a classical discussion of Socrates' approach in the early dialogues, see Geach 1966 and Santas 1972.

9. See, for example, *Euthyp.* 15d1-e2, *Prot.* 361e1-7 for interlocutors leaving, and *Gorg.* 505d1-506c4, *Prot.* 333d1-e2, *Rep.* 350d1-e3, and *Rep.* 352b2 for interlocutors refusing to continue the discussion.

10. See Russell 1959 for a classical Plato-inspired formulation of the distinction.

11. Cf. *Apol.* 31b1-c2, 36b4-d1.

12. See Ebrey, forthcoming.

13. Cf. *Apol.* 18b5-d1, *Phaed.* 70c1.

14. See Bradford Valey's cartoon (https://www.cartoonstock.com/directory/d/ds.asp), the caption to which reads: "And finally, sir, would you like your burger flipped by a PhD in Philosophy, History or English Literature?"

15. Plato's suspicion about the moral costs of wage-earning can be traced back to such early dialogues as the *Apology* and the *Protagoras*, and they shape his conception of the limited political power of the producers in the *Republic*. But it is most clearly brought out in the *Laws*, where Plato explicitly argues that the cultivation of virtue requires leisure and one's undivided attention (807d), and that the citizens of Magnesia must avoid menial work and handling money. For discussion with bibliography, see Samaras 2012 and Bobonich 2002.

16. Cf. *Stat.* 271-2; *Laws* 713–4.

17. Conditions that could potentially reduce one's motivation to pursue amusement include depression, addiction, exhaustion, and doping, and would usually be considered pathological.

18. The concept of *oikeīos* (usually rendered as "one's own" in English but also having a more technical connotation as "belonging to one's nature") plays a central role in Plato's view that each type of person in a *polis* must wholly commit to an activity that fits their capacities. I give a fuller analysis of the "one person, one job" principle and its implications in the third section.

19. For the overview of the historical and philosophical background of the figure of Callicles, see Dodds 1959, 12–14, Barney 2017. Callicles' position is echoed at *Hipp. Maj.* 304c1-5; and *Rep.* 487d1-4.

20. Throughout the chapter, I use the term "human" or "person" whenever historical and philosophical context permits such usage. I use the term "man" whenever the gender of the person in question plays a significant role in the theory under discussion, as it does in this instance. In Plato's time, as in ours, it was a commonplace view that one's proper sphere is at least in part determined by one's gender, and this analysis would usually extend to "proper amusements," whether they be conceived as restorations from work (especially when considered synchronically, within a specific period), or preparation for it (considered diachronically, over the different stages of one's lifetime). Plato himself resisted the unqualified view, arguing in the *Republic* that a person's sex is an unreliable predictor of her abilities and thus of her proper activity. Nevertheless, he considered it an empirical fact that the specific combination of proclivities and competencies relevant for success as a guardian occur in women more rarely than in men. For an influential discussion of the limitations of Plato's view about women's role in a *polis*, see Annas 1976.

21. Plato's totalitarian leanings have been sharply criticized by Popper 1945. For an influential response, see Taylor 1986.

22. On Plato's view, preparing for a practice of any single craft usually involves heterogeneous stages that build upon one another, gradually expanding one's scope and level of expertise.

23. For Socrates' self-description as one such "matchmaker," even turning pupils away from philosophy to other disciplines that better fit their talents and aptitudes, see *Theaet.* 150c1-151b5. The matchmaking feature of Socrates' activity often gets overlooked in favor of its maieutic aspect; yet he makes it clear that both are crucial for the pupil's flourishing.

24. This formulation leaves it open that the producers do not engage in an activity that has any inner worth and dignity, but rather in necessary drudgery, and that their limited "education" does not aim at making them good and happy. For discussions of the moral aspect of the producers' education (arguably amounting to little more than a training in willing obedience), see Wilberding (2012) and Jeon (2014).

25. In traditional Greek theology of fifth century BCE (which Plato's Athenian recommends for adoption in the *Laws*), these would be gods; in the *Republic*, these are forms.

26. It could be objected that in Plato's latest dialogue the *Laws*, correctly chosen, well-regulated, and properly punctuated amusements do contribute to human flourishing, and different forms of amusement must be prescribed by the legislator throughout the life-span of each citizen. Underlying the use of such institutionalized amusements are the image of a human being as a puppet of the gods (644d5, 803c2), and the view that human affairs are not worthy of being taken very seriously when considered from a nonhuman perspective (803b2, 804a-b). However, even in the *Laws* the citizens of Magnesia are not themselves encouraged to view their activities as "amusements." Indeed, many of these restorative and corrective "amusements" in the form of sports, dances, drinking parties, and festivals are presented to them as obligatory forms of

worship, traditionally considered as one of the most serious and important activities. Plato's Athenian goes as far as to suggest that each citizen must have a time table that spells out what he must do on a daily basis "from dawn to dawn" throughout the different stages of a citizen's life (cf. *Laws* 807e2-4), thus absorbing all activities that may be considered amusements into the citizen's sole proper occupation of cultivating virtue.

27. Consider the widely circulated inscription: "Arguing with a philosopher is a lot like wrestling in the mud with a pig. After a couple of hours, you realize the pig likes it."

28. For a similar argumentative strategy, see *Rep.* 342e2-347d4.

29. While the standard translation uses "evident entertainment" and "evident amusement," the Greek term *gelōs* means specifically "laughter." This is the term used at 174c3, 174d2, and 175d4. In addition to the noun form, verb and adjectival forms are also used. The dialogue contains twenty instances of such usage, suggesting that the theme of laughter is crucial for an examination of a recalcitrant interlocutor.

30. This fits the role that amusement is accorded in the *Laws*, in which the Athenian depicts a human being as a puppet of the gods (644d5, 803c2); and human affairs as not worthy of being taken seriously when considered from a divine perspective (803b2, 804a-b).

31. *Theaet.* 176b1-c5.

32. For the comic effect caused by different types of failure in self-knowledge, see also *Phileb.* 48c2-50a4. On ignorance as the cause of getting the opposite of what one wants, see for example, *Laws* 688b2-d1.

REFERENCES

Annas, Julia. 1976. "Plato's 'Republic' and Feminism." *Philosophy* 51 (197): 307–21.
Aristophanes. 1998. *Clouds. Wasps. Peace.* Translated by Jeffrey Henderson. Loeb Classical Library. Vol. 488, Cambridge, MA: Harvard University Press.
Aristotle. 2000. *Nicomachean Ethics.* Translated by Roger Crisp. Cambridge Texts in the History of Philosophy. Edited by Karl Ameriks. Cambridge: Cambridge University Press.
Aristotle. *Politics.* 1998. Translated by C. D. C. Reeve. Indianapolis: Hackett Publishing Company.
Barney, Rachel. 2017. "Callicles and Thrasymachus." In *The Stanford Encyclopedia of Philosophy*, edited by Edward N. Zalta, https://plato.stanford.edu/entries/callicles-thrasymachus.
Bobonich, Christopher. 2002. *Plato's Utopia Recast.* Oxford: Clarendon Press.
Dodds, Eric Robertson. 1959. *Plato: Gorgias. Revised Text with Introduction and Commentary.* Oxford University Press Academic Monograph Reprints. Oxford: Oxford University Press.
Ebrey, David. 2021 (forthcoming). *Plato's Phaedo: The Initiation of a Philosopher.* Cambridge: Cambridge University Press.
Geach, P.T. 1966. "Plato's Euthyphro: An Analysis and Commentary." *The Monist* 50 (3): 369–82.

Jeon, Haewon. 2014. "The Interaction Between the Just City and Its Citizens in Plato's Republic: From the Producers' Point of View." *Journal of the History of Philosophy* 52 (2): 183–203.
Lane, Melissa. 2006. "The Evolution of Eirōneia in Classical Greek Texts: Why Socratic Eirōneia Is Not Socratic Irony." *Oxford Studies in Ancient Philosophy* 31: 49–83.
Lane, Melissa. 2011. "Reconsidering Socratic Irony." In *The Cambridge Companion to Socrates*. Edited by Donald R. Morrison. Cambridge Companions to Philosophy, 237–259. Cambridge: Cambridge University Press.
Plato. 1997. *Plato: Complete Works*. Edited by John M. Cooper. Indianapolis: Hackett Publishing Company.
Popper, Karl. 1945. *The Open Society and Its Enemies*. London: George Routledge and Sons.
Russell, Bertrand. 1959. "On the Value of Philosophy." In *The Problems of Philosophy*. Oxford: Oxford University Press.
Samaras, Thanassis. 2012. "Leisured Aristocrats or Warrior-Farmers? Leisure in Plato's Laws." *Classical Philology* 107 (1): 1–20.
Santas, Gerasimos. 1972. "The Socratic Fallacy." *Journal of the History of Philosophy* 10 (2): 127–41.
Taylor, C. C. W. 1986. "Plato's Totalitarianism." *Polis: The Journal for Ancient Greek and Roman Political Thought* 5 (2): 4–29.
Vlastos, Gregory. 1991. *Socrates: Ironist and Moral Philosopher*. Townsend Lectures. Ithaca: Cornell University Press.
Wilberding, James. 2012. "Curbing One's Appetites in Plato's Republic." In *Plato and the Divided Self*. Edited by Tad Brennan, Charles Brittain, and Rachel Barney, 128–49. Cambridge: Cambridge University Press.

Chapter 11

Zhuangzi's Moral Psychology and Humor

The Playful Liberation of Self, Others, and Society

Carl Helsing

"Imagination, not intelligence, made us human."

—Terry Pratchett

"I would imagine if you could understand Morse code, a tap dancer would drive you crazy."

—Mitch Hedberg

ZHUANGZI AND HUMOR

What can the *Zhuangzi* 莊子, a Daoist text from ancient China's Warring States Period (476–221 BCE) contribute to our understanding of humor and amusement? The text itself is a collection of thirty-three chapters in three sections: the Inner Chapters (1–7), the Outer Chapters (8–22), and the Miscellaneous Chapters (23–33). Of these groups, only the first seven are most likely the work of a single individual, known as Zhuang Zhou (369–286 BCE) or "Zhuangzi" (Liu 1994, 161–172). Despite the issues surrounding authorship, the collected work is an undisputed masterpiece. As a text, the *Zhuangzi* effortlessly blends literary technique with philosophical insight, while simultaneously reveling in whimsey and wordplay. As a philosophical voice, Zhuangzi effortlessly deconstructs concepts of knowledge and language while demonstrating keen insights into the complicated human endeavor of trying to make sense of the world. Weaving throughout the collection is a mischievous—almost contrarian—spirit of humor. At the heart of this sense of humor is Zhuangzi's celebration of wandering or play (*you* 遊), an existential attitude that dissolves psychological distinctions and nurtures creative responsiveness to the world (*Dao* 道). Despite the ubiquitous puckishness running through the text, Zhuangzi never provides an explicit philosophical account of amusement or humor. Rather, Zhuangzi's thought is revealed through complex encounters that form a unique blend of philosophical reflection and narrative performance.

The Zhuangzi is well known for its humor. Earlier scholarship regards Zhuangzi as a *homo ludens* in the spirit of Albert Huizinga, a figure who stands "perpetually antithetical to any fixed category" (Mair 1983, 86). Zhuangzi's idea of playful wandering (*you* 遊) has also been compared to Gadamer's hermeneutic play, in which a subject becomes immersed in the continual to-and-fro of experience and symbolic meaning (Crandell 1983, 102). Zhuangzi's humor has been described as a critical component of psychosocial transformation (Sellman 1998, 167). In this view laughter is a means to transformation, "an alteration of one's bodily consciousness," and "a complete metamorphosis, a holo-metabolism, in which the mind and body form an integrated whole wherein being, thinking, feeling, speaking, and acting are not separable in reality or thought" (Sellman 1988, 167). Zhuangzi's use of humor is not just a dialectic, but also a process that points to a "myrialectic," in which forgetting correlative opposition allows one's self to be transformed in the processes of the way (Sellman 1988, 169–172). Recent scholarship notes the role of humor in overturning linguistic hierarchies established through correlative opposition (Froese 2013, 137–152), a topic this essay explores in further detail. The idea of overthrowing linguistic hierarchies has led other scholars to regard Zhuangzi's discourse as a unique kind of deconstruction that provides the possibility of psychospiritual transformation (Wang 2000, 352–6).

The aim of this chapter is to examine Zhuangzi's use of humor as a therapeutic linguistic strategy for treating the limitations of language and the "fixed-mind" or "complete-mind" (*cheng-xin* 成心). This involves examining the role of absurdity and understanding in humor, and how Zhuangzi's insights provide a possibility for integrating absurdity and understanding into humor. On the one hand, Zhuangzi's humor exposes the absurdity of relying on fixed distinctions, fixed models, and fixed judgments. On the other hand, Zhuangzi's humor nurtures the capacity for ambiguity, uncertainty, and exploration—in short, for playful creativity within the world. This playful creativity simultaneously nurtures and transcends individual psychological transformation. Zhuangzi's sages demonstrate how to use humor to challenge fixed views of the world, particularly views of the world that endanger life or reduce life to crude utility. Against these views, Zhuangzi's sages demonstrate how to move through life with a unique sense of amusement, using language to open creative possibilities, in a way that regards all elements of life—including ourselves—as intimate parts of life's open-ended and interdependent transformation.

MORAL PSYCHOLOGIES OF HUMOR

Before looking at Zhuangzi specifically, what makes humor so funny? The writings of Aristotle and Immanuel Kant suggest two different approaches, both worth considering here. Aristotle recognizes the role of successful understanding in wit and humor. Kant regards absurdity and a lack of understanding as a necessary precondition for humor. These approaches appear mutually exclusive, but their insights are not only compatible but also important for understanding Zhuangzi's use of humor. Zhuangzi's use of humor, I will argue, uses the contrast between understanding and absurdity to therapeutically treat the absurdities of understanding. This is not to reject understanding, but to expose the limitations of abstraction and conceptualization.

Aristotle and Witty Understanding

Historic evidence points to the existence of a (tragically) lost book of Aristotle's *Poetics* that directly addresses issues of comedy (McMahon 1917, 1–9). *On Rhetoric* provides clues regarding Aristotle's view of amusement and humor. In the text, Aristotle examines the elements of communication that accompany a sense of pleasure. Aristotle astutely notes that a sense of easily learning new things creates a sense of pleasure, and particular uses of words and language best create this sense of understanding. As is consistent with Aristotle's *Logic*, the *Rhetoric* regards understanding as something that occurs through a category or deductive reasoning (in the Rhetoric understanding occurs through the genus, in the case of the *Logic*, through predication). In both cases, we understand by identifying the categories to which things belong and the properties those categories convey. For Aristotle, the identification of shared categories creates understanding, and learning or discovering the supervening relationships leads to a sense of pleasure.

Aristotle carries this model of understanding into his writings on the use of witty humor in conversation. According to Aristotle, witty remarks (or "urbanities," as translated below), rely on creating a sense of understanding while simultaneously creating a sense of surprise. Surprise, in turn, is based on the discovery of understanding that occurs contrary to expectation (*On Rhetoric* 3.11.6; 1412a). Aristotle states:

Urbanities in most cases come through metaphor and from an added surprise; for it becomes clearer [to the listener] that he learned something different from what he believed, and his mind seems to say, "How true, and I was wrong." (Kennedy 2007, 223)

According to Aristotle, the stretches in logic that we find most pleasing are those that are neither too obvious nor too obscure, but rather those that convey an image or sense of meaning before the eyes (*On Rhetoric* 3.10.4–6; 1410b; Kennedy 2007, 219). For Aristotle, these stretches of logic often take the form of an enthymeme, an argument with an unstated premise. When confronted with an enthymeme, wit often makes use of an image or metaphor to bridge the gap in understanding. Discovery of the unstated premise creates a sense of excitement or pleasure. The mind connects the two terms of the argument under an overarching genus, which (for Aristotle) provides understanding. Thus, the best use of wit, according to Aristotle, combines a metaphor, antithesis (paradox, or a violation of expectation) with quick discovery (*On Rhetoric* 3.11.6–8; 1412a–1412b; Kennedy 2007, 223–224).

Immanuel Kant and Relief from Absurdity

Contrary to Aristotle, Immanuel Kant considers the role of absurdity in creating the sense of relief in humor. Kant's formidable work often gives the impression of a singularly focused intelligence, but Kant himself appears to have enjoyed a vibrant social life in Konigsberg. His role as a private tutor earned him entry into elite circles, where he won a reputation for wit, charm, and grace. Despite his courtly affections, he also maintained a sense of urban cosmopolitanism, keeping regular connections throughout the ranks of the city (Kuehn 2001, 114–115).

In the *Critique of Judgment* Kant examines the relationship between aesthetic representation and physical gratification. Kant is particularly interested in determining a difference between pleasures of judgment versus pleasures of physical gratification (Kant 2007, 159). Kant notes that the changing free play of aesthetic sensation affords a constant source of gratification despite not requiring judgment—hence, he claims, our ability to enjoy dinner parties (Kant 2007, 160). For Kant, humor originates with the interplay of aesthetic ideas (we might say impressions) or representations of understanding, but the pleasure results from the release of strained expectations (Kant 2007, 161). The interplay of aesthetic ideas leads to some experience of absurdity, which in turn creates a strained sense of expectation or understanding. The release of the strain, in Kant's view, results in the physical pleasure of laughter.

It may seem these models are mutually exclusive: Kant identifies the role of absurdity, while Aristotle favors understanding. It may come as some surprise that these models are not only not exclusive, but also they actually rely on a shared characteristic: the intrinsic limitations of abstract conceptualization. In Aristotle's model, the surprise and enjoyment that accompanies understanding is only possible because of the gaps in understanding. Likewise, Kant's theory of humor as the result of absurdity is also only possible due to the gaps in understanding. Unlike Aristotle and Kant, Zhuangzi observes how language creates the possibility of both absurdity and rationality. Zhuangzi plays with the contradictions that result from any conceptual distinction to show that any rational understanding can be reduced to absurdity—and that anything absurd can be made to make sense. The goal of such humor—of playing with the ambiguity between absurdity and understanding—is not to reject all understanding, but rather to demonstrate the complicated nature of conceptual understanding. The playful dismantling and creative generation of understanding is, I suggest, an important part of Zhuangzi's moral psychology, of learning to navigate a complex world of constant transformation *and* learning to see ourselves as an intimate part of that process.

Zhuangzi and the Delight in Wandering Play

Zhuangzi does not present an explicit account of humor, but the text is suffused with linguistic and conceptual play. This playfulness can be tied to Zhuangzi's attitude of wandering or play (*you* 遊). More than a sense of humor, the idea of wandering, for Zhuangzi, both describes life and serves as a psychological and existential ideal for how to live. The term *you* 遊 can be translated as either "wandering," or "play," and Zhuangzi uses the term to convey a sense of playful wandering. Zhuangzi's dialogues play with words and expectations, Zhuangzi's sages playfully wander through the world, and the world itself is an ongoing playful dynamic. The spirit of playful wandering may be understood in philosophical terms as a kind of eudaimonia, or human flourishing (Fraser 2014, 542–543). For Zhuangzi's sage, wandering nurtures an emotional capacity for flexibility and uncertainty, responding to the conditions of the world without *fixed* judgment or preference. This spirit of wandering is perhaps best embodied in the opening passages of the text, in the transformations of Kun and Peng:

> There is a fish in the Northern Oblivion named Kun, and this Kun is quite huge, spanning who knows how many thousands of miles. He transforms into a bird named Peng, and this Peng has quite a back on him, stretching who knows how many thousands of miles. When he rouses himself and soars into the air, his wings are like clouds draped across the heavens. The oceans start to churn, and this bird begins his journey toward the Southern Oblivion. The Southern Oblivion—that is the Pool of Heaven. (Ziporyn 2009, 2)

The metamorphosis of Kun and Peng beautifully exemplifies the spirit of playful transformation. Beyond merely celebrating transformation and wandering, however, the passage also notes the dependency of wandering on the transformations of the world: without sufficient water, a boat cannot float, without sufficient air, a bird cannot fly (Ziporyn 2009, 2). Making our way through the world requires nurturing our capacity to follow specific conditions that carry us safely forward. For Zhuangzi, this capacity for playfully responding to the conditions of life requires nurturing the emotional and cognitive capacities for the wandering heart-mind (*youxin* 遊心).

In classical Chinese philosophy, the locus of emotional and cognitive experience is the *xin* or heart-mind (Ames 1998, 56). In contemporary terms, we might regard the heart-mind as the conscious awareness of our emotional and cognitive experience. This awareness includes distinct emotions (joy, sadness, anger, grief, etc.), sensations (light versus dark, soft versus hard, hot versus cold, etc.), concepts (big/small, tall/short, night/day, this/that), judgments (yes/no, right/wrong, good/bad), abstract frameworks (plans, theories, models), and goals or intentions. Warring states texts frequently refer to the heart-mind as one of the senses and compare the heart-mind and the other senses to imperial officials. As officials, the senses are responsible for receiving and processing information. The heart-mind, often regarded as the central official, then uses language to identify conditions and organize experience (Geaney 2002, 84–94). In the conventional model, language, then functions as guide for direct human activity.

Zhuangzi observes, however, that simply having a clear idea and resolute determination in no way equals actual understanding. Zhuangzi humorously observes that if we regard the mind as source of instruction or insight, but we merely follow whatever is fixed in our mind (*cheng-xin* 成心), then anyone can claim to be following a wise master.

> If we follow whatever has so far taken shape, fully formed, in our minds, making that our teacher, who could ever be without a teacher? The mind comes to be what it is by taking possession of whatever it selects out of the processes of alternation—but does that mean it has to truly understand that process? The fool takes something up from it too. (Ziporyn 2009, 10)

Zhuangzi makes an important observation: our conscious awareness of experience is what it is because our emotional and cognitive processes filter and focus elements of our experience. The problem, however, is that instead of simply selecting elements of our experience, the heart-mind takes hold of distinctions and refuses to let them go. This results in the heart-mind engaging in endless struggle.

We give, we receive, we act, we construct: all day long we apply our minds to struggles against one thing or another—struggles unadorned or struggles concealed, but in either case tightly packed one after another without gap. The small fears leave us nervous and depleted; the large fears leave us stunned and blank. Shooting forth like an arrow from a bow string such is our presumption when we arbitrate right and wrong. Holding fast as if to sworn oaths: such is our defense of our victories. Worn away as if by autumn and winter: such is our daily dwindling, drowning us in our own activities, unable to turn back. Held fast as if bound by cords, we continue along the same ruts. The mind is left on the verge of death, and nothing can restore its vitality. (Ziporyn 2009, 10)

Zhuangzi's key insight here is that the same mechanisms that provide the possibility of understanding also provide the possibility of misunderstanding (Helsing 2019, 564). These processes—making distinctions, applying concepts, and comparing ideas—each have their own limitations, but they are particularly problematic when they appear as fixed determinations in our conscious awareness (when they become *cheng-xin* 成心). The fixed heart-mind clings to distinctions, labels, judgments, and objectives. The fixed heart-mind renders positions absolute and immobile. The fixed heart-mind considers itself the sole arbiter of right and wrong and is unwilling to imagine other possibilities. This creates the kind of deleterious struggle and exhaustion that, rather ironically, inhibits the heart-mind from effectively helping guide us through the world.

Zhuangzi and the Generation of Opposites

The problem is no conceptual distinction can adequately capture the entirety of experience. Any abstraction, in some sense, oversimplifies experience. Conscious identification of any element in experience necessarily involves selecting certain elements and not selecting other elements. Thus, any linguistic or conceptual distinction creates both points of understanding and gaps in understanding (Helsing 2019, 562–6). This leads to Zhuangzi's crucial insight that any distinction in experience creates the possibility of an opposing, contradictory distinction:

> There is no being that is not "that." There is no being that is not "this." But one cannot be seeing these from the perspective of "that": one knows them only from "this" [i.e., from one's own perspective]. Thus, we can say: "That" emerges from "this," and "this" follows from "that." This is the theory of the simultaneous generation of "this" and "that." By the same token, their simultaneous generation is their simultaneous destruction, and vice versa. Simultaneous affirmability is simultaneous negatability, and vice versa. What is

circumstantially right is also circumstantially wrong, and vice versa. Thus, the Sage does not proceed form any one of them alone, but instead lets them all bask in the broad daylight of Heaven. (Ziporyn 2009, 12)

In the simplest interpretation of this problem, human understanding is limited in its view of any problem or situation. We know the situation from our own point of view, not another point of view. This limited view leads to a second, more complex point, which is that linguistic or conceptual distinctions result in conceptual opposition. This is the "theory of simultaneous generation," or "speaking about the birth of opposition" (*fang sheng zhi shuo* 方生之說). Making one distinction prompts the creation of an opposing distinction. Making any "this" begs the question "what is not this?" and searching for a conceptual opposite. For example, making an abstract distinction of "light" prompts us create an opposing distinction, "dark." Making the distinction "old" prompts us to distinguish something else as "young." While these distinctions help create useful concepts (and therefore seem "reasonable"), they also contain an intrinsic absurdity: the over-simplification of experience to create a linguistic abstraction.

It is this very over-simplification that provides the capacity for Zhuangzi's sense of humor and amusement. The generation of opposites provides a means of integrating understanding and absurdity into a coherent model of humor. Any distinction, any "this" may be made to make sense from some point of view. It may be regarded as "so," or appropriate, or reasonable. However, any distinction may also be seen from the point of view of "that." It may be regarded as "not-so," inappropriate, or absurd. Thus, any one moment of humor contains both understanding and absurdity. This suggests any moment of humor also contains both excitement and relief. Aristotle observes the pleasure experienced in understanding the abstraction from experience, or the relationships between abstractions. Kant observes the relief from discovering the conceptualization is absurd. Between these two, Zhuangzi observes how any conceptual distinction may be viewed from an opposite position – and how any conceptualization may be viewed as both reasonable and absurd. When we use humor, we delight in the play of absurdity and rationality; of playfully using language to create new conceptual connections, and in demonstrating the absurdity of conventional understanding. Both of these activities rely on our capacity for seeing any distinction as either reasonable or absurd.

From this point of view, humor is the discovery of the mutual rationality and absurdity of any distinction or conceptualization. This is wonderfully captured in the humor of the late comedian Mitch Hedberg. Hedberg frequently explored the absurdities of everyday experience, revealing the competing impulses toward rationality and absurdity that resulted from viewing distinctions from multiple perspectives. Hedberg frequently commented on basic distinctions in common objects in everyday life:

> On a traffic light, green means "go" and yellow means "yield." But on a banana, it's just the opposite. Green means "hold on" and yellow means "go ahead." And red means "where the @#$! did you get that banana?" (Hedberg, 2002)

Successful understanding depends on the relationship between conceptual abstraction and contextual interaction. The same conceptual distinctions may have entirely different meanings when applied in different environments or contextual understandings. What makes sense in one environment or context becomes completely absurd in another. The contrast between what makes sense in one situation versus the possibility we have egregiously misunderstood the situation leads to a sense of surprise and aporia. Again, Hedberg observes:

> I did a radio interview. The DJ's first question was "Who are you?" I had to think, "Is this guy really deep or did I drive to the wrong station?" (Hedberg, 2002)

One the one hand, successful understanding depends on how well our conceptual representations and frameworks facilitate our interactions in the world. On the other hand, the playful reapplication of meaning leads to new possibilities of understanding the world. These new possibilities may appear absurd but also contain possibilities of meaning. Hedberg provides another example:

> If you're watching a parade, make sure you stand in one spot. Don't follow it. It never changes. And if the parade is boring, run in the opposite direction. You will fast forward the parade. (Hedberg, 2003)

The potential oppositions in perspectives—the tensions between rationality and absurdity—need not be explicit. As Aristotle notes, we enjoy the feeling of drawing comparisons and creating a sense of understanding. At the same time, the ability to discover reasons behind alternate or competing conceptualizations often raises questions about why the initial distinction was held in the first place. This creates a sense of aporia, of "being lost," and wondering at the rationality of any conceptualization. Thus, any conceptualization provides the basis for both "this" and "that," for both rationality and absurdity.

EXAMPLES OF THERAPEUTIC HUMOR IN ZHUANGZI

Now we can better see how Zhuangzi uses humor to therapeutically treat fixation and nurture an open, receptive psychological attitude. The simultaneous experience of rationality and absurdity is not only humorous but also creates an aporetic experience. The sense of disorientation prompts us to redirect our conscious attention back to the conditions of the situation. This reorientation helps nurture an attitude of receptivity to possibility. We no longer seek to enforce our limited understanding of the world. We become better able to let our understanding be shaped by the interactions of the world. By demonstrating the limitations of understanding through humor, Zhuangzi creates the possibility of learning to better accept these limitations, and to view our understanding as more limited and conditional.

Forgetting Things and Being Useless

The first step in this therapeutic treatment is "emptying" or "fasting of the heart-mind" (Helsing 2009, 567). In contemporary terms, we might describe this as releasing fixed distinctions, fixed concepts, and fixed intentions. We see this need for emptying or "fasting" in a conversation between Yan Hui and Confucius in chapter 4. In the Confucian *Analects*, Confucius regards Yan Hui as his favorite disciple and frequently lauds Yan Hui for his resolute dedication to ritual propriety. In Zhuangzi's fictional encounter, Yan Hui presents Confucius with his plans for correcting the behavior of the ruler of Wei:

> I have heard that the ruler of Wei has reached the prime of his life and become quite autocratic in his ways. He makes frivolous use of his state without seeing his error. He thinks nothing of the death of his people—nationfuls [sic] of corpses fill the marshes, clumped in piles like bunches of plantains. The people there are utterly without recourse . . . I wish to take what I have learned from you and to derive some standards and principles from it to apply to this situation. Perhaps then the state can be saved.
>
> Confucius said, "Ah! You will most likely go and get executed!" (Ziporyn 2009, 24)

In response to Yan Hui's inquiry on how best to cure the evils in the nearby state, Confucius unexpectedly tells him to forget his careful plans, as they will only bring him into danger and ruin. Thrown off guard but still determined, Yan Hui presents a collection of carefully considered strategies to Confucius. Confucius effortlessly dismantles Yan Hui's rebuttals, demonstrating how each approach ultimately leads to failure. Yan Hui ultimately relents and asks Confucius how to succeed. Confucius (speaking for Zhuangzi) describes emptiness as "fasting of the mind," (Ziporyn 2009, 25). Yan Hui, thoroughly confused, is finally receptive to a different approach:

Yan Hui said, "What is the fasting of the mind?"

Confucius said, "If you merge all your intentions into a singularity, you will come to hear with the mind rather than with the ears. Further, you will come to hear with the vital energy rather than with the mind. For the ears are halted at what they hear. The mind is halted at whatever verifies its preconceptions. But the vital energy is an emptiness, a waiting for the presence of beings. The Course alone is what gathers in this emptiness. And it is this emptiness that is the fasting of the mind. (Ziporyn 2009, 25)

The humor in the passage rests on the audience's understanding of Confucius and Yan Hui. The Confucian *Analects* regard self-cultivation and benevolence as cornerstones of restoring social stability. The Confucian values of filial piety, ritual propriety, and benevolence extend through familial and political relationships to create political, economic, and social stability. Thus, a sage, by demonstrating virtue and benevolence, can inspire others to similarly virtuous behavior. While the *Analects* themselves warn against following rulers who do not follow the Way, Zhuangzi's portrayal of the Confucian project is not without a legitimate basis. The Confucian project emerged with the growing demand for skilled administrators during the Zhou dynasty, which happened to coincide with the rise of competing territories and imperial ambitions. In this manner, the Confucians attempted to maintain a sense of social stability and humane governance despite the rapidly changing conditions. Thus, when Confucius bluntly torpedoes Yan Hui's careful plans for moral reform, Zhuangzi presents a scene that is absurd *and* completely reasonable.

The exchange between Yan Hui and Confucius also provides a clear model for therapeutic practice. When confronted with the realization that his goal of teaching moral virtue to an authoritarian ruler is absurd (despite being perfectly reasonable from his initial point of view), Yan Hui reconsiders his project and asks Confucius how to actually respond to the dangers of political court life. Confucius explains that by emptying his mind of preconceptions, Yan Hui can better attenuate to emerging circumstances. In addition to helping Yan Hui avoid potential dangers, this attention to transformation creates a sense of stillness and peace. By no longer trying to force his plans on the situation, Yan Hui gains the capacity to creatively respond to the needs of the situation.

Zhuangzi also uses humor to help dislodge reductionist views of others, to help understand how different methods of moving about in the world may be equally viable. In chapter 4, Carpenter Shi and his apprentice travel to Crooked Shaft in the state of Qi. Upon their arrival they behold the great tree, broad enough to shelter several thousand oxen, measuring a hundred spans around, and towering above the hills. There are many sightseers, but the master carpenter passes through without sparing the tree a glance. The carpenter's apprentice, struck by the magnitude of the mighty specimen, exclaims he has never seen timber of such beauty and asks his master why they pass without stopping. Carpenter Shi replies the tree is too old and gnarled to be of any use! Anything made from its bulk would fail—boats would sink, coffins would rot, vessels would break, doors would sweat sap, and posts would be eaten by worms. He declares the tree completely useless.

> Back home, Carpenter Shi saw the tree in a dream. It said to him, "What do you want to compare me to, one of those *cultivated* trees? The hawthorn, the pear, the orange, the rest of those fructiferous trees and shrubs—when their fruit is ripe they get plucked, and that is an insult. Their large branches are bent; their small branches are pruned. Thus do their abilities embitter their lives. That is why they die young, failing to fully live out their natural life spans. They batter themselves with all the vulgar conventions of the world—and all the other creatures do the same. As for me, I've been working on being useless for a long time. It almost killed me, but I've finally managed it—and it is of great use to me! If I were useful, do you think I could have grown to be so great?" (Ziporyn 2009, 30)

The passage presents multiple instances of humor that utilize the generation of opposites to create both understanding and absurdity (this is in addition to the general playfulness of the language, which further suggests the conditional nature of meaning). First, the apprentice mistakenly deems the gnarled tree "useful" (*yong*用); he believes himself clever for his crude understanding but is quickly reprimanded by the master carpenter, Second, the sacred tree rightly chastises Carpenter Shi for passing judgment based on the carpenter's perspective of what is useful. Despite being deemed "useless," and therefore "no good," the tree's way of living is perfectly "useful" to the tree (and as a humorous aside, this is the only passage I know in the history of philosophy where a man loses an argument to a tree, and rightly so). Third, the sacred tree criticizes the Confucian program of self-cultivation. The Confucian program appears "useful," but Zhuangzi fears the lives of eager young scholars are cut short by the machinations of court, their "virtue" reduced to disposable forms of utility by early dynastic lords. Finally, the idea of working on being useless is itself absurd but also recognizes an important truth—as described in Heinrich Böll's oft-adapted short story, "Anecdote Concerning the Lowering of Productivity" (Böll 1995, 628–630).

Ironically, Zhuangzi's point is not that we should strive to be useless in the eyes of others: this is simply another way of defining ourselves in terms of fixed utility. A passage from chapter 20 recounts the story of the useless tree, but then raises the example of a useless goose:

> When he left the mountains, he lodged for a night at the home of an old friend. His friend was delighted and ordered a servant to kill a goose for dinner. The servant said, "There is one that can crow and one that cannot. Which should I kill?" The host said, "Kill the one that cannot crow." (Ziporyn 2009, 84)

The point is not that we should strive to be useless in the eyes of others, but that we should change and adapt to the changes of life as necessary. The passage continues:

> I would probably take a position somewhere between worthiness and worthlessness. But though that might look right, it turns out not to be—it still leads to entanglements. It would be another thing entirely to float and drift along, mounted on only the Course and its Virtuosity—untouched by both praise and blame, now a dragon, now a snake, changing with the times, unwilling to keep to any exclusive course of action. Now above, now below, with momentary harmony as your only measure—that is to float and drift within the ancestry of things, which makes all things the things they are, but which no thing can make anything of. What then could entangle you?" (Ziporyn 2009, 84)

In each of these cases, Zhuangzi uses the binary oppositions that result from fixed judgments to reveal the weakness at the heart of any universal judgment: that no distinction or judgment can adequately address the myriad possibilities of the world. Any fixed distinction or judgment provides the basis for an opposing position. Attempting to defend that distinction or judgment as *the only universally proper position* or the superior position rapidly becomes absurd.

This is particularly true when those definitions and judgments refer to systems of utility. When we allow ourselves to be defined by our usefulness to others, we become reduced to objects that are simply subsumed into schemes of means and ends. Or we reduce others to simply being the means by which we achieve our own ends. Either case results in using language to divide the world into objects, and then reducing the meaning of those objects into mere utility. Along with the danger to living beings there is a real sense of loss here. Affixing labels and passing judgment obscures our ability to appreciate others for their own playful creativity. Why not wonder at the gnarled, twisting limbs of the tree? Why not be amazed by its age and size? Why not rest against its trunk and enjoy its shade?

Wandering and Imagination

Creative responses to life depend on turning our attention away from preconceived frameworks of understanding and instead reexamining our conditions without judgment or expectation. This means finding possibilities of action in our surrounding circumstances. This means using language to make temporary distinctions and to explore possibilities as they emerge. Consider the example of Huizi and the gourds, from chapter 1:

> Huizi said to Zhuangzi, "The King of Wei gave me the seed of a great gourd. I planted it, and when it matured it weighed over a hundred pounds. I filled it with liquid, but it was not firm enough to lift. I cut it in half to make it a dipper, but it was too large to scoop into anything. It was big and all, but because it was so useless, I finally just smashed it to pieces."
>
> Zhuangzi said, "You are certainly stupid when it comes to using big things . . . How is it that you never thought of making it into an enormous vessel for yourself and floating through the lakes and rivers in it? Instead, you worried that it was too big to scoop into anything, which I guess means our greatly esteemed master here still has a lot of tangled weeds clogging up his mind!" (Ziporyn 2009, 7)

Zhuangzi again uses the humorous contrast between what seems reasonable and what seems absurd to disrupt our fixed understanding of the world. Zhuangzi leads us into this uncertainty with the rapid vacillations between Huizi's attempts to use the gourd and his failures. Huizi's frustration leads him to destroy the gourds, which—from his point of view—seems reasonable. This act of destruction, however, is completely absurd, and results in losing a real possibility for moving about in the world. Zhuangzi's humor relies on the tension between what seems reasonable and absurd, and then uses the open space created by the confusion to reorient Huizi's understanding of the world.

However, Zhuangzi's passage also raises an important problem: what is the difference between helpful possibility and harmful possibility? When is possibility harmful? The challenge here is similar to the question about humor: Why shouldn't we practice derisive humor? What in Zhuangzi directs us away from derisive humor? For the sage, the heart-mind must learn to explore possibility without reducing others to mere instruments. Zhuangzi's sages excel in disrupting conventional judgments and redirecting conscious attention to the flux of experience. This is important for individual creativity and flourishing, but this is also important for broader social flourishing:

> Yang Ziju went to see Lao Dan, saying, "here is a man, ambitious and quick, aggressively proactive, with a profound comprehension of things and a capricious intelligence, who studies the course without fatigue. Can such a man be compared to a clear-sighted sovereign?"

Lao Dan said, "Compared to a sage, he is a petty official or a diviner bound to his craft, laboring his own body and terrorizing his own mind. The beautiful patterns of the tiger and the leopard bring on the hungers that kill them; the monkey's grace and the dog's rat-catching bring on the leashes that bind them. Can these be compared to a clear-sighted sovereign?"

Yang Ziju, jolted as if kicked, said, "I beg to ask about how a clear-sighted sovereign governs."

Lao Dan said, "When a clear-sighted sovereign rules, his achievements cover all the world, but they seem not to come from himself. He transforms all things and yet the people do not rely upon him. There is something unnamable about him that allows all creatures to delight in themselves. He establishes his footing in the unfathomable and roams where nothing at all exists." (Ziporyn 2009, 51–52)

Again, Zhuangzi uses creative wordplay to imagine a scenario where an ambitious young scholar seeks reassurance that he follows the path of virtue. Contrary to providing constructive criticism of the aspiring scholar's progress, Lao Dan (the purported and oft-disputed author the *Dao De Jing*) capsizes the entire project of self-cultivation. Instead of leading to harmonious relationships and social flourishing, the scholar's attempts will see him consumed and destroyed by the very political machinery he hopes to guide.

In each of these cases the best possibilities are those afforded by mutually open-ended, responsive relationships. In Zhuangzi's view, we must learn to react to the world around us, instead of reducing the world into a series of fixed distinctions. This reduction is a reduction of the open-ended possibilities afforded by the ever-transforming processes of life. Life itself must remain an open-ended system of possibilities, instead of a closed system of instrumentality. Ultimately, this requires sufficient courage to relinquish the desire to mechanize the world or control the world through frameworks of instrumentality.

MODELS OF HUMOR

These stories demonstrate how Zhuangzi uses wordplay and the juxtaposition of opposites to disrupt our fixed understanding of the world. The recognition of simultaneous rationality and absurdity creates a moment of aporia, of being lost. This moment of confusion the critical element necessary for drawing human attention or awareness back to the emerging conditions of life as a process of transformation. By disrupting our conventional understanding of what makes sense and what does not, we have to turn our attention back to the world and reexamine where we are and what we are doing. Aporia challenge us to turn our attention back to the active transformations of the world and find creative possibilities within the flux of experience.

Looking at humor through the "birth of opposites," we can construct a model of humor that integrates both reason and absurdity. From Zhuangzi's perspective, any conceptual distinction can give rise to binary opposition. Any distinction, concept, or judgment may be deemed either reasonable and correct ("that's it!") or absurd and incorrect ("that's not it"). Zhuangzi uses the juxtaposition of conventional rationality and absurdity to create a complex experience of humor. Zhuangzi attacks fixed positions that prevent us from engaging the world as a complex, ongoing process of transformation. Zhuangzi uses the juxtaposition of opposites ("that's it" and "that's not it") to create a simultaneous experience or rationality and absurdity. The simultaneous experience of rationality and absurdity creates a sense of surprise and confusion, but we also experience delight and relief. On the one hand, we delight in discovering the conceptual relationships between absurdity and rationality. On the other hand, we experience relief from recognizing the absurdity of fixed distinctions between the rational and the absurd. This release creates new possibilities for receptivity and creativity: receptivity to transformation, and playful wandering in the world as a process of continual transformation.

Zhuangzi takes particular delight in recognizing the absurdity of language itself and enjoying the constant interplay of conceptual frameworks and possibility. In this manner Zhuangzi's juxtaposition of opposites also reveals the limitations of all understanding. From Zhuangzi's point of view, all conceptual understanding of the world is limited, due to the imperfect mapping of concepts onto experience. Any concept can, theoretically, be rendered absurd when considered from the "wrong" perspective. Anything absurd can, theoretically, be rendered sensible when considered from the "right" perspective. This suggests that the process of conceptualization itself is fallible and should be regarded in good humor. Our capacity for abstraction should be accompanied by an acceptance of the limitations and potential absurdities produced by conceptualization. This realization leads to the deep, far-reaching sense of humor that extends through the text of the Zhuangzi—every moment of the text deploys language in a way to unseat the comfortable relationship with fixed meaning. Contrary to finding the lack of fixed meaning in language problematic, Zhuangzi revels in the possibilities afforded by limitations of language. We are no longer standing on fixed ground but gliding on changing possibilities of meaning.

Liberating Humor

What distinguishes Zhuangzi's use of liberating humor from derisive humor or humor as oppression? For Zhuangzi, the issue is whether or not our sense of humor, our capacity for wandering and play, extends the possibilities of continual play. By surrendering our desire to control a situation and reduce the situation to merely individual utilitarian ends, we gain the ability to continue participation in the play of the situation. This actually means actively following certain possibilities and rejecting other possibilities, with an eye for possibilities that will present continued opportunity for play.

The therapeutic liberation of humor applies to both an individual and social sense. In an individual sense, humor liberates the human mind (the heart-mind, or human consciousness) from harmful fixations: from clinging to views that harm one's self or others; from gross oversimplifications that reduce others to mere utility or the means to ends; and from goals or objectives that continually bring the subject into self-destructive conflict with others. In a social sense, humor liberates

What makes Zhuangzi's humor noteworthy is that the resolution to the apparent contradiction is in fact, simply a return to the normal state of affairs—if we understand the normal state of affairs as living in a world of constant change that requires us recognize the limitations of our understanding. Liberating humor asks us to reconsider our understanding in relation to the world, instead of forcing the world to conform to our understanding. This approach to humor asks us to surrender our egocentric and utilitarian appropriations of the world, and to better respond to the needs of our circumstances. Zhuangzi's statements are liberating in the sense that he constantly disrupts the human tendency to divide and organize the world into discrete categories that can then be used in fixed patterns of understanding. Zhuangzi's creativity, absurdity, wordplay, and whimsy are all remedies to a world of humorless instrumentality, where everything exists for the sake of a predetermined and limited purpose.

Derisive Humor

Derisive humor also functions by using absurdity and rationality. In this case, however, the idea of the other as equal participant is what feels "absurd" (to the speaker). This idea of the other as equal or intrinsically valuable is then attacked by applying a derisive distinction. In the case of derisive humor, however, the idea of intrinsic value in the other is regarded as absurd, while the idea of the other as inferior is what feels "right" or reasonable to the speaker. The key part of this is the derisive distinction reduces the other to a fixed conceptual object whose only purpose is to serve as means to reinforcing a fixed end. The other serves as an object in the conceptual hierarchy of the speaker, and the derisive humor serves to reinforce the position of the other as below that of the speaker.

Nowhere is this more apparent or harmful than in the derisive humor of stereotypes. Crude stereotypes are used repeatedly in humor to denigrate others. These stereotypes emerge from arbitrary binary distinctions between what is "normal" and what is not. These distinctions are, in turn, often based on localized structures of power and control. All of these reduce the subject of the joke to an object; the setup of the joke promotes (in a very limited sense) a question or uncertainty—while the resolution of the joke reduces the subject to an object—an object to be used for the pleasure of the comedian or the comedian's dominant culture.

Derisive humor fails because derisive humor relies on an arbitrarily a limited view of "how things should be," "the way things are," or "that's it." In actuality, the distinctions or concepts used to support derisive humor are often easily shown to be absurdly limited and hypocritical. The greatest limitation of derisive humor, however, is that derisive humor attempts to reinforce fixed norms and values that actively fail to respond to the world as a world of continual change. By contrast, liberating humor rejects closed systems of meaning, enabling us to explore new possibilities. Derisive humor eliminates possibilities by forcefully imposing closed systems of meaning.

Amusement

This approach to humor also provides a new way to look at amusement (often defined simply as a state of experiencing humor). Derisive amusement derives satisfaction from cruelty. Derisive amusement "plays" with the world by dividing the world into component parts and finds pleasure in manipulating those parts in ways that eliminate the possibilities of others while enforcing one's power over others. Derisive amusement uses others as sources of entertainment—particularly when the entertainment in question "tests" the victim. This reduces the subject to a mere object; whose abilities and possibilities exist for being used by the perpetrator.

We can contrast this reduction with an open-ended theory of amusement—a theory in which none of the elements or variables of the equation are regarded as superior, in which all members function as nondiscrete sources of possibility. Open-ended amusement "plays" in the world without seeking to control the world. Open-ended amusement delights in the possibilities of the situation but without reducing those possibilities to mere instrumentality. This is distinctly related to the interplay of rationality and absurdity. For Zhuangzi, life is a constant source of both "that's it" and "that's not it," of reason and absurdity. A healthy sense of amusement results from accepting the world as a process of change. New possibilities emerge in every situation, develop, resolve, and then blossom again in the next moment. In summary, Zhuangzi's sages have an emotional capacity for sustained suspension of certainty. The capacity for suspending certainty allows the sage to consider possibilities and be entertained by possibilities—and to understand which possibilities are sustaining, interdependent possibilities. This "wandering heart-mind" replaces the "closed heart-mind," and the sage nourishes the ability to continually engage possibility.

CONCLUSIONS: HUMOR AND SOCIAL MORAL PSYCHOLOGY

This moral psychology of humor, based on Zhuangzi's attitudes and writings, offers important insights to how we conduct ourselves in contemporary affairs. Humor and amusement play important roles in our relationships with the world around us, with others, and with society at large. In each of these cases, we see benefits of being able to relinquish the problems related to fixation: we can relinquish tired concepts that no longer illuminate new possibilities; we can relinquish judgments that lead to pointless disputation; we can discover the points of correspondence that lead to misunderstanding; and we can identify possibilities that sustain different-but-interrelated approaches to human flourishing.

Zhuangzi's humor can also helps create a healthier relationship with language, where we use language, but realize its limitations. Zhuangzi asks, "Where can I find someone who has forgotten words, so that I might have a word with them?" (Ziporyn 2009, 113). As noted by Terry Pratchett, imagination is a central facet of human experience: our capacity to imagine and postulate new ideas creates intricate possibilities for interacting with the world. As Mitch Hedberg notes, what may be completely meaningful in one context may drive us completely insane in another. If we insist on clinging to rigidly narrow interpretations of language and the signals used to create meaning, we will inevitably stumble into confusion and chaos. As Goya somberly noted, the dreams of reason can indeed produce monsters (Goya, 1969).

Finally, a Zhuangzian sense of humor has its own sense of comedy and tragedy. In this approach to humor, we can laugh at the absurdities of reason because we can live despite our misunderstandings. This does not mean that reason cannot cause tragedy—reason provides ample material for tragedy. Rather, this means that if we can recognize and accept the limitations of understanding, then life can be more forgiving of our mistakes. This forgiveness is not the forgiveness of a rational being or the forgiveness of divine compassion. Rather, this forgiveness is the give of a world that allows space for failure while simultaneously providing new opportunities for living. In this model, the tragedy of human life is our continued attempt to control the world and subsume the world to a given set of ends, which in turn reduces the world's capacity to forgive human mistakes—to the point where life no longer possesses the flexibility to accommodate the mistakes of human understanding.

Finally, we can see here how Zhuangzi's sense of humor is not merely an individual linguistic therapy. Zhuangzi's sense of humor emerges from a spirit of playful wandering that views all life as a form of playful wandering. As we play within life, exploring possibilities, life is a process of constantly exploring possibilities. Within this idea of life as constant play, Zhuangzi fearlessly celebrates a vision of all life delighting in the capacity for living *as* a part of the process of transformation. Here we see that Zhuangzi's spirit of playful, wandering humor is possible not in spite of the uncertainty of the world, but because of the continual possibility of the world:

> Tian Gen roamed along the sunny slopes of Mt. Yin, until he came upon a nameless man on the banks of the Liao River. He said to him, "How is the world to be managed?"
>
> The nameless man said, "Away with, you boor! What a dreary question! I was just about to go chum around as a human being with the Creator of Things. When I get tired of that, I'll ride off on a bird formed from the unkempt wisps of air, out beyond the six extremities of the known world, roaming in the homeland of nothing at all, thereby taking my place in the borderless wilds. Why do you come here to bother my mind with this business about ordering the world?"
>
> But Tian Gen asked the same question again. The nameless man then said, "Let your mind roam in the flavorless, blend your vital energy with the boundless silence, follow the rightness of the way each thing already is without allowing yourself the least bias. Then the world will be in order." (Ziporyn 2009, 50)

REFERENCES

Ames, Roger T. and Henry Rosemont. 1998. *The Analects of Confucius: A Philosophical Translation*. New York: Ballantine Pub. Group.

Aristotle. 2007. *On Rhetoric: A Theory of Civic Discourse*. Translated by George A. Kennedy. 2nd ed. New York: Oxford University Press.

Böll, Heinrich. 1995. "Anecdote Concerning the Lowering of Productivity," in *The Stories of Heinrich Böll*. Translated by Leila Vennewitz. Northwestern University Press.

Crandell, Michael Mark. 1983. "On Walking without Touching the Ground: 'Play' in the Inner Chapters of the *Chuang-tzu*," in *Experimental Essays on Chuang-tzu*. Edited by Victor H. Mair, 101–24. Honolulu: University of Hawai'i Press.

Fraser, Chris. 2014. "Wandering the Way: A Eudaimonistic Approach to the Zhuāngzǐ." *Dao: A Journal of Comparative Philosophy*, Vol. 13, no. 4: 541–65.

Froese, Katrin. 2013. "Humour as the Playful Sidekick to Language in the *Zhuangzi*." *Asian Philosophy*, Vol. 23, no. 2: 137–52.

Geaney, Jane. 2002. *On the Epistemology of the Senses in Early Chinese Thought*. Honolulu: University of Hawai'i Press.

Goya, Francisco. (1799) 1969. "El sueño de la razón produce monstruos," *Los Caprichos*. New York: Dover Publications.
Hedberg, Mitch. 2002. Strategic Grill Locations (Live). Comedy Central (Recorded Jan. 1, 1999).
Hedberg, Mitch. 2003. Mitch All Together. Comedy Central (Recorded December 9, 2003).
Helsing, Carl. 2019. "The Wandering Heart-Mind: Zhuangzi and Moral Psychology in the Inner Chapters," *Dao: A Journal of Comparative Philosophy*, Vol. 18, no. 4: 555–575.
Kant, Immanuel. (1970) 2007. *Critique of Judgement*. Translated by James creed Meredith, edited by Nicholas Walker. Oxford: Oxford University Press.
Kuehn, Manfred. 2001. *Kant: A Biography*. New York: Cambridge University Press.
Liu Xiaogan. 1994. *Classifying the Zhuangzi Chapters*. Ann Arbor: The University of Michigan, Center for Chinese Studies.
Mair, Victor H. 1983. "Chuang-tzu and Erasmus: Kindred Wits," in Experimental Essays on Chuang-tzu. Edited by Victor H. Mair, 85-100. Honolulu: University of Hawai'i Press.
McMahon, Philip A. 1917. "On the Second Book of Aristotle's Poetics and the Source of Theophrastus' Definition of Tragedy." *Harvard Studies in Classical Philology*, Vol. 28: 1–46.
Sellman, James D. 1988. "Transformational Humor in the *Zhuangzi*," in *Wandering at East in the Zhuangzi*, edited by Roger T. Ames, 163–74. Albany: State University of New York Press.
Wang, Youru. 2000. "Philosophy of Change and Deconstruction of Self in the *Zhuangzi*," *Journal of Chinese Philosophy* Vol. 27, no. 3: 345–360.
Ziporyn, Brook. 2009. *Zhuangzi: The Essential Writings*. Translated by Brook Ziporyn. Indianapolis: Hackett Publishing, Inc.

Chapter 12

Starting from the Muses
Engaging Moral Imagination through Memory's Many Gifts
Guy Axtell

1. INTRODUCTION: MOTHER OF THE MUSES

In Greek mythology the Muses—patron goddesses of fine arts, history, humanities, and science—are portrayed as the nine daughters of Zeus and Mnemosyne; she, the earthly goddess Memory, is of the race of Titans, older still than Zeus and the other gods of Olympus. We sense the Muses' presence in the expressive arts, but more widely in any study which we aspire to be good at. Hesiod felt his Muses in the hills of Mount Helicon where he purports to have both tended sheep and honed his skills as an oral bard. They inspired his poems including *Theogony* and *Works and Days*. In these poems, the Muses' first home is Mount Olympus, where they are favorite daughters of Zeus. When the gods are at peace and leisure, they bring a "mirth" and "gladdening of hearts" which then extends outwards to humankind. Mnemosyne's gifts to us are her daughters, and the comforts and joys they each bring. As Hesiod writes, "Every man is fortunate whom the Muses love; the voice flows sweet from his lips" (West 1988, 96–97).

When a bard sits his audience down aside a fire or addresses a crowd in a more formal public setting such as a festival, storytelling customarily begins, as we see in the proems to Hesiod's two great works, with a sort of ritual act of calling upon the Muses. In the Invocation of the Muses section which begins *Theogony*, Hesiod has the Muses collectively reply to the humans who piously call upon them; they encourage these beseechers to seek through them not only artistic inspiration and delight but also knowledge and wisdom:

> We know how to tell many believable lies, But also, when we want to, how to speak the plain truth . . . So start from the Muses: For when they sing for Zeus

Father they thrill and delight the great mind deep in Olympus, telling what is, what will be, and what has been . . . until these thundering Halls of Zeus shine in his laughter! (West, 1988, 26–28, 36–37)[1]

While a strong positive *pathos* (shared values and concerns) is created between bards, singing with a lyre, and their listening audience, "invoking" the Muses also functions to strongly enhance these poets' *ethos:* their credibility and authority *for* their audience. However humbly they might give credit to the goddess for the truth and beauty of their words, they are establishing the storytelling as a sacred event, insinuating that epic tales are of divine origin, and confirming to their audience that poets, as keepers of cultural memory, are both honorable and wise. Since the Muses of poetry and story/history, through the will of Zeus, have the ability to memorialize the deeds and achievements of some but deny it to others, this power for all practical purposes is in the hands, or in the voice, of the poet. The power of cultural memory and the authority of those able to transmit it is quite apparent in the *Odyssey* (BK VIII, 512–514) where Odysseus entreats King Alkinoos' blind court poet to remember him alongside other heroes of the Trojan War; he even first butters him up to this request by proclaiming in the king's presence, "All men owe honor to the poets—honor and awe, for they are dearest to the Muse who puts upon their lips the ways of life" (Fitzgerald 1998, 159).

But connections of the arts and sciences to memory are much richer than emphasis on social functions of storytelling allows us to see. Hesiod's genealogical myth of Mnemosyne and her daughters runs much deeper. In "The Mother of the Muses: In Praise of Memory," Clara Claiborne Park (1981) points out that "to make the Muses the daughters of Memory is to express a fundamental perception of the way in which creativity operates . . . The Muses, for Hesiod, inspire all those arts of communication that inform, delight, civilize, and link us with the past and with our fellows" (West 1988, 56). The relationship between memory and such fields as epic poetry, history or music and dance is easily recognizable to moderns. Each requires quite serious study and practice in order to achieve any degree of proficiency, and "mastery" is probably a relative term. Oral storytelling certainly served functions of codifying a people's sense of identity; the epics, though they encompass not just a human but a supernatural or spiritual world, and human-divine interaction, help create "tradition" (literally, "to hand down") and moral lessons and exemplars. But commemoration, even in an oral culture running back through Homer centuries earlier than Hesiod, is not the only, even if it is the most apparent, value. What these poets knew who invoked the Muses with their audience, was that remembering, forgetting, and imagining should *each* be esteemed as, in Hesiod's words, "gifts of the goddesses." Such is the healing powers of the arts in ancient thought. Not only rememberings (commemoratings, memorializings, celebratings) but also forgettings and imaginings are appreciated in the Athenian golden age as divine "gifts."

Each of these three, this chapter will argue, holds some direct bearing on the development of moral emotions.[2] We will examine ways that amusements, broadly understood, engage with the economy of memory, and function to educate the moral emotions. The moral economy of memory and representation is an important focus of study for moral psychology, philosophy of emotions, and philosophy of imagination. We will seek to naturalize the generous activity of the Muses by examining the economy of memory, and the ways that amusements engage with it at the same time that they engage the moral imagination.[3] While my initial examples of the moral value/disvalue of rememberings, forgettings, and imaginings are mostly drawn from classical Greek and Chinese cultures, these points I will suggest may also be applicable to the best design of networks and computer games, and to what Chris Bateman (2018) terms cyber virtues and vices.

Humor excuses much, especially when presented as only personal musing, or as a play for the annual City Dionysia. For example, the all-male stage actors and audience of the plays performed in the Athenian amphitheater could easily choose to ignore such ironies as women running the city better than them in *Ecclesiazusae (Assembly of Women)*; they could similarly take it as ridiculous that their wives forcing their cooperation and compromise with the Spartans through using a sex-strike against them in *Lysistrata*. Yet these comic "absurdities" were at least lessons in imaginative perspective-shifting, and in the possibilities of more cooperative or win-win thinking, generally. Even if the audience would not likely take them as seriously suggesting radical moral and/or political reform, it is clear that the value of good satire includes the ability to utilize cultural differences to critique one's own culture's assumptions.[4] It is important to our thesis of humor's contribution to the development of moral emotions that humor, and not just tragedy, epic, or philosophy, can investigate "universal" concerns and insights: those that reflect on the human condition, or life lessons.

In Aristophanes' *Ecclesiazusae* for example, conceptual incongruities arise as utopian dreams collide with unquestioned moral traditions and political institutions.[5] For when Athenian women come in charge of the city's ruling Assembly (purportedly as a strategy of last resort since nothing *else* has worked), they immediately begin to propose major utopian-*qua*-egalitarian reforms. The greater the moral and cognitive dissonance that satire instigates, the more that these incongruities work to create humor.[6] So satire and not just tragedy, or epic, or philosophy, can lead people to reflect upon "universal" questions. Very likely, it was in order to rebut the opinion that all wisdom is in the more traditional forms that Aristophanes elsewhere has one of his characters bravely declare, "Comedy, too, can sometimes discern what is right. I shall not please, but I shall say what is true" (Aristophanes 2013, 32, lines 500–501). But the moral dissonance the audience of Aristophanes *Ecclesiazusae* will experience, and the moral incongruity which produces comic humor, is also a fine example of amusing yet thought-provoking satire:

Praxagora: I want all to have a share of everything and all property to be in common; there will no longer be either rich or poor; [. . .] I shall begin by making land, money, everything that is private property, common to all . . .
Blepyrus: But who will till the soil?
Praxagora: The slaves. (Aristophanes 2013, lines 590–591 & 597–598 & 651)

2. REMEMBERINGS

a. Commemoration and Competition

The commemoration of greatness in Greek and Roman cultures of antiquity illustrates how central their own cultural history was to them.[7] Narrative structure implicates memetic connections: a story must itself be remembered, something often aided by metered verses sung with accompaniment of a musical instrument. Sacred narratives or mythology provided the bulk of narrative content for the arts to work with, but there were also statues and commemorations of many sorts. What is unique is the ways that the Greeks sought to recognize and remember greatness of many kinds. Orators, painters, sculptors, musicians, poets, and stage choreographers, no less than champions in physical contests and Pan-Hellenic games, might vie for special recognition. Competitions in martial, but also plastic and performing arts were of such interest to the Athenians that if they couldn't hope to achieve cultural immortality in the way of ancient heroes who interacted with the gods, the Greeks still saw themselves as competing for honor and glory under the constant gaze of those gods from above. More practically, success might well mean having their names inscribed in stone as winners, and as benefactors of the city, and receive "meals and a pension" (as Socrates, after his conviction, tells the jury that as teacher and benefactor of Athens, he deserves "far more than punishment").

Both pride and shame can be the basis for remembering, and imagination can motivate but also distort pride and shame. Hesiod's *Works and Days* begins with a mythologically cast distinction between "good" and "bad" eris. Hesiodic "good eris" creates a kind of jealously or strife "between potter and potter" which is "good for people." Bad eris he associates with no such positive work ethic, but rather with ambitions of killing, of war, or of mastery over others. Bad jealousy or strife, we also learn, is not respectful of Themis (Divine Law) or her civilizing daughters (Justice, Order, and Peace); by its disrespect it shows its allegiance instead with calamity of all sorts, mythologically (and moralistically) depicted as the frightful "children of Night": Thanatos; Nemesis; the vengeful Furies, the Keres or battlefield goddesses of cruel and unnatural death, and many more.[8]

In the Athenian golden age, the arts flourished and winners of competitions of all sorts were commemorated and remembered in ways meant to add their achievements to a cultural memory that is partly historical but also extends back to a mythological past of gods and heroes. In "Homer's Contest," an essay written shortly after *The Birth of Tragedy*, Friedrich Nietzsche skillfully explains just how *agonistic* (competitive; combative) Greek society was. Those bloodlusts which predominated in the earlier Homeric age and in that of the Mycenaeans featured in Homeric epic, remained ever-present. Nietzsche also recounts several historical instances of people being remembered for shameful, savage, pettiness, hubristic actions. The potter vying with potter were not just over the pots themselves but over the paintings that adorned them, common examples of which include depictions of Olympic games, or instead of fairly gruesome acts of *hubris* in mythology, such as Achilles dragging Hector's dead body behind his chariot. This contrast reflects the moral message of this same thin line between striving for achievement and committing an act of *hubris* deserving the wrath of the gods.

The Greek genius and the achievements of the golden age Nietzsche attributes in no small part to the invention of formalized contests, competitions which served to redirect or "channel" our aggressive drives and baser emotions. But the struggle never ends; the attempt to tame or civilize the baser instincts and ancient bloodlust is never secure. In any age, the closeness of the one eris to the other needs to be acknowledged not just by society as a whole, but by each individual as he or she copes with it. Moral development in part just is its successful maintenance of this line by the individual, who in turn draws upon cultural memory in the form of exemplars of both good and bad eris.[9]

b. Museums and Cultural Memory

Besides Zeus' shining halls, the Muses are seen as potentially present to any human setting where creative and artistic excellence are fostered or specific crafts (*techne;* τέχνη) like astronomy, history, or medicine are pursued. But their more formal earthly home is the "museum" itself, originally meaning "shrine to the Muses." The politics of museums can serve as a prime example of amusements that directly involve us in moral debate over cultural memory and its ownership. When a museum's collections have a history stemming from war, colonialism, or economic and cultural dominance, their leading narratives have come under scrutiny. Today, for example, there is ongoing debate about the ethics of collecting artifacts such as native people's bones, and African or native people's rituals ornaments. Attitudes toward museum holdings appear to be in flux. The older "white man's burden" rationale of removal for the sake of preservation and appreciation is increasingly challenged by persons who identify with groups whose cultural memory is on display and found to be presented with a certain "master" narrative. The most high-profile case in point is the long-standing debate concerning whether the British Museum should maintain its ownership of the Parthenon Marbles or submit to pressure to repatriate them to their native Greece. That these were, until only recently, widely referred to and identified as the "Elgin Marbles" after the colonial appropriator Thomas Bruce, Seventh Earl of Elgin, who removed them from the Parthenon and Acropolis (he claimed with consent of the Ottomans who ruled Greece at the start of the nineteenth century) and sold them to the British government, is itself part of the long-standing battle over how they should be remembered. The renaming of the marbles by their name of origin rather than collector may be a significant step forward, even while the museum maintains its stance against demands for their repatriation.

This of course is but one instance of the debate over cultural memory, identity, and the modern museum. As Graham Black (2011) points out in "Museums, Memory, and History,"

> The process by which communities and nations remember collectively itself has a history. For museums, as for the official memory written by historians, selectivity has been a key element. The core criticism of museums as instruments of the state is that the version of the past they have given form to is based on the selective collection, preservation and presentation of evidence of past human society. (415)

"Preserving-saving" is for some a euphemistic phrase for confiscated property. Black writes in the backdrop of a repatriation-of-antiquities movement which has been gaining strength over recent decades. The key critical concern he identifies is the prioritizing of elites:

> Objects relating to wealthier classes have a far higher likelihood of survival . . . [I]n the process of collecting this material, museums both create knowledge and manipulate it, and through interpretation and transmission they define its relative importance or authority. Meanwhile, the silences in a museum's collections and narratives is just as revealing. What goes unacknowledged, accidentally or purposely "forgotten"? (Black 2011, 421)

Supporters of the repatriation movement, including groups of native peoples, see a return of artifacts as a symbolic means of healing a past wrong, and a kind of restitution for earlier humiliation. In this sense, it allows forgetting of wrongs, insofar as museum collections much like trophies from safari, were the handmaids of colonialism. Although focused on the more overt case of Hitler's confiscations and plundering of art during World War II, the book and film, *The Monuments Men* has in an indirect way spurred thinking about what distinguishes the colonial-era acquisition of certain high-profile museum collections from mere exploitation. The response to demands for repatriation of antiquities is typically one that concedes the colonial background, but bids people to set this aside as now historical, and to join in the educational ideals of the "universal museum": One should be able to experience all things in one place, under one roof. The "return" of artifacts presupposes the fiction that the activists are owners of particular cultural traditions and reflects cultural particularism or segregation.

3. FORGETTINGS

The passage of time and the availability of amusements and interests in arts, literature, or science greatly aids our ability to cope with, and to recover from distress or sufferings of our own. Hesiod speaks of the *emotion* of amusement in terms of "respite from cares" through "care-free hearts" moved by song, story, and other a-musements (no-troublings/cares). Attention-diverting pleasures, whether of arts, science, or simply of humor or good conversation with friends, are forgettings which grant repose to persons from distress, anxiety, fear, or grief. As early as Solon's *Prayer to the Muses* (sixth century BCE), scholars have pointed out, the gifts of Muses were understood to consist "not only in the grief-destroying power of song but also in the persuasion and the 'intellectual' achievement of the king who succeeds in talking the parties of a lawsuit into a peaceful settlement of their conflicting claims" (Allen 1949, 64).

On the social scale, forgetting and forgiveness allow for the ebbing of cycles of vengeance and the re-emergence of social compacts and the mutual benefits of trust. Dan O'Shannon (2015) in this connection notes the old saying, "Tragedy plus time equals comedy." The value of *safe distance*, he suggests, "allows us to enjoy pain on several levels. There may be a conscious or unconscious element of relief in laughter, as in the sudden realization that we can be close to this experience of harm and yet not be hurt" (7).[10] Apollo is a god associated with healing, and if this were only through the actual medical arts then the poets would not be depicted so often in the company of the Muses, and as having Thalia, the masking and unmasking Muse of comedy and humor, as his most genuine romance. Thalia, whose name is etymologically connected with "flourishing" and "joyous," is a goddess not just of theater but more generally of laughter and joyful play (perhaps ironically, though, for a god some feminists describe as a "master rapist").

But mocking humor and even Socratic irony was a contentious issue in the new Athenian city-state, as it was taken by many to connote anti-democratic values or traits of character. Yet our human *aptitude* for laughter, and the benefit we derive not just from theater but from arts and sciences is mythologically an *aphthonos*, or "generous activity" of the gods. This aptitude or capacity is a gift-bestowed on humankind, a gift depicted as stemming from the divine laughter instilled in mighty Zeus by his loving and ever-surprising daughters.

Words inspired by the Muses are classically associated with peace and calm, and with the social rewards of sweet, soft words in contrast to harsh, contentious ones. Indeed, like Homer and Hesiod, Aristophanes within his own poetry (*Frogs*, performed 403 BCE) finds time to laud the poets, and by extension, a broader range of arts for many of what moderns would call "prosocial" sentiments and achievements.

> Look how right from the start the noble poets have been useful—been teachers: Orpheus taught us initiations and avoidance of bloodletting, Mousaious taught divination and cures for sickness, and Hesiod, the working of the soil and the seasons of harvest and plowing. (O'Neill, 2013)

Forgetting, to the extent that it allows a rebuilding of trust, is a unifier of discordant aims. One literary example of this aspect of the healing power of the arts is the *Aeneid*. Greek and Roman poet often engaged in etymological "play" with the names and associations of the gods, and here Virgil juxtaposes Juno's grudges and plans for vengeance with the memory actively fostered by the Muses, who are of such a nature that they seek *concordia* and work through concordant purposes. As Alex Hardie (2007) in "Juno, Hercules, and the Muses at Rome" comments,

> "Mindful anger" and its corollary in revenge is of course a very old idea (indeed the homophone endings *memorem* . . . *iram* might be designed to recall the sound-similarity of Greek *menis* ("anger") and *mnēmnō* ("mindful"); anger, in other words, is inherently endowed with a long memory). Juno's "mindful anger" evidently has to do with the goddess' capacity for harbouring grudges, and it is recognisable, in terms more immediately applicable in the civic sphere, as the standard political fault of *mnēsikakein* ("harbouring grudges") . . . Juno's

inability to set aside former *causae irarum* in the interests of general harmony is a fundamental component of her discordant character within the poem. (571–572)

Martha Nussbaum and others who appreciate tragedy's contributions to educating moral emotions will agree with the Greeks and with Aristotle (and contemporary psychology) that the experiencing of negative emotions of grief and suffering is not without purgative and educative value.[11] Nussbaum's book *Anger and Forgiveness* (2018) provides rich historical and literary examples of overcoming cycles of violent retribution and of the zero-sum or loss-loss thinking the fuels it. While acknowledging anger some inevitability, she tries to show how it is often a confused and damaging moral emotion.

Ancient tragedies dealt deeply with universal themes of retribution and grief, and Nussbaum's own main literary example of virtuous forgettings is Aeschylus' tragic trilogy, *The Oresteia,* which is known to have won first prize at the Dionysia festival in 458 BCE. The trilogy is named for the central character Orestes, who sets out to avenge the murder of his father Agamemnon by his own (undoubtedly abused) mother, Clytemnestra. Vengeance or vendetta and justice, and the emergence of law out of a more primitive system of vendettas, are its central themes as Nussbaum articulates them. But what she finds especially insightful are trilogy's concluding scenes. The slaying of Clytemnestra and her lover by Orestes does not end the cycle of violence, but unleashes the Furies, divine avengers, to pursue and punish Orestes for his act of matricide. The justice of their retribution on Orestes is eventually brought to trial before the gods, with wise Athena aiding the pardon of Orestes and proclaiming that matters of retribution or punishment shall henceforth be settled in court rather than be carried out personally or outside of law. But to undergird this societal shift in the conception of justice, one which quelled endless cycles of retaliation and analogized them to a curse, Athena actually renames the force from the Furies. She names them the Eumenides, meaning the "gracious ones," which in effect disconnects justice from backward-looking retribution and attaches it to a broader set of forward-looking concerns including social stability, the welfare of the polis and its citizens, and the healing of wounds. *The Oresteia* concludes on these surprisingly optimistic themes of renewal and of moving beyond cycles of vendetta-justice, and to further ensure that the audience is ushered out into the streets in a high mood of revelry, the audience would have seen a short comical satyr play to conclude the evening's official festivities.

The healing power of time and of the arts as diversions and sources of amusement, connects with psychological study of the *fading affect bias* (FAB), which refers to the demonstrated greater dwindling of unpleasant compared to pleasant emotions in autobiographical memory. We appear to have an instinct to heal, since the FAB is recognized since a ubiquitous emotion regulating phenomenon in autobiographical memory. Ritchie et al. (2015), for example, disclose studies showing that positive affect fades slower than negative affect. "Results suggest that in tandem with local norms and customs, the FAB may foster recovery from negative life events and promote the retention of the positive emotions, within and outside of the USA" (278). Affective fading is generally greater for negative events/memories than for positive events/memories, but this greater dwindling of unpleasant compared to pleasant emotions is impacted by other traits. Dysphorics and those with depression or anxiety disorders show a smaller fading affect than nondysphorics.

We could also find ancient Chinese examples of successful and failed forgettings.[12] One of the most famous plays of China is *The Peony Pavilion*, a tragi-comedy of the human condition written in the Ming style by Tang Xianzu, who lived contemporaneously with Shakespeare and is sometimes referred to as the 'Shakespeare of China'. The play features a young woman, Miss Du, who falls asleep in a peony field. In the dream sequences typical of the Ming style (often shared in modern Peking opera), she meets and falls in deeply love with a young, handsome scholar. This young man Liu is real, but she has never met him and upon awakening to find his memory but a dream, she develops an all-consuming lovesickness, and a utopian desire for a kind of pure, unfettered love that would have been impossible in the characters' structured society. At the end of the first act Miss Du, unable to forget, eventually mourns herself to death. But in the second act Liu, passing on foot years later through the garden where she is buried, learns her story through a self-portrait she had left before dying. Liu falls into a love with the dead girl so genuine that the Flower Goddess and the Judge of Hell eventually get involved and conspire to resurrect Miss Du in order to fulfill what is seen as a destiny that time and circumstance had unjustly prevented. The two characters' inability to forget initially brings them great sorrow, yet through the power of their virtuous forgetting of the rigid social roles and codes, true love in the end prevails.

To conclude this section, let us consider some of the criticisms of amusements as aids to psychological well-being. Marx allowed that humans have an intrinsic need to engage in some creative activity, but he portrayed retreat into constant amusement as a dysfunctional response to one's state of alienation. As one contemporary historical material puts it,

> Only in the bourgeois world has the idea become the norm that the primary purposes of art are the self-expression of the artist and the entertainment of the public. . . . With entertainment, the artist compromises his self-expression to pander to the tastes of the masses so that he or she can make a living. At the same time, with the control by big business of most of the mass media that

entertainers depend on, entertainment has often played a reactionary role in dumbing down the masses' view of the world and encouraging escapism as an alternative to class struggle. (O'Shea 2015)

Escapist withdrawal through endless amusements might give one a sense of individual autonomy, while in reality leaving individuals more isolated and less motivated or equipped to find the solidarity with others. Other critics of big media have worried that we are, in Neil Postman's terms, "amusing ourselves to death" (1984), and they sound a Huxleyan warning of its goal of pacifying its consumers and keeping them glued to advertising or political agendas. Amusements and the forgettings they allow might be sought as compensation for a deficit of opportunities for meaningful choices and genuinely human relations.

These criticisms of amusements deserve serious reflection. But if contemporary amusements like video games are "escapes" from reality, they are rarely *only* so. They are less passive than many give them credit for, and today's youth do not demote virtual realities or contrast reality and fantasy as past generations have. Contemporary amusements and virtual worlds are, but are not *only*, "escapes" from troubles. With Jean Baudrillard, today's youth tend to accord reality to simulations along a spectrum, and reject the Platonic binary of one's being either "in reality" or "under illusion." Years ago, when I presented to my students "The Matrix" movie's choice between "taking the red or the blue pill," uncomfortable truth or pleasant medicated illusion, they almost unanimously vowed they would take the red pill no matter how far down the rabbit hole they might fall. It seems to me not merely anecdotal that today by comparison many more of my students, when presented with the Matrix or "The Experience Machine" thought experiments that have been staples of introductory philosophy classes for decades, will respond that while truth and freedom are values, their decision would also turn on just how badly "reality" sucks.

4. IMAGININGS

According to contemporary enactivists and narrativists like Daniel Hutto and Peter Goldie, the emotions have a structure that is "ripe for narrativity" (Hutto 2006, 17).[13] Many scholars have described how vital stories are to our sense of individual identity and collective belonging. Some go further to assert and develop the educative value of stories, which may present conflicts and dilemmas that spur critical reflection. Larry Hill (n.d.), a Seneca storyteller, writes,

> Our stories were us, what we knew, where we came from and where we were going. They were told to remind of us of our responsibility, to instruct, and to

entertain. There were stories of the Creation, our travels, our laws. There were legends of hard-fought battles, funny anecdotes—some from the smokehouse, some from the trickster—and there were scary stories to remind us of danger, spiritual and otherwise. Stories were our life and they still are.[14]

Let us briefly return to Nussbaum's work, since she has been one of the strongest and most eloquent proponents of the benefits of literature and narrative imagination for moral development. In *The New Religious Intolerance* (2012) she discusses how sympathetic imagination makes others real for us:

> A common human failing is to see the whole world from the point of view of one's own goals, and to see the conduct of others as all about oneself . . . By imagining other people's way of life, we don't necessarily learn to agree with their goals, but we do see the reality of those goals for them. We learn that other worlds of thought and feeling exist. Nussbaum calls on educators to counter new and old forms of intolerance "through deliberate cultivation of the imagination." (143–144)[15]

The "participatory imagination" she takes as a primate inheritance, but as one inviting us to see others as intelligibly pursuing human goals. The participatory imagination can raise awareness of what John Rawls (1996) calls the "burdens of judgement" (154–158), and to this extent support tolerance and mutual respect (what Rawls terms reasonable pluralism). For empirical support, Nussbaum (2012) cites the studies of Daniel Batson as showing "that vivid imagination leads, other things equal, to helping behavior" (146). She also holds that with the development of empathetic (moral) out of participatory imagination, people learn to "move in a direction opposite to that of fear. In fear, a person's attention contracts, focusing intently on her own safety, and (perhaps) that of a small circle of loved ones. In empathy the mind moves outward, occupying many different positions outside the self" (146).[16] This shift from contracting to expanding moral attention aids development of moral judgment and cooperative, win-win strategies of problem-solving. Empathy she concedes can have its own narcissism, and partiality can also be a "pitfall of imagination." But the directional difference from contracting to expanding one's moral attention show imagination as, on balance, "valuable as an antidote to fear's narcissism" (Nussbausm 2012, 146). Nussbaum's stance is one that draws not just on literature, but on psychology and on John Dewey's pragmatism. Dewey (1944) held that reason is an imaginative capacity, and proclaimed art and imagination to be "more moral than moralities" (350). Habit, imagination, and judgment are intimately related; "the faculty of imagination has the ability to make things present which were previously absent" (148, my italics).[17] Other pragmatists like Steven Fesmire

(2010) credit Dewey for framing a theory of ecological imagination that is compatible with contemporary cognitive research.[18]

But there is also a skepticism or pessimist that runs contrary to this optimism about the benefits of narratives that we have seen Nussbaum and others express. Skepticism may begin with a political realism about cultural or collective memory, and proceeds from there. Andrew Leutzsch investigates these conflicting views in *Historical Parallels, Commemoration and Icons* (2019) One focus of the study is the inflationary erecting of monuments and other ways that historians, professional or amateur, "prefigure the future by constructing the past" (152).

> [A]rchives store and destroy; and historians select and ignore sources—sometimes accidentally, sometimes on purpose but always because all of them are embedded in a discourse and in a net of connotations, which tells them and us what matters and what does not ... Memorials are both an indicator and a factor of the political discourse—they represent history and contribute to the making of it. [As Reinhart Koselleck puts it], "To commemorate the deceased belongs to human culture. To commemorate the fallen, violently killed, those who in battle, civil war or war died, belongs to political culture." (116)

Leutzsch acknowledges the politics of memory, but remains optimistic about historical narrative. "Whereas the contingency of the future compels us to consider what might come next, the past makes us reflect about why events transpired as they did and contributes to the reduction of the future's contingency."[19] But other authors are still more critical of the "historical fallacy," and of the value of narratives in pursuing epistemic goods of knowledge and understanding. On this minority report, storytelling and self-deception often go hand in hand.

As James Baldwin observed in a much-discussed 1970 exchange with Margaret Mead about identity, race, and moral sentiments, "What we call history is perhaps a way of avoiding responsibility for what has happened, is happening, in time" (Papova 2017).[20] Perhaps the fullest recent development of pessimism about the moral and cognitive value of historical narratives, is Alex Rosenberg's *How History Gets Things Wrong: The Neuroscience of Our Addiction to Stories* (2018). Rosenberg critiques our long-standing reliance on autobiographical, biographical, and historical narrative, presenting numerous examples of its unreliability. The narrativization and moralization of events typically go hand-in-hand, and most often our stories re-enforce us/them divisions. So much are they a reflection and re-enforcement of group biases that they undermine history's pretention to provide real understanding of the past, present, or future.

Rosenberg argues for three provocative claims counterpoint to Dewey and Nussbaum: "that our confidence in history, our taste, our need for it, indeed, our love of history is almost completely hardwired, that history is all wrong, and that its wrongness is the result of the later evolution of what was originally hardwired . . ." (Rosenberg 2018). Nussbaum's narrative optimism and Rosenberg's narrative pessimism are two contrary moral appraisals of storytelling, two contrary responses to the narrativist-enactivist claim that the emotions have a structure that is ripe with or for narration. We need not feel bound to choose between them; Rosenberg's critique of history, even if it is not overstated, may not carry over to the value of narratives which recognize themselves as fictional.[21] We can anyway take this "ripeness" as a mixed blessing. For the pro-educative and the skeptical perspectives on the moral value of narratives have at least this in common: they each tell us that we need to "Stop feeding the wrong wolf"; that is, we need to distinguish bad from good eris and accept responsibility for the problems of the world. There is a concept of German origin in recent use, *Gestaltungskompetenz*, which perhaps deserves recognition here in order to reinforce the educative potential of the moral imagination. It is a feminine noun term for the competency to shape the future; this "shaping skill" is one both of analyzing present problems and applying forward-looking problem-solving; it is a *creative* competence to shape the future.[22] Since shared stories, shared amusements, and shared humor often function as a social lubricant, their ability to support the evolution of social cooperation should be unsurprising.

5. CONCLUSION

Hesiod's theme of there being "two Eris-goddesses on earth" (West 1988, 37–38, lines 11–14) was, for Nietzsche, "one of the most noteworthy Hellenic thoughts and worthy to be impressed on the newcomer immediately at the entrance-gate of Greek ethics."[23] So too, Nietzsche adds, "if we remove the contest from Greek life, then we look at once into the pre-Homeric abyss of horrible savagery, hatred, and pleasure in destruction" (Nietzsche 1977, 145–146). Contests of all sorts allowed the Greeks to channel their aggressive drives into great and works and memorable achievements. This is the good *eris* at work, the kind in which potter competes with potter for excellence, playwright with playwright. But as Nietzsche insists, the line between motivating and "hateful" envy is quite thin; both for individuals and for groups, it can be difficult not to cross over into spite and odium, too often with dire consequences.

So how can amusements involving rememberings, forgettings, and imaginings better serve critical thinking and other pedagogical functions through actively engaging the moral imagination? How can they be examples of good and not bad *eris*? These questions I suspect need to be asked with respect to the design of computer games and human-machine relationships of all kinds. Posing them helps us further identify what Chris Bateman (2018) terms the cyber virtues/vices which we encounter in relationship with games and online groups/networks.[24] Relational virtuosity does not stop with relations only between human, or between humans and animals, but extends to human-machine relations as well. And Aristophanes was right: humor or comedy can also tell truth; it can, as he has Aeschylus say of *all* the poets, "rouse the citizenry to strive to equal" them, and to emulate the hero-types. We would be better off in the study of amusement had the ability to engage universals of the human condition and to provoke reflective morality never been ceded to only the "serious" poetic forms of epic and tragedy. Given also that use of humor and of computers contributes to student-focused learning, it is important that the educative potential of laughter and of amusements more generally be brought to the fore. "Funny is the new deep," as Steve Almond (2015) puts it, and we have here endeavored to connect this with the ability of amusements, whether associated with remembering, forgetting, or imagining, to throw light on our human foibles, and to balance competitive games with the encouragement of cooperative strategies of problem-solving. We end, then, in agreement with Percy Shelley (1821) that, "A person to be greatly good must imagine intensely and comprehensively."

NOTES

1. I here take liberty to slightly combine lines from what are said to be two pro-ems (1–35 and 36–115).

2. Another collection which focuses on how information is often filtered, selected, and rearranged to support a single narrative is A. Leutzsch (ed.), 2019.

3. See also the Paola Ceccarelli, Silvia Milanezi, and Lea Grace Canevaro, and Catherine Darbo-Peschanski chapters in the excellent collection edited by Luca Castagnoli and Paola Ceccarelli, *Greek Memories* (2019).

4. Whether Aristophanes truly meant them as such, and why and how the audience could partake of the play but then go back to daily political life without any genuine moral impact, are two questions we must set aside.

5. For more direct connections between imagination and utopian-dystopian hopes and fears, see Darko Suvin, *Defined by a Hollow* (2000).

6. In these respects too, *bemusement* might be just as important as amusement, since bemusement perhaps more clearly brings in the universals of the human condition, putting in ironic focus our human frailties and biases, and our inability to see them.

7. In a recent collection, *Greek Memories: Theories and Practices* (2019, 151) Mirko Canevaro writes, "In fact, memory of the past, of the laws, of the culture, even of the day-to-day life of the city was a necessary attribute of the Athenian citizen."

8. Greek justice was becoming heir to Themis, with her balanced scales. As early as Pindar (fifth century BCE) the daughters of "wise-counselled" (*euboulos*) Themis/Justitia were girls whose names meant such things as "Good Order," and "Peace."

9. Nietzsche places the philosophers within, rather than above, this competition. The philosophers invent a "new kind of agon" (competition) which they describe as truth and wisdom-directed, but which also explains how a figure like Socrates could inspire resentment. Nietzsche thinks of philosophers such as Plato, Thales, and Xenophanes as actively competing in and expecting to win "Homer's Contest."

10. See also Andrew Jordan and Stephanie Patridge, this volume, on Aristotle's claim in the *Politics* (VIII.3) that "Amusement is for the sake of relaxation, and relaxation is of sweet necessity, for it the remedy of pain caused by toil . . .," and on their development of Aristotle's account of *eutrapelia* as a social virtue.

11. For recent philosophical and psychological research on these topics see Michael Brady and other chapters in Laurie Candiotti (ed.) 2019 collection *The Value of Emotions for Knowledge.*

12. For more on humor, laughter, amusement and pleasure in Chinese tradition, see especially Michael Nylan's rich work, *The Chinese Pleasure Book* (2018). On smart humor in Zhuangzi in particular, see Axtell 2016, Dull (Helsing) 2012 and this volume, Moeller 2017, and Sellmann 1998. On connections with the concept of relational virtuosity discussed below, see the works of Peter Hershock and Roger Ames.

13. For discussion of the "narrative alternative to theory of mind," see Shaun Gallagher (2006), esp. 224, and Hutto's response. See also Goldie, 2012.

14. Relatedly, *Psychology Today* recently highlighted humans as storytelling animals. "We thrill to an astonishing multitude of fictions on pages, on stages, and on screens: murder stories, sex stories, war stories, conspiracy stories, true stories and false. We are, as a species, addicted to story. But the addiction runs deeper than we think. We can walk away from our books and our screens, but we can never walk away from story."

https://www.psychologytoday.com/us/blog/the-storytelling-animal/201205/creatures-story

15. Nussbaum's focus is not unconnected with our previous discussion of good and bad eris. J. S. Mill (1859) for example discusses in *On Liberty* (Chapter One) "the *odium theologicum,* in a sincere bigot" as being "one of the most unequivocal cases of moral feeling."

16. In a tradition going back at least to Francis Bacon, contemporary authors such as Herman (2017) emphasize how fiction "increases the range of our vicarious experience and behavioral options." Fiction can design events and characters to provoke us to reflect on, say, generosity or threat, or deception and counterdeception. And it efficiently evokes our intense emotional engagement without requiring our belief" (Herman 2017, 5). See also Breyer (2019).

17. Dewey wrote that "only gradually and with a widening of the area of vision through a growth of social sympathies does thinking develop to include what lies beyond our direct interest: a fact of great significance for education."

18. Fesmire 2010, 189 quoting Dewey, *Art as Experience*, LW 10:348. On imagination, knowledge, and emotion see Any Kind and Peter Kung (eds.) *Knowledge through Imagination* (2016). On narrative see Harrellson (2012). Building on his earlier *Dewey and Moral Imagination* (2003), Fesmire (2012) explains how relational thinking not just in American pragmatism but also in much Eastern thought helps us better perceive the relational networks in which finite lives are embedded. Ecological thinking, as it enters into our deliberations about private choices and public policies, is a function of this sort of imagination. It aids moral awareness and serves as a tool of responsibility-through-action. "Ecological imagination is here understood as relational imagination shaped by key metaphors used in (though not necessarily originating in) the ecologies. That is, imagination is specifically 'ecological' when key metaphors and the like used in the ecologies organize mental simulations and projections. Our deliberations enlist ecological imagination when these imaginative structures (some of recent origin and some millennia old) shape what Dewey calls our dramatic rehearsals" (2012, 213). On William James' distinction of the "crude" and "subtle" emotions, and the higher moral relevance of the latter, see Axtell (2017). James, I think, was right to notice in *Principles of Psychology* "how unexpectedly great are the differences between individuals in respect of imagination." Dewey's developments of moral imagination seems to reflect this as well as James' view that "No matter how emotional the temperament may be, if imagination be poor, the occasions for touching off the emotional trains will fail to be realized, and the life will be *pro-tonto* cold and dry" (1981, 704; 1088).

19. Leutzsch, 3. He continues that "Almost-forgotten or sleeping history can be revived to legitimize an imagined future in a political discourse today." Analyzing historical analogies as they appear in narratives, iconography, movies, journalism, and so on "enables us to understand how history and collective memory are managed and used for political purposes and to provide social orientation in time and space."

20. According to Maria Papova's assessment, when the storywriter and playwright James Baldwin said, "*We made the world we're living in and we have to make it over*," he was exploring the paradoxical ways in which we imprison ourselves even as we pursue our liberty. One the one hand, "we can only make a broken world over if we first closely examine its parts—that is, its pasts—and take responsibility for the conditions as well as the consequences of its brokenness. And yet, too often, we flee and burrow in the comforting certitude of our history, which is not the same as our past, no matter how false and hubristic such certitude may be" (Papova 2017).

21. We can take the many theories of humor traditionally on offer, as O'Shannon (2015) does, as best seen as "parts in search of an elephant": "when we gather these basic theories together, it begins to look as though people have been approaching comedy from different directions. Some theories concerning the comedy's content, others are based on the feelings that arise from the comedic experience, and others are process-related" (10).

22. One sees this new "heroic" virtue exemplified, for example, in the *Tomorrowland* movie characters Casey Newton, an optimistic teen who refuses to accept technological determinism and the easy moral rationalizations for inaction it supplies, and Athena, the more-human-than-most-of-us android who recruits just such dreamers and innovative can-doers as Casey and the young (pre-jaded adult and "realist") Frank Walker.

23. Nietzsche reminds us that while envy, jealousy, or strife might translate Eris for both Goddesses, Hesiod's point is that they have quite *different* moral dispositions. "For the one, the cruel one, furthers the evil war and feud! This bad eris, as the elder, gave birth to black Night." Many of the miseries sent to humans through Pandora's "jar" are of this kind. Zeus however is said to have placed the other Eris upon the roots of the earth and among men as a much better one.

24. Bateman (2018) finds it scarcely surprising that "fake news," infotainment, and still more overt propaganda "thrives in systems that discourage fidelity and thus minimize productive community" (109). Fidelity, which is what binds us to other humans and their shared practices, is a prime virtue that we need today: "fidelity is founded on the promise (literal or figurative) to be part of something and thus to foster knowledge within that community (whether we are talking sports, research, art, crafts, or anything else). Cyber-fidelity would therefore apply whenever our robots aided our commitment and our communities without simultaneously engendering our dependency . . . What I'm calling cyber-fidelity is another name for what Ivan Illich calls *convivial tools*: technology that empowers individuals within their communities, rather than creating dependence and dividing or destroying community" (110; 137).

REFERENCES

Allen, Archibald W. 1949. "Solon's Prayer to the Muses." *Transactions and Proceedings of the American Philological Association* 80: 50–65.

Almond, Steve. 2015. "Funny is the New Deep," In *Humor: A Reader for Writings*, edited by Kathleen Volk Miller and Marion Wrenn. Oxford; Oxford University Press.

Aristophanes. 2013. *Ecclesiazusae (Assemblywomen), Frogs,* and *Acharnians.* Translated by Eugene O'Neill, Jr. In *Delphi Complete Works of Aristophanes (Illustrated).* Delphi Classics.

Axtell, Guy. 2016. "Moral Learning, Imagination, and the Space of Humor." Unpublished conference paper, accessed https://www.academia.edu/28958914/Moral_Learning_Imagination_and_the_Space_of_Humor

Axtell, Guy. 2017. "The Emotions in James' *Principles of Psychology*." In *William James, Moral Philosophy, and the Ethical Life: The Cries of the Wounded.* Jacob Goodson (ed.). Lanham, MD: Lexington Books.

Bateman, Chris. 2018. *The Virtuous Cyborg.* London: Eyewear Publishing/Squint Books.

Black, Graham. 2011. "Museums, Memory and History." *Cultural and Social History* 8(3): 415–427.

Brady, Michael. 2019. "Learning from Adversity: Suffering and Wisdom." In Laurie Candiotti (ed.) *The Value of Emotions for Knowledge*. London: Palgrave Macmillan, 197–214.
Breyer, Thiemo. 2019. "Self-Affection and Perspective-Taking: The Role of Phantasmatic and Imaginatory Consciousness for Empathy." Springer Nature B.V. Published online https://doi.org/10.1007/s11245-018-9627-4
Candiotti, Laurie (ed.). 2019. *The Value of Emotions for Knowledge*. London: Palgrave Macmillan.
Canevaro, Mirko. 2019. In Castagnoli, Luca and Paola Ceccarelli (eds.), *Greek Memories: Theories and Practices*. Cambridge: Cambridge University Press.
Castagnoli, Luca and Paola Ceccarelli (eds.). 2019. *Greek Memories: Theory and Practice*. Cambridge: Cambridge University Press.
Dewey, J. (1944). *Democracy and education: An introduction to the philosophy of education*. New York, NY: The Free Press.
Dewey, John. *Art as Experience* (*Later Works, Vol. 10*). 1969–1991. All references to Dewey are to *The Collected Works of John Dewey*, edited by Jo Ann Boydston, 37 vols. Carbondale: Southern Illinois University Press, 1969–1991.
Dull, Carl J. 2012. "Zhuangzi and Thoreau: Wandering, Nature, and Freedom." *Journal of Chinese Philosophy* 39(2): 222–239.
Fesmire, Steven. 2003. *John Dewey's Moral Imagination: Pragmatism in Ethics*. Bloomington, IN: Indiana University Press.
Fesmire, Steven. 2010. "Ecological Imagination." *Environmental Ethics* 32(2): 183–203.
Fesmire, Steven. 2012. "Ecological Imagination in Moral Education, East and West." *Contemporary Pragmatism* 9(1): 205–222.
Gallagher, Shaun. 2006. "The Narrative Alternative to Theory of Mind." In Richard Menary (ed.) *Radical Enactivism: Intentionality, Phenomenology, and Narrative*. Amsterdam: John Benjamins Publishing, 223–230.
Goldie, Peter. 2012. *The Mess Inside: Narrative, Emotion, and the Mind*. Oxford: Oxford University Press.
Halliwell, Stephen. 2008. *Greek Laughter: A Study of Cultural Psychology from Homer to the Early Christians*. Cambridge: Cambridge University Press.
Hardie, Alex. 2007. "Juno, Hercules, and the Muses at Rome." *The American Journal of Philology* 128(4): 551–592.
Harrellson, Kevin. 2012. "Narrative Pedagogy for Introduction to Philosophy." *Teaching Philosophy* 35(2): 113–141.
Herman, David. 2017. *Storytelling and the Sciences of Mind*. Boston: MIT Press.
Herman, David. 2017. *Storytelling and the Sciences of Mind*. Boston: MIT Press.
Hesiod. *Works and Days & Theogony*. Translated by M.L. West. Oxford: Oxford University Press. 1988.
Hill, Larry. Seneca storyteller quotation accessed http://www.indians.org/welker/stories1.htm.
Homer. *The Odyssey*. Translated by Robert Fitzgerald. New York: Farrar, Straus and Giroux, 1998.
Hutto, Daniel D. 2006. *Narrative and Understanding Persons*. Cambridge: Cambridge University Press.

James, William. 1981[1890]. *Principles of Psychology* (2 volumes). Cambridge, MA: Harvard University Press.
Kind, Amy and Peter Kung (eds.). 2016. *Knowledge through Imagination.* Oxford: Oxford University Press.
Leutzsch, Andreas (ed.). 2019. *Historical Parallels, Commemoration and Icons.* London: Routledge.
Mill, John Stuart. 1859. *On Liberty.* https://www.utilitarianism.com/ol/three.html.
Moeller, Hans-Georg. 2017. *Genuine Pretending: On the Philosophy of the Zhuangzi.* New York: Columbia University Press.
Nietzsche, Friedrich. 1977. "Homer's Contest." In *The Portable Nietzsche,* edited and translated by Walter Kaufmann. New York: Penguin books.
Nussbaum, Martha. 2012. *The New Religious Intolerance: Overcoming the Politics of Fear in an Anxious Age.* Cambridge, MA: Belnap Press/Harvard University Press.
Nussbaum, Martha. 2018. *Anger and Forgiveness: Resentment, Generosity, Justice.* Oxford: Oxford University Press.
Nylan, Michael. 2018. *The Chinese Pleasure Book.* New York: Zone Books.
O'Shannon, Dan. 2015. "What are You Laughing at?" In *Humor: A Reader for Writings,* edited by Kathleen Volk Miller and Marion Wrenn. Oxford; Oxford University Press.
O'Shea, Rupert. 2015. "Marxism, Materialism and Art." In Defence of Marxism blog, https://www.marxist.com/marxism-materialism-and-art.htm
Papova, Maria. 2017. "The Muse of History." Accessed at https://www.brainpickings.org/2017/01/23/the-muse-of-history-derek-walcott/
Park, Clara C. 1981. "The Mother of the Muses: In Praise of Memory." *The American Scholar* 50(1): 55–71.
Plato, *Phaedo.* Translated by Benjamin Jowett. Accessed at The Internet Classics Archive, http://classics.mit.edu/Plato/phaedo.html
Plato. *Philebus.* Translated by Benjamin Jowett. Accessed at The Internet Classics Archive, http://classics.mit.edu/Plato/philebus.html
Postman, David. 1984. *Amusing Ourselves to Death: Public Discourse in the Age of Show Business.* New York: Elizabeth Sifton Books.
Rawls, John. 1996. *Political Liberalism.* New York: Columbia University Press.
Ritchie, T. D., T. J. Batteson, A. Bohn, M. T. Crawford, G. V. Ferguson, R. W. Schrauf, and W. Walker. 2015. "A Pancultural Perspective on the Fading Affect Bias in Autobiographical Memory." *Memory* 23(2): 278–90.
Rosenberg, Alex. 2018. *How History Gets Things Wrong: The Neuroscience of Our Addiction to Stories.* Boston: MIT Press.
Sellmann, James D. 1998. "Transformational Humor in the Zhuangzi." In Roger T. Ames (ed.), *Wandering at Ease in the Zhuangzi.* Albany: SUNY Press, 163–174.
Shelley, Percy. 1821. *A Defence of Poetry.* Accessed 12/25/2019, https://www.poetryfoundation.org/articles/69388/a-defence-of-poetry
Suvin, Darko. 2000. *Defined by a Hollow: Essays on Utopia, Science Fiction and Political Epistemology.* Oxford: Peter Lang.
Trivigno, Franco V. 2019 forthcoming. "Plato on Laughter and Moral Harm." In Franco V. Trivigno and Pierre Destreé (eds.) *Laughter and the Ancients.* Oxford: Oxford University Press.

Index

absurdity, 81, 115, 119, 190–93, 206–7, 213
aesthetics, 6, 66, 72, 73n3, 122–23, 125, 151, 153, 164–66n1, 192
affordance, 13, 20–28
amusement: benign appraisal, 66, 68–72; as emotion, 1–3, 8–9, 15, 48–49, 57, 78; etymology, 32, 41, 48–49; seriousness, 5, 49, 76, 167–68
anger/angry, 2, 5, 8, 15, 19, 22–23, 40, 78, 82, 97, 134–35, 137–38, 140, 143–45, 184, 194, 218–19
anxiety, 15, 68, 70–71, 218, 220
apology, 54, 77, 97, 102, 109, 121
aristocrats joke, 45
Aristophanes, 7, 131, 174, 213–14, 218, 225
Aristotle, 6, 8, 55, 151, 153–60, 164–65, 166n3, 166n6–9, 171, 191–93, 196–97, 219
attention, 4, 36, 41, 46–49, 55, 57–58, 79, 155, 158–59, 171, 185n15, 198–99, 201–4, 217, 222
attitudes, 4–6, 8–9, 15–16, 39, 41, 45, 48, 58, 68, 70, 73n9, 75–81, 83–86, 88–89, 91n12, 92n15–16, 97, 109–14, 117–25, 126n13, 127n19, 151–53, 155, 164–65
autoethnography, 3, 32, 36

benign violation theory. *See* humor, benign violation theory of
blackface, 113–14, 116, 118, 122
Brooks, Mel, 5
bully, 16–17, 19, 25–26

Carlin, George, 87–88, 91n14
Carroll, Noël, 4, 14–15, 45, 66–72, 73n1, 73n6, 74n9
Chaplin, Charlie, 69
Chappelle, Dave, 88
Charles, Larry, 75, 83, 85, 88, 91n10
child/children, 24, 68, 84–85, 90n2, 108, 154, 168–69, 173–74, 211
Cho, Margaret, 111
CK, Louis, 114–15
Cohen, Ted, 80, 102, 152
Colbert, Stephen, 116–17
The Colbert Report, 116, 131–32, 134, 139, 145–46
comic amoralism, 4, 65–66, 73n1
comic amusement, 15, 67, 71–72, 152
comic immoralism, 4, 45, 65–66, 73n4
comic moralism, 4, 45, 65, 68, 71–72, 73n6, 84
Confucius, 198–99
context, 25, 27, 31, 38, 49, 54–55, 57–58, 76, 78, 80–81, 84, 86–89, 109,

231

114–19, 121–22, 152–56, 158–65, 172, 186n20, 199, 207
cooperation, 3, 15–18, 24–28, 213, 222, 224–25
coordination, 3, 24–27, 116
Curb Your Enthusiasm, 14
cynicism, 97, 99–101, 134, 139–40

The Daily Show, 6, 131–32, 134, 139, 142, 145–46, 147n7
Daoism, 7, 189–90, 203
deception, 18–19, 25–26, 41, 49, 223, 226
Dewey, John, 7, 222–24, 226n17–18
disgust, 2, 14–15, 24, 91n11, 139–40
distraction, 4–5, 7, 41, 46, 49–50, 52, 55–58, 158, 160, 176

education, 46, 57–58, 81–82, 139, 155, 178–79, 181, 186n24, 213, 217, 219, 221–22, 224–25, 227n17
embarrassment, 16, 78, 100–102, 124, 126n16, 181
emotion: capacity for, 193–94, 206; competing, 140; contagious, 16, 19, 26; content/structure of, 13, 18, 20, 22, 25, 28, 137, 221, 224; control of, 21–22, 81; enactive account of, 3, 13–14, 17–18, 20, 23, 25–28, 29n5; negative, 15, 47, 51, 134, 136–45, 164n4, 217–20; positive, 46–52, 54–55, 57, 70, 72–73, 77, 133, 136–37, 140–43, 145, 220; theories of, 13, 18–20, 22, 25, 28–29, 47, 57, 70
empathy, 58, 71, 81–82, 114–15, 123, 222
entertainment, 16, 39, 90n2, 187n29, 207, 220–22
eudaimonia, 155–56, 193

fading affect bias, 217–20
fear, 15, 18–22, 24, 47, 78, 83, 134, 195, 200, 208, 217, 222, 225n5
Flanagan, Owen, 100–101, 104n4, 145
Foot, Phillipa, 96–97, 103

Freud, Sigmund, 37, 65–66
Full Frontal, 131

Gadsby, Hannah, 75
gender, 17, 35, 118, 139, 156, 186n20
Gimbel, Steven, 2, 77, 83, 90n1, 110–11, 117, 119, 121–25, 127n19–22
Gottfried, Gilbert, 59n1
Greene, Joshua, 53, 135

Haidt, Jonathan, 53, 135–36
Hedberg, Mitch, 189, 196–97, 207
Hesiod, 7, 211–12, 214, 217–18, 224, 228
Homer, 7, 154, 212, 215, 218, 224, 226n9
humor: adaptive/maladaptive theory of, 11, 31, 33–34, 37, 40, 47; anti-Semitic, 89, 95; benign violation theory of, 8, 14–19, 25, 28n1, 38, 41, 70, 125; black humor. *See* humor, gallows; derogatory, 6, 16, 107–25, 126n2, 127n23; ethnic, 39, 123, 127n21; gallows, 4, 69–70; homophobic, 39–41, 80–81, 89, 114; incongruity theory of, 8–9, 14–15, 18, 67–68, 70, 163, 213–14; mocking, 5–6, 19–20, 26, 86–87, 89, 102, 104, 110–11, 115, 118, 157, 173, 183–84; offensive, 17, 28n1, 38, 98, 114, 117, 124, 157; parody, 76, 82; political, 5–6, 16, 37–38, 40, 131–46, 183; potty, 24; prank, 5, 82–83, 85–86, 91n13; racist, 5, 16, 39–41, 45, 59n2, 76, 80–81, 90, 102, 112–17, 122–23, 126n4, 159; rape, 5, 65, 75–76, 87–88, 90, 92n15, 122, 147n4; sarcasm, 33, 37, 97, 99–101; satire/satirical, 5–6, 9, 16, 25, 37, 58, 76, 89, 110–11, 114, 116–17, 126, 131–46, 213–14; self-depreciating, 85, 90, 115, 126n2; sense of, 3, 31–34, 36–37, 57–58, 90, 96–97, 99–101, 152, 162, 165, 190, 196, 204–5, 207–8; and seriousness, 1, 5, 7, 16, 23–24, 37, 49, 55–56, 75–76, 78–86,

88–90, 91n3, 91n5, 91n15, 92n16, 101–3, 133, 144, 157, 165, 171–76, 179, 180, 182, 184, 213; sexist, 4, 16, 39–41, 45, 65, 76, 80, 90, 92n15, 118, 120, 126n4, 132; slapstick, 92n16, 151; transphobic, 80

incongruity theory. *See* humor, incongruity theory of
insult/insulting, 16–19, 24, 33, 38, 77, 200
irony/ironic, 40, 91n11, 114, 173, 185n6, 195, 200, 213, 218, 225n6

James, William, 7, 19, 227n18
joy, 2, 18, 47–48, 137–38, 140, 194, 211, 218
just joking defense, 3, 31, 37–38, 40, 75, 89, 172

language, 3, 7, 15, 22, 34, 39–40, 110–11, 117, 163, 173, 189–91, 193, 194, 196, 200–202, 204, 207
Last Week Tonight, 6, 131
Late Night, 131–32
laughter, 3, 35, 48, 159; and amusement/humor, 5, 35, 48–49, 54, 57, 69, 75, 88, 110, 126n14, 151, 159–64, 166n4, 166n8, 183, 212, 218, 225, 226n12; cheap, 132; contagious, 18–19, 24, 26–27; Duchenne, 119–20, 166n4; enactive, 24–25; forced, 3, 13–20, 26–28, 126n15; permissibility/morality of, 6, 59n2, 78, 88, 97, 102, 109, 119, 121, 126n13, 127n19, 133, 151, 153, 158–59; philosopher exhibiting, 172, 182–84; pleasure of, 192, 217–18; as response, 32, 34, 37, 75–77, 80, 88, 112, 117, 121, 140, 142, 144, 147n7, 153–54, 157, 174, 187, 207; spontaneous, 19–20, 25–27, 41, 98, 120; translation of, 187n29
Letterman, David, 101
Lewinsky, Monika, 101–2

Manne, Kate, 114, 123, 125
merited-response argument, 4, 66–72, 73n5
misogyny, 114, 120, 123, 125
Modern Times, 69
moralistic fallacy, 68, 73–74n9
Morreall, John, 8–9, 78, 80–83, 91n8
Muses, 7, 211–12, 215, 217–18

Nanette, 75
Noah, Trevor, 132, 142, 147n4
norms/normative, 3, 7, 14–16, 24–28, 31–32, 39–40, 51–52, 73n2, 110–11, 114, 118, 131, 151, 153–54, 156, 159–62, 164–65, 164n9, 206, 220
Nussbaum, Martha, 217, 222–24, 226n15

The Office, 59n1
Oliver, John, 82
The Opposition, 131
outrage, 6, 82–83, 89, 131, 132, 139–40, 143–44, 146

Plato, 7–8, 111, 171–84, 185n15, 185n18, 186n20–21, 186–87n25–26, 221, 226n9
play, 7, 14, 16, 25, 28, 33, 35–38, 48, 55, 57, 68, 70, 78, 82, 121–23, 156–57, 160, 172–73, 177, 181–82, 189–90, 192–94, 196–97, 203–8, 218
political correctness, 40
positive psychology, 33
Postman, Neil, 41, 221
power, 4, 25, 27, 37, 40–41, 111, 124, 173, 176, 181, 183–84, 185n15, 206, 212, 218–20
practical joke, 76, 100–1
practical wisdom, 5, 101
prank. *See* humor, prank
Prinz, Jesse, 6, 13, 20, 25, 28n4, 133–38, 140–41, 147n6
privilege, 89, 121, 175
pun, 7, 151, 161–62
punching down, 88

racism. *See* humor, racist
Real Time, 131
roast, 6, 16
Roberts, Robert C., 8–9

satire. *See* humor, satire/satirical
sense of humor. *See* humor, sense of
seriousness. *See* humor, seriousness
sexism. *See* humor, sexist
Silverman, Sarah, 166n2
The Simpsons, 14, 158
Slote, Michael, 99–101, 104n4, 135
slur, 112–14, 116–17, 120, 126n12
Smuts, Aaron, 45, 67, 126n13, 127n19
sociolinguistics, 3, 31–32, 36, 40
stereotype, 35, 39, 65, 80, 83, 88, 91n6, 102–3, 113–16, 126n9, 127n20–21, 205–6

teasing, 33

tickling, 14, 49, 70
The Tonight Show, 132
Tosh, Daniel, 87
Trump, Donald, 6, 109, 132–33, 142, 147n4

vice, 73n2, 97, 155–56, 158–60, 213, 225
virtue, 6–7, 55, 59n10, 90, 97, 113, 153–60, 164–65, 166n5–6, 167n10, 174, 181, 184–85, 187, 199–200, 214, 219–20, 225, 228n22
voting, 6, 132–33, 140, 145

Weekend Update, 131
Wolf, Michelle, 6, 109, 113, 125
Wolf, Susan, 97, 100

Yankovic, Weird Al, 82–83, 91n9

Zhuangzi, 7, 189–91, 193–208

About the Contributors

Guy Axtell (PhD, University of Hawai'i, Manoa) is a comparative philosopher with interests in psychology, and in emotional and narrative aspects of identity. He is a Radford Honors College Faculty Fellow, and there teaches (would be) popular courses with modules on critical thinking through humor, moral imagination in Zhuangzi, and the art and reason of political cartooning.

Catherine Evans Davies (PhD, University of California at Berkeley) is Professor Emerita of Linguistics from the English Department at the University of Alabama. She identifies as an interactional sociolinguist and her research has been in the areas of humor, cross-cultural interaction, and Southern American discourse.

Ralph DiFranco (PhD, University of Connecticut) is an Instructor in the Department of Philosophy at Auburn University, and an affiliated member of the Expression, Communication, and Origins of Meaning research group at the University of Connecticut. His main research interests are at the intersection of expressive communication and applied ethics, including topics such as derogatory expression by means of nonlinguistic symbols, images, and jokes.

Carl Helsing (PhD, Southern Illinois University) specializes in the study of classical Chinese philosophy (particularly Daoism and Confucianism), comparative philosophy, and philosophies of moral psychology and language. His scholarship explores emotional, cognitive, and linguistic experience in classical Chinese texts and the interactions of these models with social, political, and environmental thought. He currently teaches courses in philosophy and religion for High Point University.

Andrew Jordan (PhD, University of Washington; JD, University of Michigan) is a Faculty Fellow at the University of Michigan Law School. His research interests are in the areas of virtue ethics, philosophy of humor, legal philosophy, constitutional theory, and contract law.

Rasmus Rosenberg Larsen (PhD, University at Buffalo, SUNY) is an assistant professor of philosophy and forensic epistemology at the University of Toronto Mississauga. His research interests include theoretical and applied issues in value theory and philosophy of science.

Oksana Maksymchuk (PhD, Northwestern University) is a scholar, poet, and translator. Her work has been supported by the National Endowment for the Humanities, the National Endowment for the Arts, and the Fritz Thyssen Foundation. She is the Writer in Residence at the Institute for Advanced Studies at the Central European University in Budapest.

Brian Mondy (PhD, University of Miami, FL) is senior lecturer in philosophy at the University of Minnesota-Rochester where he has taught since 2012. He looks forward to being able to safely return to attending comedy clubs, since his streaming services are running dry.

Andrew Morgan (PhD, University of Virginia) is visiting assistant professor of philosophy at the University of Alabama at Birmingham. His work aims to draw out the implications of ethical theory for the philosophy of language and vice versa. This has encompassed research projects on inner speech, moral language, slurring, and online linguistic communities. He is an affiliated member of the Expression, Communication, and Origins of Meaning research group at the University of Connecticut.

Tristan Nash (PhD, University of Wales Trinity Saint David) is a senior lecturer in philosophy at the University of Wales Trinity Saint David. He has published work in the areas of applied ethics and the philosophy of religion.

Stephanie Patridge (PhD, University of Washington) is a professor of philosophy at Otterbein University in Westerville, Ohio. She is the coeditor of Aesthetics: A Reader in the Philosophy of the Arts (2017, Routledge). Her research areas are in virtue aesthetics, the philosophy of humor, and the philosophy of games.

Alan Roberts (PhD, University of Sussex) is policy researcher at the United Kingdom's Government Office for Science.

About the Contributors

Brian Robinson (PhD, City University of New York) is assistant professor of philosophy at Texas A&M University-Kingsville. His research focuses on moral psychology and philosophy of language. Part of the intersection of these two fields is in the moral psychology of humor and amusement. He is an inveterate punster, which he swears is more than just some antics. He lives in South Texas near the beach, which he enjoys when he can get there.

David Sackris (PhD, University at Buffalo, SUNY) is the chair of the philosophy program at Arapahoe Community College. His research interests focus on value theory broadly construed.

Daniel Shargel (PhD, City University of New York) is an associate professor of philosophy at Lawrence Technological University. His research is primarily in the philosophy of mind, philosophy of cognitive science, and philosophy of emotion. He has developed an enactive theory of emotional content, and he is currently developing a theory of how emotions fit into an account of moral judgement based on reinforcement learning.

Nathan Stout (PhD, Tulane University) is lecturer in the Program for Medical Ethics and Human Values at the Tulane University School of Medicine and Medical Ethicist in the Southeast Louisiana Veterans Health Care System, U.S. Department of Veterans Affairs. His work is broadly interdisciplinary, spanning the fields of ethical theory, moral psychology, biomedical ethics, the philosophy of medicine, and political philosophy.

www.ingramcontent.com/pod-product-compliance
Lightning Source LLC
Chambersburg PA
CBHW032038300426
44117CB00009B/1111